ON THE BRINK

CHARTER PARTIES
& AGREEMENTS FOR
FREIGHT
OFFER
BILLS OF LADING
INWARD

Charles Fox

ON THE BRINK

*The Story of G. C. Fox
and Company—A Quaker
Business in Cornwall Through
Eight Generations*

'This world of ours and worlds unseen
And thin the boundaries in between'

CHARLES FOX

ZULEIKA

First published 2019
by Zuleika Books & Publishing
Thomas House, 84 Eccleston Square
London, SW1V 1PX

British Library Cataloguing in Publication Data

A catalogue record for this book is
available from the British Library

ISBN: 978-1-99-962329-6

Designed by Euan Monaghan
Printed in England by CPI Group (UK) Ltd, Croydon CRO 4YY

*Frontispiece: Detail of a nineteenth-century
filing cabinet, which stood for over 150 years in the
office of G. C. Fox & Co. (see Chapter 2)*

CONTENTS

LIST OF ILLUSTRATIONS

FOREWORD

by Philip Marsden
Author of *The Levelling Sea* (2011)
and *Rising Ground* (2014)

IN THE MIDDLE of the eighteenth century, a Quaker merchant called George Croker Fox arrived in Falmouth. The business he set up there, G. C. Fox & Co., continued to trade under the same family name for over 240 years. During that time, the Fox family not only sustained the firm but ensured that it remained at the centre of the town's commercial life. The Foxes were ship agents and victuallers, merchants of fish and timber, coal and flax.

But the family's interests spread far beyond waterfront trade. In the early nineteenth century, Cornwall was in the midst of a mining boom which offered not only huge financial rewards – and risks – but required a constant flow of innovation and technology to extract, process and export the minerals. The Foxes were involved in foundries and small harbours as well as Falmouth's Polytechnic Society where scientific matters were discussed and applied. The Foxes too were writers, painters and gardeners. Around Falmouth remains a ring of lovingly planted Fox gardens. They were also honorary consuls for dozens of countries, from the United States to Colombia, the Ottoman Empire to Sweden.

Charles Fox, one of the last of the firm's family directors, has spent years sifting through the records to assemble a portrait of G. C. Fox & Co. What he presents is not so much the account of a business as the view of an entire world. Falmouth in the late eighteenth and nineteenth centuries was one of the spinning hubs of the British Empire, and the Foxes were in the middle of it. The stories collected here include shipwrecks and diplomacy, fishing calamities and bonanzas. They deal with the often bruising conflict between deeply held Quaker convictions and the often freebooting maritime enterprise. They are history at its most absorbing – tales of individuals' adventures and triumphs, of humility and courage from another age, of men and women clinging to beliefs and ideals while trying to keep afloat.

PREFACE

Towards the end of the twentieth century, after eight continuous generations of business, the two main strands of G. C. Fox & Co. were sold and passed out of family ownership. This book is a personal memoir of the contribution made by the company to trading in Cornwall for over three centuries.

I CHOSE THE title 'On the Brink' for a number of reasons. Falmouth is on the brink of the English Channel and the Atlantic Ocean, both areas of sea which represent opportunities for any business involved in maritime industries. Less obviously, the Foxes, like so many Quakers, were astute businessmen, but the strength of their Christian morality acted as a brake: they were in this way often on the brink of being tempted into shady adventures. Somehow they were able to stand firm. Connected to this and perhaps most importantly, their view of mankind's time on this planet was that we are all on the brink of something much more exciting: the best is yet to be. This went hand in hand with their concepts of stewardship, with seeing good in all things, and with helping others.

No doubt it was these attitudes that brought them to the brink of this life and the next.

Looking back to the late 1970s, when I became actively involved with the firm, perhaps G. C. Fox & Co. was on the brink of another adventure. On the one hand there was the feeling of a well-run establishment, which had survived so many vicissitudes, but on the other hand there was a question mark over the future of such family businesses.

Now living in the twenty-first century, we can see that what was once one of the busiest trading centres in the northern hemisphere has since become the destination of cruise ships; and the tall-masted sailing ships for which G. C. Fox & Co. acted are now the essence of ocean races. Anything else to do with historic boats has become the pride of maritime museums. The firm's signal station on The Lizard is now a house; and the Foxes' foundry at Perranarworthal (famous for its cutting-edge technology), their timber depots in Penryn, and their fishing cellars around the coast of Cornwall, have also been transformed into homes. Their tin-mining tracks are now bicycle trails; their mines are of archaeological significance; their gardens, which were once mere repositories for plants being introduced to this country, are now tourist destinations, or have fallen victim to urbanisation; and the seeds the Foxes sowed in the world of education, especially the arts and sciences, have now borne fruit in the evolution of a university.

The story of a company which was something of an enigma, and of how its strengths and weaknesses were handled, has now become the focus of this book.

Don't be like the people of this world, but let God change the way you think. Then you will know how to do everything that is good and pleasing to Him.

Romans 12, verse 2

INTRODUCTION

IF YOU VISIT the National Maritime Museum in Falmouth, after you have gazed at all the hanging boats, admired the panoramic views from the top of the tower and, at high water, peered at the underwater views from the bottom of the tower, you can find on the second floor an area called the Cornwall Galleries; and here in one small corner there is a motionless figure standing behind a desk. This is the re-creation of the office of a nineteenth-century ship agent whose business, in inverse proportion to the exhibit, was to have far-reaching effects throughout Falmouth and far beyond the brink of Falmouth's bay.

On the Brink is a response from the last senior partner to those who have asked for something on the history of G. C. Fox & Company. The earliest records for this business go back to the mid-seventeenth century. At that time the Foxes were trading as merchants, but over the following 300 years they went on to become involved in a variety of commercial and industrial undertakings in

1

Cornwall. Their move to Falmouth in the mid-eighteenth century came 75 years after the port's establishment as a Packet station (initially serving La Coruña and Lisbon) and it coincided with the growing expansion of the international mail service to the West Indies and destinations on the eastern seaboard of the American colonies. They became the leading ship agents and were known internationally as 'Foxes of Falmouth'. They were recognised as men of business, entrepreneurialism and, above all, strong moral values; and their lives affected the course of history both locally and throughout the county.

The book is based on the rich archive of business correspondence, documents, copybooks and letters at my disposal. Sadly, and frustratingly, much was lost. In 1872 there is a partners' minute which says

'We have sold to Howe & Co. Exeter & J. H. Jackson Marlow Road our old paper i.e. six old copy books (excepting two in each decade as samples) up to 1850 old accounts, and newspapers etc.'

They also sold some business papers and journals belonging to Fox Hamilton and Co. and Fox Price and Co.

In July 1877 they were at it again. Howard Fox, my great-great-uncle, records

'OLD LETTERS – In order to make room and lessen the weight on our floors we agreed to sell all our old letters, for waste paper, received up to the end of 1867 reserving one letter from each year as a memento…. the letters filled 60 sacks weighing about 70 cwt nett.'

Thankfully, Howard, who supervised this task, did not do it very well; it has been fun finding ancient documents wrapped up in more ancient documents – which were often auction posters. The sorting of this mass of archive material was one of my first tasks at G. C. Fox & Co., when in the late 1960s as a holiday job I spent a fortnight in the strong room, going through several very heavy metal deed boxes, and listing the contents, mostly vellum paper conveyances conserved in chalk.

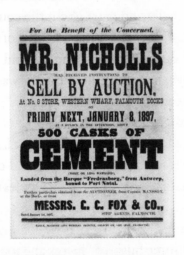

An auction poster dated 1897 which had
been used to wrap up old documents

Ten years later, after I joined the firm and was looking at ways in which I could make myself useful, I squeezed into a boiler suit one day, and negotiated a narrow staircase which was overflowing with the contents of an attic. For the next three months I spent every working hour in the roof amid a jumble of memorabilia: old photographic prints, many with shattered glass, of tall-masted sailing ships, and of kings, queens and presidents of all the countries which members of the family had represented in a consular capacity. Scattered around them were stacks of files and piles of books: old letter books, journals and dictionaries, and more recent books with inviting titles such as *The Elements of Export Practice* and *The Principles of Marine Law*. To encourage and discourage me, there were unread books on famous shipping companies and family businesses. There was a motley collection of old ships' parts: masts, anchors and anchor chain, and of fishing nets, lobster and crab pots, ropes, flagpoles, and moth-eaten flags. There were damaged chests of drawers and captains' chairs waiting to be mended, two deckchairs made from a design one of the partners had seen on a cruise, long forgotten, a clock, a pair of oars, some outboard engines, all broken, and a collapsed rubber dinghy. There were chests, sacks and suitcases, containing the discarded effects of ships' crews, a briefcase full of spirits – clearly contraband, numerous pots of old paint, a vast quantity of gash timber, and a swordfish bill. Everything was covered in decades of dust and everywhere there was evidence of bats, rats, mice, silverfish, spiders, flies, pigeons and seagulls, many dead and others very much alive. I must have removed about three tons of rubbish; and amongst it there were old documents and letters, most of them loose but some tied up in pink linen ribbons, and many with their stamps neatly removed by a pair of over-enthusiastic scissors.

So I have, over more recent years, performed a similar task to that undertaken by Howard, with an even greater weight of files 'disturbing', as Barclay Fox puts it in his Journal, 'the dust of generations in hunting thro' old ledgers'.[1] I just hope that I have been reasonably selective, and that what has been preserved and catalogued will be of interest to future researchers.

Based on earlier research and already in print, or accessible on the world-wide web, there is a wealth of material which I have chosen not to revisit in this current project. For those who are interested in a full social commentary on Victorian life in and around the Fox family and its businesses in Falmouth, there are no better accounts to read than the diaries of Caroline and Barclay Fox.[2] There are lesser-known but equally delightful unpublished journals, such as 'George Fox of Tredrea and his three daughters' by H. Crewdson, 'Our childhood at Perran' by E. Crewdson, 'Jottings from Alfred Fox's Diaries', 'Two Homes' by Elton Fox and 'Late Harvest' by Ellen Bosanquet. There are countless potted biographies and obituaries and regular genealogical accounts, in which, to simplify matters, I have concentrated only on the main players.

Family research is complicated: there are some who married twice within the Society of Friends and inevitably within their own extensive cousinage. To compound this, my great-great-grandfather, Alfred Fox, had 12 children, and thereby my grandfather and his siblings had

---

1   R. L. Brett (ed.), *Barclay Fox's Journal 1832–1854* (Bell & Hyman, 1979; re-printed with additions by Cornwall Editions Ltd, 2008), p. 148.

2   *Barclay Fox's Journal 1832–1854*; Wendy Monk (ed.), *The Journals of Caroline Fox 1835–1871* (Elek Books Ltd, London, 1972)

nearly 100 first cousins. There is no known evidence of the family being related to George Fox, the founder of Quakerism[3] who lived from 1624 to 1691, but unhelpfully for the researcher his name recurs in every generation, in his honour. For clarity, both first and second names are used, where known.

For those whose literary interests have a different focus and who appreciate historical facts as well as good literature, there is an abundance of pamphlets, papers, and newspapers which more than adequately narrate the histories of various Cornish industries in which the Fox family has invested, such as the pilchard fishery business, Perran Foundry, the Kennall Vale Gunpowder Company, the Lizard signal station, the Falmouth Towage Company and Falmouth Docks (in 1860 the sum of £40,000 was contributed by the Foxes to its construction). The Falmouth Polytechnic Society was founded in 1833 by Caroline Fox and her sister Anna Maria; and in 1835 it became the Royal Cornwall Polytechnic Society, which has its own library containing many Fox-related publications. The Foxes provided their skills and a steady line of chairmen for many other Falmouth organisations, notably schools.

In the family archive there are scrapbooks of headline

---

3   In recording the death of George Henry Fox (1845–1931), the weekly Quaker magazine *The Friend* noted a triple coincidence in connection with his death and that of George Fox, the founder of the Society of Friends. It is a strange detail that both Georges died on Tuesday 13 January, both were buried three days later on 16 January, and in both cases their deaths took place in the first year of a new decade, respectively 1691 and 1931. (*The Friend*, 23 January 1931)

news over many years (the wreck of the *Flying Enterprise* was one – see Chapter 5), interspersed with obituaries and the accounts of marriages. Some of the latter go on for pages with details not just of those who attended, but also what they wore, and what presents they gave.

For the ardent researcher there is the treasure trove, of all things connected to the maritime history of Cornwall, to be found at the National Maritime Museum in Falmouth. There are also many publications on specialist subjects such as shipwrecks, smuggling, fishing, mining, and every type of boat that has ever sailed the sea. Consequently, I have not delved into technicalities. These are better left to the specialists. I have, as is my habit, skated around many of the topics, all of which would make interesting books in their own right. Despite the abundant primary sources, I have not written in detail about, for example, every ship's arrival, every towage job, every wreck, every timber transaction, every catch of pilchards, every mineral extraction, or every bit of machinery which was fabricated at Perran Foundry. Rather than dwell on such minutiae, what I have endeavoured to do is to give the reader a feel for a family business, run for over 300 years by men with both strong Christian ethics and at the same time, no doubt very stressfully, high business acumen. There is an appendix which list the different partners and partnerships.

I have tried to describe the quiet evolution of the firm, responding to changing technology and a variety of different circumstances through many generations, from the simple mercantile exchanges of early days to international recognition for the Foxes' knowledge of shipping and diplomacy as consuls. It is an account of effective entrepreneurship constantly adapting to need.

There may be some who would have liked to see a dry chronological account, but because so many different enterprises were running concurrently, the book is divided into topics, which I hope will make it easier to absorb. When using quotes, the original texts remain unchanged, even in the occasional archaic spelling, which I feel adds a certain magic. For example, in the 1770s the word 'claret' was sometimes spelt with two 't's; and 'wall-nutts' sound instantly more flavoursome.

With *On the Brink*, I enter the story at a late stage. This would not have happened had it not become clear as the pages took shape that I had to include the firm's conclusion, in which I had a part to play. For that personal, and not illustrious, intrusion on the past, and probably an excessively liberal sprinkling of personal anecdotes and observations, due warning is given.

Everyone knows how irksome it can be to read nature notes which are more about the observer's emotional response to his observations than about *what* he observes. But I do this frequently; and the reason is because on balance opinion is what gives reports colour. The resultant book falls somewhere between the two stools of a storyteller and an historian. But maybe this will bring life and humour to this account of part of Cornwall's history, an account which otherwise might appear to have been wrapped forever in mothballs.

On the whole, however, I have striven to stick to the evidence and be objective, even if, it must be emphasised, history has no more validity beyond the written evidence on which it is based.

I trust my ancestors would forgive me for writing this book, and not just because of any faults of misrepresentation. There is another reason. In 1962 the company celebrated – albeit three years in arrears, as it later transpired – the bicentenary of its existence in Falmouth.[4] But if there is one characteristic that comes across more than anything else in the Fox family, it is a complete disregard for marking any achievement, or for celebrating anniversaries, or for any self-congratulatory gestures. Salesmen's bluff and advertising the company for commercial reasons were a different matter: the partners owed it to the business and its employees to do their very best for its survival. But the idea of boasting, or flaunting wealth, was alien to the Foxes; and my sincerest hope is that this book is never seen as an example of that. It is simply my record of a very small company with a long reach; and it is also a small book which I have been working at for a long time.

---

4   This date was based on evidence available at that time. But subsequent research in the archives has revealed that there is evidence of George Croker Fox trading from Falmouth in 1759.

1

THE MERCHANT

THE NAME FOX is not Cornish, though the earliest records we have indicate that by the mid-seventeenth century members of the Fox family were trading as merchants in Fowey, a harbour on the south coast of Cornwall. However, to put things into a healthy perspective at the start of this book, the following story needs to be told. I have a friend whose modest appearance and manner belie the fact that he comes from an old and distinguished Cornish family living near Falmouth: his surname is the only clue. One day I was discussing with him the advent of a container terminal in Falmouth. For several years this was a strong possibility in which my father Philip Fox, for one, had invested heavily. 'Falmouth has always been a commercial port,' I argued forcibly, not thinking particularly of the contribution the Fox family had made in this way since the 1750s, nor even thinking that Falmouth may have had a history before that time. 'Oh no, it hasn't,' retorted my friend. 'It wasn't when we came here in 1170.'

So much for all those who prospered through their connection with the Falmouth Packet Service, or later as a result of the Industrial Revolution, and who thought they were something more than Johnnie-come-latelies.

In his *Genealogical and Heraldic History of the Commoners of Great Britain and Ireland* (later known as 'Burke's Landed Gentry', published between 1833 and 1838), John Burke stated that the numerous families of Fox residing at that time in the west of England sprang from one common ancestor, Francis Fox of Wiltshire. It is said that he migrated to St Germans in 1645 'during the commotions of the Civil War', and in the following year married Dorothy Kekewich, a member of a Cornish branch of a noted Exeter family. More tenuous is Burke's claim that Francis was closely connected to another more celebrated Wiltshire Fox: Sir Stephen Fox, the politician, founder of Chelsea Hospital and father (from his second marriage in his late 70s) of both the first Earl of Ilchester and the first Baron Holland).[5] More recent research has established that Francis Fox (1606–1670) was the son of Henry and Edith Fox of Devizes, and probably had little or no connection to the political dynasty.

After their marriage, Francis and Dorothy moved into

---

5   It has often been asked in particular if Sir Stephen Fox's grandson, Charles James Fox (1749–1806) – the politician and crony of the Prince of Wales, later George IV – was a relation. I cannot imagine a man less Quaker in his expansive countenance, or in his habits and temperament, but I like the coincidence that, like many Quaker Foxes, Charles James Fox was firmly, and very influentially, opposed to the slave trade. The alleged connection may have come about partly because in the early nineteenth century George Croker Fox (III), of Grove Hill House, took out a coat of arms which was based on Sir Stephen Fox's escutcheon. Earlier generations of the family were, in Richard Hingston Fox's helpful words (written in 1907), 'too severe in their unworldliness to be likely to give attention to arms-bearing'.

Catchfrench, the Kekewich house near Liskeard. According to Burke, Francis and his family joined the Society of Friends soon after its establishment in Cornwall, some sharing 'in the sufferings that awaited its early members, on account of the stand which they so resolutely and successfully made for liberty of conscience'. Members of Francis's family who were most affected included his younger son James, who was imprisoned in the Bridewell at Exeter in 1683 'on account of his religious principles' and three years later left England altogether to settle in Philadelphia, where descendants of other family members who had accompanied James and his family on the ship *Desire* still live.[6]

Francis's elder son, also Francis, remained in St Germans but amongst the next generation it seems that there was some rationality for the Foxes to move increasingly further west, to where the English Channel meets the Atlantic Ocean. One of Francis the younger's sons by his second wife Tabitha (née Croker), known as George Fox of Par, also married twice. It is from these two marriages, the first in 1719 to Mary, 'daughter of Edward Bealing, merchant, of Penryn' and the second in 1726 to Anna, 'daughter of Philip Debell, merchant, of East Looe', that many of the Fox families throughout the South West originated. Many Foxes were to set up business in Plymouth as ship agents, and merchants in timber and chemicals.

Edward, the eldest son from George's first marriage

---

6   For more information about the American branch of the family, see *Growing with America: the Fox Family of Philadelphia*, by Joseph S. Fox (2006).

to Mary Bealing, moved to Wadebridge in North Cornwall; and from him stem the Fox families of Wadebridge, Perranarworthal, Exeter, Kingsbridge, Plymouth and Wellington. Outside the scope of this book but a nonetheless fascinating topic is the famous textile business of Fox Brothers of Wellington. Before the First World War they had a few thousand employees, and were responsible for inventing the colour khaki. After the Second World War, however, the business entered a time of decline, until comparatively recently when it was bought by Deborah Meaden who, very much in the name of British manufacturing, has set about its resurrection.

A further subject of interest is the medical line of the family, spearheaded by Edward's half-brother Joseph (1730–1801). He was the product of George's second marriage to Anna Debell and although tangentially, and very movingly, he does come into our story (see Chapter 3), he became a surgeon. His three sons entered the medical profession in London and in Bristol and became eminent in and in treating those who were then known and described as insane.

Meanwhile, another half-brother to Edward by the same marriage, George Croker Fox (1727–1782), was to set up shop in Falmouth in 1759 'for the greater conveniency of any foreign Business'. Although over the years the name of the firm changed with the initials of the partners (see Appendix), it became known as G. C. Fox & Co., passed through eight generations, and still continues today, albeit under different ownership and name, and no longer at 48 Arwenack Street but altogether more suitably within Falmouth Docks.

These two half-brothers, Edward and George, combined their talents wherever possible. In due course, and in the nature of many non-conformists, they and their descendants collaborated most successfully within their own sect: for example, Fox Brothers in Wellington made use of the ship agency in Falmouth for the export of their woollen products. More significantly, when the threat of French invasion was at its most serious at the height of the Napoleonic Wars, Robert Were Fox (senior) took the precaution of sending money bills to his cousin Thomas Fox in Wellington, to be exchanged for cash should the need arise.

In the early days, and certainly in Fowey before the Foxes moved to Falmouth, they were traders as much as ship agents. Fish and fish-oil feature on every page of the letter books but in amongst all the fish there were other commodities: tea, salt, oats, corn, wheat, flour, barley, flax, coals, iron, 'tyn', rum, brandy, wines, 'extreme good red or white port', tanned hides, leathers, bricks (as used by the Foxes for their properties in Falmouth and Wadebridge), mahogany, elm, deals, 'wallnutts', raisins, beef, pork, muscovado sugars, butter, pitch, tar, turpentine, cordage, hemp, and, in August 1770, George Croker Fox records 'a couple of Spanish Pointing Dogs'. With everything travelling in sacks, barrels, bushels, bundles, pipes and firkins and, presumably just on deck, there must have been a high incidence of tainted goods. George Croker Fox's sister Tabitha, who seems to have been left in charge of the Par office shows some concern in this respect, writing to a Mr Arch on 4 January 1770:

'I doubt I shall be obliged to return the price of wrapping calicoe it being so much spotted that it will not sell if the spots are such as will not come out in washing but if thee canst send what is clean thee mayst send 2 pieces by the next opportunity'.

Should the reader be wondering, soap does indeed make its appearance. George Croker Fox, writing to a cousin on 31 January 1756, says

'Inclosed thee hast my draft on Henton Brown & Son for £12. 7. 4. wch pays thee for the 4 boxes of soap if I am not much mistaken when thee wert here at the time the soap was landed thee desirdst I would take it if suitable & saidst thee hadst a large parcell by the Bristol ship.'

Ships with names such as *Fox, Mickey, Providence, Lovely Nelly, Felicity, Adriatick* and *Little Dick* went to and from every part of the globe, and not just in Europe and the Mediterranean, at the mercy of weather and the inconvenience of both war and piracy: 'I much fear the Phoenix is taken', George Croker Fox writes in March 1760. At one point things have reached such a pitch that he recommends a friend 'undertake a journey on his own bottom', whatever that means. In a copy book bound in vellum, which is cracked with age, George went doggedly on with a quill, one letter after another:

'by the last mail I was favoured with a letter from thy house at Naples intimating their inclination

16

to be concerned in a cargo of summer and winter fish.'

'I flatter my self her cargo wilt meet an advantageous sale.'

'I see that thee were not inclineable in any bananas.'

and

'I have before me yr favour of the fifteenth in reply to which the price I gave you for my iron was the very lowest farthing I could sell for.'

At a time when farthings were common tender perhaps it should also be mentioned that by today's standards the firm was also trading in not insignificant sums of money, amounting to the equivalent of many thousands of pounds. These high values are never recognised (Quakers were fully aware of the dangers of serving God and mammon) and as if to underline his modest attitude to business George Croker Fox was always in the habit of referring to his 'little vessel'. The following entry also has a throwaway character:

'June 9th 1770 I can't put my hand on the little bunch of diamonds being mislaid but when it comes to hand I will send it thee.'

and an entry of a personal nature from the summer of 1771 shows not only concern for his dress but also his modest Quaker tastes, and sobriety in all things great or small:

> 'In answer to thine I don't like the buttons thee hast sent me therefore desire thee to send me some others but thee need not find me any Greens Blues Whites or Claretts – I generally wear what are full cloth colours.'

(Gentlemen's outfitters made a very good living in any port.)

He had escaped the criticism of Voltaire, who had observed that even then some Quakers, 'enriched by the industry of their parents became desirous of enjoying honours and of wearing buttons and ruffles', and presumably, as a result, felt guilty at being called Quakers.

Others did not.

What comes across from George Croker Fox's letters is a man who was totally scrupulous, patient and consistently polite in all his dealings. But if crossed, he had no hesitation in stating unemotionally, which is a rare gift, what his emotions were. The fact that the letters were written in the first person singular, and mostly signed by George himself, and revealingly with a hint of an Elizabethan curlicue, is impressive; and it suggests perhaps more of an industrious sole trader rather than a roaring partnership which later issued circulars starting 'G. C. Fox & Co. beg to inform' or 'We beg to inform'. It is an odd paradox of shopkeeping that success is often accompanied by an unnecessary degree of obsequiousness ('May

I ask what is your pleasure?' etc); and in 1781 a circular was sent out by the company ending,

> 'We therefore take the freedom to hand thee our respective Signatures at foot, and to return our Friends our best thanks for the kind preference of their past commands (and attention to such of the concerns of our late Partnership as were intrusted to their care) intreating a continuance thereof to us as long as our conduct may merit their Partiality.'

Today we live, somewhat deplorably, in what might be called an 'I' culture, but that apart, nothing succeeds like straightforward 'I' messages, such as to be found in the early letter books.

George Croker Fox consistently refers to his good and trusted friends all over the world. Many of these were members of the Quaker fraternity. But as for the rest of his contacts, either this means he was naïve or, more likely, it means that in the eighteenth-century days of snail-mail, a man's word was his bond, in stark contrast with today when even a handshake can result in one less finger. Alternatively, it could mean that hundreds of traders did indeed come to Falmouth and, as a certain Captain Snellman later records, 'went to see Mr Fox'.

2

THE SHIP AGENT

SHIP AGENCY WAS always the mainstay of the business, especially when Falmouth, from about 1700 to about 1850, was one of the busiest ports in the northern hemisphere with, as a circular issued by the business in 1843 proclaims, the harbour having 'the great facility...of ingress and egress at all times'. In 1854 Robert Were Fox (II) wrote to the Secretary of State in Washington and said, 'vessels at this port ride at their anchors in a capacious and safe roadstead'. To quote from my book about Glendurgan, the family's home on the Helford River near Falmouth:

'Falmouth is one of the largest natural harbours in the world; it is the first and last port of call in the English Channel; and until the advent of the steam train it handled all the incoming and outgoing mail for most of northern Europe. In addition, the French wars caused overseas trade to be concentrated here, rather than risk running the gauntlet of enemy shipping further up the channel. On occasions Falmouth was so busy that it was possible to walk from one side of the harbour to the other – if you could see it

21

– stepping from boat to boat. One day in the winter of 1847 Alfred counted 190 vessels in the bay alone.'

To put this in perspective, 120 ships in the bay, and 40 arrivals a day, just after the evacuation of Dunkirk in 1940, was more unusual, 'choc-a-bloc' as my grandfather Cuthbert Fox wrote in a letter dated 27 June of that year. The arrival of 40 to 50 ships a day in the nineteenth century was not uncommon. Boarding clerks stood with their telescopes levelled on the bay and at the first sign of a sail agents competed fiercely to win the job. In his autobiographical *Life and Letters of Admiral Sir B. J. Sulivan*[7], the author refers to the journals of his father-in-law, Captain James, who lived at a house near Mylor, and how captains visiting Falmouth were often entertained to dinner at his house. These included, it is recorded *en passant*, in some cases before they became famous:

'Israel Pellew, James Saumarez, Sir Peter Parker, Horatio Nelson, George Cockburn, Thomas Free-

---

7   *The Life and Letters of Admiral Sir Bartholomew James Sulivan, KCB, 1810–1890* was intended as an autobiographical memoir. However, Sulivan only completed the first chapter of his reminiscences, taking his story up to 1829, when as a 19-year-old midshipman he had recently joined the crew of H M sloop *Beagle* at Rio de Janeiro, on the ship's first voyage before she was joined for the second voyage in 1831 by her most famous passenger, Charles Darwin. The rest of Sulivan's life story was told by his son Henry Norton Sulivan, based on his father's and others' letters and documents, and published in 1896, six years after the Admiral's death.

mantle, James Macnamara, Isaac Coffin, and Edward Hamilton.'

From an independent source this corroborates the Fox papers which relate what a lively place Falmouth must have been round about 1800. It was the heyday of the famous Falmouth Packet mail business, about which others have written copiously. It lasted from roughly 1688 to 1851, and G. C. Fox & Co. as well as being ship agents, also acted as postal forwarding agents. Think too of the competing ancillary businesses: for a start, all those whose businesses began with the letter 'B' and who banked, brokered, baked, butchered, built and buried.

It was only after the railway came to Falmouth in 1863 that its full effect on the Packet business was felt: before then its proponents were optimistic. The notice to a public meeting as early as 1836 reads,

'This meeting is fully impressed with the important advantages which must result to the general interests of the kingdom by the establishment of a direct Railway communication from Falmouth to the Metropolis, by causing the very earliest delivery of the Government Mails and Dispatches, and more particularly to this County, by giving greater facilities to the conveyance of passengers, and the transit of its valuable productions and importations, and ensuring the permanent stability of the Packet Station on this port.'

Little, however, did anyone know how useful trains were going to be for the transport of fish.

G. C. Fox & Co. had its own gigs and boarding boats. Nowadays, boats with engines give no idea of how perilous it must have been to come alongside a ship in a boat under sail, and how skilled were those who helmed them. It was difficult enough in calm weather, and additionally several boats would have been competing to be the first to board a vessel and win the business.

Lloyds Agency Sailing Gig off St Mawes.
Alexander Kay Branden. Oil on canvas, mid-nineteenth century

From some memoirs written about 100 years ago here are a few extracts which describe the business at perhaps its liveliest:

'Three or four look-out men sat on the hedge with their telescopes every day to tell Fox's office about the shipping.'

'In the old days (i.e. before the introduction of steam tugs) the vessels arriving at Falmouth were boarded by the clerks of the various shipping firms (Fox & Co., Broad & Sons and Lashbrooke & Hunt being the principal ones) in long boarded gigs[8] which might be seen racing either rowing or sailing through and out of the Harbour to get to the vessels first – It was often of advantage to be the first on board, as the Captains, if they had no special Agent or reason for applying to any particular firms would give their business to the representative arriving first…In the days of the old Black Sea fleet of wooden vessels of all nations, carrying principally corn, Wilson Lloyd Fox remembers as many as 83 arriving in one day and about the same numbers arriving the following day – It is impossible to describe and difficult to imagine the babel of tongues, noise & apparent (not real) confusion in Fox & Co.'s office in those times of stress and business pressure.'

'The Captains and the Sailing vessels came ashore in their own ships and boats with 2 or 4 or 6 men and rowers in each of all nationalities in the Custom House Quay for hours until the Captain went on board their vessels again. Spanish Italian Greek and other sailors often wearing clothes of bright colours and being a picturesque collection & sometimes there were rows and fights between them.'

George Henry Fox records in 1874:

---

8   G. C. Fox & Co. flew a red flag marked with the letter 'F', and Broad and Sons flew a blue flag marked with the letter 'B'.

'Robert [*Barclay Fox II – his cousin*] met us near the Union & handed me a note announcing Captain Nicolo Figari's death in the office, about 3. Some noisy sailors had been bothering the consulate for their discharge. One of them said something derogatory of Camogli his native place & he rushed at him and put him (a big fellow) out at the back door. He barely reached the Italian room when he fell without a word.'

Meanwhile, numerous clerks were expected to stay rooted to their Davenport desks. These desks were of a certain height and necessitated the use of sit-up-and-beg type stools, each with a fender of spindles, not unlike the captain's chairs which were littered around the office, but on long legs. In one hand the clerks held a cylindrical rule about 18 inches long and an inch in diameter, and in the other a pen, or in the early days, a quill. The result of all their endeavours speaks for itself: it forms much of the raw material for this book.

The incoming letters in the nineteenth century reached Falmouth, so Howard Fox records, by coach from Plymouth.

'The London post was delivered about 3 p.m. The bag of Fox & Co.'s letters was brought to Wodehouse Place for our father to sort and read for the firm. The clerks were too busy with Customs etc business and settling ships orders and accounts to answer letters until after ten. So that all London and most other letters were answered after 7 p.m.'

In the office there was an early nineteenth-century piece

of furniture which takes four men to move. It is divided into drawers, with some elegantly inscribed, in the colour of parchment, as follows:

Foreign post
Large post
Small post
Forms of invoices
Forms of offers
Ruled post
Agreements
Blank charter parties
Memoranda
Letters to answer
Notepaper
Envelopes
Passports
Forms of bills of lading
Pens
Charter parties' agreement forms
Freight
Bills of lading inward
Bills of lading outward
Account sales
Accounts current
Receipts
Bills
Invoices
Policies of insurance
Telegraphic messages

Then there are pigeon-holes, each with a fretted arch bearing letters of the alphabet, for ships' mail; and at the bottom of this handy cabinet there is a small safe, lined with lead. This piece of furniture has since entered a new life, containing different types of string, elastic bands, staples, picture hooks, cotton reels, light bulbs, batteries and candles. But the habit of putting ships' mail into alphabetized compartments continued into the twenty-first century; and was extended to include office departments and senior members of staff, all neatly labelled with Dymo tape. Some of these later pieces of furniture comprising pigeon-holes, in various office makeovers also became upgraded into accommodating flags, and then more recently, I am sorry to report, into domestic use as boot lockers.

It is difficult to define the work of a ship agent, often confused with a shipping agent; and once when I had rather pretentiously explained to someone that my work was 'in shipping' (misheard as 'chipping') we had a mysterious conversation about slate quarries in the North of Cornwall, and how remarkable it was that it took me only twenty minutes to drive there each day, in my very powerful car.[9] A ship agent looks after ships when they come into port; a shipping agent wraps up things. A poet named Anna-Christina Gilmore wrote a poem which in essence says that whatever your problem is, 'call the agent'. Its last verse aptly goes

9   More recently, someone owned up to me that she had no idea the family business was based on biscuits, after the famous brand. I did not rush to correct her, ever hoping that I might glean more to add to my list of misinformation on the Fox family, and thinking that an alternative title to the book might be 'Was it biscuits?'

'At every single port you'll find an agent.
If your gangway is too short, call the agent.
He's the scapegoat on the quay
Trying to calm a consignee
Whose goods fell in the sea.
Who'd be an agent?'

A ship agent normally has to deal with several regular procedures, on behalf of the ship, its owners or charterers. This involves the pilots, the harbour master, the Customs, immigration and port health; and in many cases we were, to our consternation but their convenience, held to be as answerable to port officials as to our principals. In addition to these mandatory tasks the ship agent can be asked to help with the following: ship's stores, spare parts, fuel, disinfestation, crew changes and travelling arrangements, crew's wages, and sick crew (including at least one seaman who wanted to be cured of impotency). But he might also be asked to perform any task under the sun, some of which are best left to the imagination. My father had to cope with a cargo of dead giraffes. To the potential intrigue of archaeologists in a thousand years' time it was finally decided to pop them down a disused tin mine, an idea quite a few people and revered organisations have also had for the disposal of rubbish. A job I recall from the time of the mackerel fishing bonanza in the late 1970s and early 1980s was when the ship agency was responsible for a floating population of about 5,000 sailors on board a number of Eastern Bloc ships. To celebrate 60 years of Soviet rule, we were asked to distribute 60 red roses to each ship. In those days at the end of the 1970s, it was hard to find in Falmouth a dozen red roses let alone 600; but we persevered, and on a gale-laden wintry day a quay punt, full of roses, left Customs House Quay, each delivery to be hauled on board by a heaving line.

As an observer as well as the agent, I wondered what there was to celebrate. I had heard about the penalties at home for anyone who misbehaved, and I knew the conditions on board some of these ships. For example, because fish filleting is a sedentary job, the headroom on that particular deck was severely restricted; accordingly, air pollution was not. George Fox of Par had talked about 'stinking fish'; and 'the odour was unutterable', Ellen Crewdson later recalled, in the memoirs of her childhood, about the curing cellars and the 'unctuous flooring' at Portreath. I also knew about Russian wages. In the dry cleaners ashore I would watch the crew inspecting the price tags on the sleeves of coats to be collected, mistakenly thinking they were for sale, and at such reasonable prices. One day I learned that some ships were going to be fined a few hundred pounds for throwing rubbish overboard and allowing it to drift on to the local beaches. Because we knew the dire consequences of this, and because we were aware of the size of the fine, we were in the event able to arrange a preferable solution: that the crew came ashore in their free time and, armed with some plastic sacks, cleaned up the beaches themselves. This proved to be a very good exercise in public relations.

An unforgettable job was in the early 1980s when a transatlantic liner was delayed in Falmouth Bay for a week. For us, this represented a huge amount of work dealing with not only the regular business of the ship, but also a very large number of dissatisfied passengers. The ship arranged two gangways, one for the ship's business and one for the passengers, and used two different corresponding quays in Falmouth. Again, as with the red roses, we were challenged: having to find coaches and Cornish pasties for 1,000 passengers in a hurry, for example.[10]

The same episode illustrated how much it is possible to achieve when one is really under pressure. Having been told that there was never ever any likelihood of Newquay becoming an international airport, suddenly it was possible to charter a jumbo jet to take a whole crowd of impatient passengers to New York. This was an instance of the small airport, as opposed to port, with the long reach; and in its way that flight proved to be inaugural.

On some days during the transatlantic liner's enforced stay, G. C. Fox & Co's agents had to be on board at 6.30 a.m. When the quay punt came alongside the ship, there was a steward standing in the gangway with a tray of rolled-up napkins, which looked as though they were destined to go ashore until I saw behind him another steward with a jug of coffee. This was breakfast (never have bacon baps tasted so delicious) as only Americans know how to organise: an essential start to an effectual working day.

Occasionally accused of using a steamroller to crack a nut, Americans nevertheless have to be admired for their

---

10   It was on this occasion that I was able to persuade some Americans late at night that the 'mysterious little lights' they detected running alongside our quay punt, just below the surface of the water, were laid on by the ship owner to guide us back to the ship in foggy conditions. This fib, if circulated to the rest of the world, can only be to that shipping line's advantage, if to the disadvantage of phosphorescence.

ability to think laterally. In order, for example, to deliver a spare part to a ship, they would work out that it was cheaper to charter a helicopter than slowing down a super tanker, diverting course, paying pilotage and harbour dues, and quay punt charges, etc.

Germans are also ultra-efficient: on spotting the agent approaching in his quay punt they would lower a lifeboat, start the engine in mid-air, and then speed alongside the quay punt, collect the agent, speed back to the side of the ship and then haul the lifeboat back on board. This compares very favourably with the more regular rope ladder dangling over the side of a ship. It is a matter of acute timing as to when you step from the prow of the quay punt on to the ladder. Accidents did happen – sadly sometimes fatal. On one occasion the author broke his hip and femur, not an experience he wishes to repeat.

Some ships had no idea about safety, or seamanship. It is unfair to say which Third World country it came from, but once there was a ship wishing to go from the Bristol Channel to Falmouth. He asked a Dutchman to show him the way. All went well until going around the Lizard peninsula the Dutchman turned to port. A mile behind, the following ship did the same and, as the Cornish are wont to say, 'fetched up' on a rock.

If you, as a stranger, walk through the woods which border the National Trust's garden at Trelissick, leading steeply down to the banks of the River Fal, you will sometimes be surprised, through the branches of the trees, by a surreal scene: the topsides of a ship, weirdly stretched out like a stretch-limo. The estuary is a ria and the water here is very deep: it can accommodate vessels of considerable size. In 1927 the ship agency had the job of looking after an earlier cruise liner which had been laid up temporarily in the River Fal: the Peninsular and Oriental Steam Navigation Company's S. S. *Bendigo*, as described in George Henry Fox's diary entry on 4 November.

'Cuth[bert] brought out to tea Mr White (& his wife) of the P. & O. Service at Falmouth re repairs to Bendigo with 1160 settlers (passengers) put back from Las Palmas to Truro River for transfer of passengers to Balranald bound to Australia.'

A more vivid account is found in the memoir of one of those passengers, who was travelling on the outward voyage of the *Bendigo* to join her son in Western Australia. Having sailed through the Bay of Biscay, one of *Bendigo*'s propellers broke, and on arrival at the next port, Las Palmas in the Canary Islands, it was found that the other propeller was damaged. The steamship was ordered to return to Falmouth for repairs and her passengers endured a nightmare return journey when they 'encountered a storm, in which the crippled steamer behaved like a bird with a broken wing' and was so badly damaged that it required three tugs to tow the ship into Falmouth. It is small wonder that the passengers viewed with dread the prospect of a third crossing within a month of the Bay of Biscay 'in its winter fury'.[11]

All the passengers, together with their luggage, were transferred in Falmouth to P. and O.'s sister ship, S. S.

---

11   Quoted in Chapter 5 of *My Nixey Family*, by Jonathan Nixey (published online at www.blackleadking.org.

Balranald. The cargo, which included six aeroplanes bound for Cape Town and several motor cars (reportedly Mercedes) must have stayed on board the *Bendigo*. Following the transfer, the ship went into the Docks, where it was repaired and 'the cargo replaced in such a manner by Falmouth stevedores that there was room for another 100 tons'.

Apart from dramatic events like this, and one or two other exceptions, ships laid up the River Fal would be mostly awaiting orders. Human nature being what it is, if a ship is left unattended, within a short time opportunists will be on board, swarming over the ship like ants, and again like ants removing whatever they can, as happened in former times with shipwrecks. For this reason, G. C. Fox & Co. employed watchmen, and also a sub-agent called Peter Newman who looked after the ships laid up the River Fal. The delivery of the watchmen's wages by taxi and boat made a pleasant outing for the office staff.

Falmouth is the first and last port of call in the English Channel and there must have been many occasions when ships made use of the shelter and protection afforded by both the River Fal and its tributaries. For centuries too, there had been trading from Tregony, higher up the river, no doubt importing and exporting some of those commodities mentioned in the early letter books of G. C. Fox & Co. Along the creeks which feed into the river there are the vestigial fields of cottagers who grew fruit, and who continue to do so. Two hundred years ago it is unlikely that Vitamin C had been defined, but sailors knew that to combat scurvy a supply of fruit was essential, hence perhaps that little-known expression 'to orchard a ship'.

When Alfred Fox came to the fishing village of Durgan in 1821, perhaps the first thing he observed were the orchards everywhere. At the same time, he must have seen the fish being brought ashore and watched the donkeys, with their panniers full of fish, ambling off to market.

3

THE MEETING HOUSE

WHEN I WAS about five and had been farmed out to stay with my great-aunt and her husband Romney, a partner in the firm, I was one morning trying to help by picking up my uncle's briefcase. Unfortunately, and as I have so often since experienced, the lid was not shut and the next moment there were about a hundred important-looking documents and letters sliding over the polished floor. I thought I was going to be in serious hot water, until my much-loved uncle appeared, said 'Now that doesn't matter in the slightest', and shovelled them all back in again. The office was just a place where the partners went each day, and was always mentioned in rather reverential terms, but perhaps this was the first moment when it entered my head that there was something different about my family and its attitude to business.

If this were a book about businessmen of any other Christian denomination, this chapter might well be titled 'The Church' or 'Chapel'. But I like 'The Meeting House' for a variety of reasons. In the first place it is factual: it was, and still is, the name for the Quakers' place of worship.

Howard Fox recalls,

'George Henry Fox also sat on the front seat by his father (the old brothers having taken independent seats further back – the men then sat under the windows in the N. E. side of the old meeting house and there was a sounding board over the gallery and 3 windows at the S. E. end) – opposite Uncle Charles – a rather fastidious man…as boys we used to get restless to give Uncle Robert (who was accustomed to break up the meeting by shaking hands with his next neighbour on the women's side) a hint but in the end we came to the conclusion that he kept us waiting all the longer.'

His sister Rachel Tuckett expands

'Our morning assembly was very interesting, the dear active labourers of the heavenly vineyard spoke to my heart…'

Secondly, 'The Meeting House' has all the innuendos of coffee houses where men met to conduct their business – as indeed were the origins of Lloyd's underwriters. In the Quaker Meeting House at Come-to-Good, I once noticed a bright red book lying on the desk. Red is an executive colour; and it should be pointed out that, for all their gentle ways, Quakers have always been renowned for their resolve and their ability to respond quickly and efficiently to the problems of this world – and to the alternatives of the next – as we shall see.

Interior of Come-to-Good Quaker Meeting House, near Truro
Photograph © William Fox

Thirdly, it is what Quakers did: they were good at meeting people, and at every level, be it a road-sweeper, or the Queen of Portugal on an official visit. With a natural charm they would elevate the one and humanise the other. Furthermore, they were proficient at making sure that practical deeds met spiritual needs: good works with faith as much as faith accompanied by good works. As discussed elsewhere the concept of stewardship was important to them; and this pervaded their own needs for provision as much as others. When a party of distant Quaker cousins decided to go and meet the Czar of Russia in an attempt to stop him from being nasty to the Turks, they first loaded up in Paris with a quantity of furs, the forerunner of the modern Arctic jacket.

Fourthly, 'meetings' were to the Quakers the very fabric

of their business. In reading through the minutes of the different companies in which the Foxes were involved there seems to be a multitude of meetings, ever since the early days of George Croker Fox (I). In those days these meetings were about the business of being a merchant. In subsequent times the meetings were more about investments, share-holdings and dividends: pages and pages of accounts, and commissions, and percentages, and partners' drawings. In the course of over 300 years there have been about 20 dif-ferent articles of partnership; there is an appendix for those who are interested in this sort of detail. With each new partnership there are supporting agreements, memoranda, deeds of appointment, consultancy agreements, deeds of variation and supplemental partnership deeds. As a new partner was introduced often he would initially be given only a small percentage of the shares, such as in one partic-ular agreement 'two-75ths' (Quakers were extraordinarily commercial in their dealings with relatives). Similarly a partner being phased out into retirement would enter a consultancy agreement. The following entry from the min-utes of a partners' meeting in July 1962 seems today rather academic, and puzzling: under points 'needing consider-ation' was 'the pension position and future of the Partners when they grow old' (it is an interesting question to ask any God-fearing Quaker about his or her future). There were also a great many meetings following the death or retirement of a partner. This is because, on such occasions, a partnership is automatically dissolved. Accountants and solicitors made money, not so much a consideration then as it is now: they charged relatively less and the firm had more reserves. It must also have been quite helpful that one of Alfred's sons, Wilson Fox, had married twice into the Rogers family and practised as a solicitor in their company, Reginald Rogers and Son.

Again looking back, this time at the working life of my father, who was the archetypal businessman, his routine was centred around one meeting after another. They were the stuff of life to him, probably because he had such a good analytical mind; and he had the patience of a Quaker. Although this gave the appearance of being productive, it should be noted that he was mostly unpaid for his time. In this way he may have performed a valuable service to the community, e.g. the Harbour Board, the Pilotage Commission, the Sail Training Association, Cornish Seamen's Benevolent Trust, the Royal National Lifeboat Institution, the Royal Cornwall Yacht Club, the Institute of Chartered Shipbrokers, and several travel organisations, etc. His involvement with these organisations was good for public relations and there is the very Quaker, and Biblical, instruction to 'cast your bread upon the waters, for you will find it again after many days'.

But fifthly, and perhaps most significantly, 'The Meeting House' underlines the title of this book: Quakers sit 'on the brink'. In other words, they are in their element where the two worlds meet:

'This world of ours and worlds unseen
And thin the boundaries in between.'[12]

---

12   From the hymn 'The Lord is King!', words by Josiah Conder, 1824.

Without any implications of spiritualism or the occult, this in fact was very much the way of the Celtic Christian: it was a matter of course that the divine should accompany every aspect of his life, and not just on Sundays, or when he is hatched, matched and dispatched. As an illustration of this, in 1877 the *West Briton* talks about Robert Were Fox (II) in his obituary as 'being earnest in the search after truth, whether revealed from on high, or in the relations of human polity, or in the reign of law in the material world'.

There was a branch of the Fox family living and working in Plymouth and some of them entered the medical practice. His exact relationship to the family has never been confirmed, but a certain Dr Fox was once walking home late one night when he stopped to hear a church clock strike midnight; and the clock struck 13. Suddenly he became aware of a man standing by his side; and the man said, 'Did you hear that?' 'Yes,' said Dr Fox. 'Very strange.' The two men bade each other 'Goodnight' and parted. Months later Dr Fox woke up in the middle of the night and said to his wife, 'I have to go to Bodmin.' 'But', said his wife, as wives are wont to state the obvious, 'it is the middle of the night.' 'I know that', said her husband, as husbands are wont to respond, 'but I must go.' He saddled his horse, rode down to the river, woke up the ferryman, crossed the Tamar and then galloped through what was left of the night until very early in the morning he arrived in Bodmin. Here he found the town to be astir. 'What is going on?' he asked. 'Well, there is to be a hanging today in half an hour's time, unless the condemned man can produce his alibi.' 'Oh, I would like to see the fellow', said

Dr Fox. 'Well, that's him being led up to the stage now,' whereupon Dr Fox recognized the condemned man as the one who had stood next to him outside the church when the bell had struck 13; and the condemned man recognized his alibi.

Quakers liked to meet with God: they loved this sort of divine intervention and anything which had numinous qualities. But this also meant that, in accordance with Biblical instruction, there were certain activities they did not do, or tried not to do: swearing, blaspheming, heavy drinking, etc. In 1755 George Croker Fox (I) wrote 'In Chancery, George Croker Fox one of the People called Quakers doth affirm', etc. This opening proclamation, identifying his sect, was his way of explaining why he would not swear on the Bible or on any occasion, but it was also a remark which gives tacit understanding that the word 'Quaker' was originally a term of mockery. There were some pastimes which for many were unthinkable on a Sunday: card playing, dancing and theatre. This was on top of keeping the day of rest sacred by refraining from work, an issue which had caused consternation amongst both Methodists and Quakers in the fishing industry: less religious fishermen from East Anglia had come sailing down to fish off the Cornish coast on every day of the week.[13]

---

13   It seems odd that this should have become such an issue when it is pointed out in *The Catechisms of George Fox* by Stephen W. Angell that for a Quaker 'the term "Sabbath" is no longer primarily a reference to a day of the week, but to an inward attitude of rest and peace' – on any day of the week. (See quakertheology.org/issue-9-angell-02.htm)

There was of course the view taken by some that if the pilchards were stupid enough to shoal on Sunday then they should be duly punished, and that being caught in a seine net was as much their own funeral, as it was for a ripe fruit to be picked. After all, one of the Fox family had once opined that 'a pear is at its best for twenty minutes during which time it may be seen to glow with a peculiar radiance by all those who care to look at it'. The opportunity of a lifetime has to be grabbed within the lifetime of that opportunity. In 1871 a poet – and punster – from Penzance had put this all into a poem. Who Mr Foster is remains unknown.

' 'Tis a terrible thing these "schools" of fish
Mr Foster – sir, I devoutly wish
You'd kindly say, what education
Would be vouchsafed, sir, by the nation,
To pilchards on the Sabbath day,
Which in our seas begin to play?
We know they're meant by the Power on high,
To help us save for our bye-and-bye;
They mean fresh meat, and fuel, and health,
And cosy hearths, – to some, mean wealth,
To all, they're welcome – and yet 'tis Sunday;
Why couldn't they wait twelve hours! Till Monday!!
My friends, the Power that sent them here,
Wished you to keep them – don't you fear!
Like the manna which Moses brought down for the
    Jews,
It was picked at the moment, they dare not refuse!
Yet conscience may prick you – let me tell you a way

To punish the fish for arriving this day,
First "shoot" everyone – don't miss, 'tis "in seine";
Then "take them all up" for your duty is plain:
They've broken the Sabbath!! One cannot endure them
And having done this, you will very soon "cure" them!!'

One cannot help thinking that, unlike manna, pilchards did occasionally make an appearance on the Sabbath. This was evidently as difficult to resist, as it was for anyone who wanted to rescue his ass or his ox from a pit, on the Sabbath. In the end there is some sympathy for the Martha-like directness, and faith, of those who were simply desperate to make enough money to put bread on the table, even if they were not putting the Kingdom of Heaven first. Another poet, this time from Cadgwith, in 1907 wrote 'THE SEINER'S PRAYER':

'Lord, let me catch a school of fish
So large that even I
When talking of it afterwards,
Will have no cause to lie.
And let the weather be the best
That I can ship them East and West.
Send me a buyer who'll pay the freight
And furnish luggers free,
And then, Lord, put the prices up,
And I'll contented be.'

The Quaker view of pilchards shoaling on a Sunday is unclear, but if nothing else, Quakers were sensible and could, like the poet who came from Cadgwith, be refreshingly straightforward.

They also had intuition.

One learns to distrust those who dress in a certain way: the cut of a collar, or the height of a heel, for example. These little signs are often impossible to rationalise. Similarly there is a certain type of writing which again for no apparent reason arouses suspicion. Perhaps it was to impress, but in a distinctly flowery hand one of the Falmouth ship agents in 1880 wrote to G. C. Fox & Co. as follows:

> 'In reply to your communication of yesterday's date, we beg to inform you that we have never been asked to sample a cargo on the Sabbath day, neither have we done so, and are glad to learn from Messrs Broads that you join in the arrangement not to do so.'

It seems as if the finger of the one who assumes he is accused is turned, and 'doth protest too much'. In a contrastingly straightforward style of writing, however, there is an added note in which G. C. Fox & Co. own up to being only as pure as the driven slush:

> 'Wm Broad saw GHF & RF allowed that on one occasion they had sampled a steamer on a Sunday but gave his word that they wd not do so again. So all are agreed.'

So much for Pharisaical behaviour amongst the Falmouth ship agents.[14]

The Meeting House gave Quakers a set of boundaries in which to do as they pleased, and curiously, as with another well-known Christian sect, the Amish community, there comes with that a degree of freedom. Unlike today, they were not going to kow-tow to the pressures and whims of society, but rather to what they felt, and had been told, was pleasing to their Maker, and therefore to them as well.

But it must have been a struggle, and there were indeed those who fell from grace, such as a young lady who eloped (a word not in much use today): she climbed out of a bedroom window at beautiful Meudon and rode off into the night with a soldier, no doubt on a snowy white steed. Perhaps, too, he was French, which would have added to the allure, and heightened the scandal. [15]

I do not know what became of them.

Most readers will be familiar with the world of the eighteenth or nineteenth century as portrayed by the power of the television in dramas and romances, and how frustrating life must have been, especially to Quakers who

---

14 Samples of cargoes, especially of grain, were taken in order to be sent to markets in London, and presumably elsewhere. From these samples an entire cargo could be sold and orders for the vessel in Falmouth would then be issued to proceed to a port of discharge. It was not always the easiest of tasks: George Henry Fox records G. C. Fox & Co. prevailing on Broads to send down one of their own men, who said afterwards that 'he had to get down to the cargo through a ventilator!' (Diary, before 1907)

15 Meudon, at Mawnan near Falmouth, was used to house French prisoners-of-war during the Napoleonic Wars.

were not allowed to marry outside their sect. But at the same time it must have been exciting. There was plenty of forbidden fruit; and you do not have to look very far to discover that Quakers were, and are, the perfect audience for stories of aberration. They have never had confessionals, but have always been understanding, patient, tolerant and loving.

In the face of temptation, it is no wonder that as a start to the day, morning prayers were *de rigeur*; and among the business letters to each other and to their Quaker connections, there is often a page or two of preamble focusing on their gratitude for the gift of life and all its blessings. For example:

'Much of our comfort and satisfaction, my beloved cousin I believe consists in this, being strengthened to do the right thing in the right time; and oh that our views may be more and more turned this way even after a suitable Disposition to know the Divine Will and strength to perform it.'

But the one which stands out as being appropriate for this particular narrative is the memoir written by Alfred Fox's sister in 1817:

'We had to take leave of our dear Alfred, before we went to bed, for some weeks' separation as he has to set out on the following day for London per coach, my darling brother tho' thou art so frequently divided from us by distance how often do I desire for thee as for myself that the omnipotent Pilot may always guide thy little barque & that thou may'st cooperate with Him.'

So often this is a recurring theme: the concept of being sent into the world for a relatively short time, as much on a little barque as in a 'Moses basket'; and there to do one's best to follow God's will, and to return to Him. In this way Quakers were both on the brink of this world and the next. The one influenced the other: to do good to mankind and to be conscientious stewards were a necessary part of the journey, as was divine instruction. Perhaps at this point the reader needs to be reminded that, as much as anywhere else, life in Cornwall nearly 200 years ago had its dangers: disease, such as cholera, which Alfred Fox had noted in his journal, infant mortality and premature death, industrial accidents, ship wrecks, and war. Charlotte Fox recalls 'wounded soldiers, who had come from the battle of Corunna' passing her home in carts or chairs and 'presenting a sickening comment on the woes resulting from war'. She continues:

'I remember too, watching from our nursery window a poor man swimming backwards and forwards before the house, with, I think, his clothes in his mouth, vainly endeavouring to escape the fearful press gang watching to seize him as their prey.'

Nor was the Fox family immune: Alfred had seven of his children all with whooping cough at the same time, and as many claims on his purse as he could 'conveniently meet', he wrote to his cousin Edward in 1844. Piracy, smuggling, the white slave trade, the evils of alcohol and other addictions were also commonplace. One of the more uncivilized characteristics of so-called civilizations is that prosperity and affluence go hand in hand with poverty, and often exploitation, and slavery. In the nineteenth century there were those who went hungry; and there were thousands who starved to death.

Meanwhile there was plenty of opportunity for the devout.

This is well illustrated by a touching story involving Alfred Fox's wife, Sarah. It is included in its entirety for other reasons. It gives a very good flavour of Falmouth in the days of town criers. It describes a time when some of its populace were prospering and others were destitute. It shows a typically Quaker absence of judgement and more the keenness to take advantage of a very clear opportunity to do good to our fellow men.

'Wodehouse Place
Falmouth   11th month 1882

In the beginning of the year 1870 I lost a roll of Bank notes under the following circumstances. They were Tweedy's local notes £5 – there were nine rolled up together and they were new and stiff. I went across with them to the Post Office where I exchanged one of them and then putting them in my reticule went up Well Lane to see a poor woman, and whilst talking to her extracted from the reticule under my cloak a trifle to give her. At Market Strand I had to pay a bill but the notes were not in the reticule. I hurried back to the poor woman not doubting they were on her kitchen floor but alas! they were not there. I went to the Post Office and then to the Bank to see if they had their numbers but local notes were not numbered. What was to be done? Happily in my dismay I saw Blanche and Sophy in the street and on telling them my distress the former suggested to have them cried! I consented although very hopeless as to the results. However I left it in their hands having company at home and I hastened back in sad discomfiture… I told them to offer £5 reward and they did so, and in less than an hour they were recovered – they had been picked up by the wife of a poor man out side the bank and must have been entangled in my dress when I went to Market Strand. The man was a drinking person and they were living in a furnished room in dirt and misery – but on receiving the reward which was wealth to him he at once resolved to raise himself out of the slough into which he had fallen. He got himself tidy clothes, they got a room and furnished it and entered on the trade with all the help of his wife of mending umbrellas and china and thus maintained themselves respectably. He assured me only a few weeks ago that he had given up drink from that time of finding the notes nearly thirteen years ago and that he had been greatly helped by what the young lady did to him and should never forget her words – she put "a Band of hope" in to his hands with the words "God has put it into my heart to try and do thee good". "I have shown" [*he said*] "that band of hope till it was worn to shreds and although I never saw her before or since I could never forget her words." '

This absolute commitment to a Christian way of life governed all the Foxes' business dealings, as much as their social lives. Henry Scott Holland's words, so often a source of comfort at funerals, talk about how as a ship disappears from our view over the horizon, so it is welcomed into someone else's view. The theology of this may be questionable, but it still is another aspect of the fascination Quakers had for all good things beyond, as well as within, the brink, and the concept of Heaven in particular. Equally, there is for so many a fascination for what enters into our immediate worlds from over the brink of the horizon. The owner of a house progresses from his house into a garden; and businessmen go out of their offices and explore the boundaries. Unlike maps which show no partiality for either land or sea, there are hardly any paintings of Falmouth that look towards the horizon of the hinterland: they focus on the distant brink, beyond the sea. Not mined in Cornwall, but within Alfred Fox's collection of minerals there would have been a sample of lapis lazuli; and its colour, ultramarine, means 'beyond the seas' (perhaps this is because sea is not really a pink-blue, in spite of Thomas Hardy's words 'and purples prinked the main'). For Quakers, as much as any potential business beyond the seas, such as the remote possibility of mining lapis lazuli in Afghanistan, the brink also represented a Heavenly destiny. This might have been what Sir Francis Drake described in a prayer as 'the horizons of our hopes'. It begins,

'Disturb us, Lord, when we are too well pleased with
     ourselves,
When our dreams have come true
Because we have dreamed too little,
When we arrived safely
Because we sailed too close to the shore.'

But there are some interesting observations to be made. One of many unsaid Quaker tenets is to see good in everyone, even if it is to the detriment of one's judgement. There were, however, exceptions. On 29 September 1722 George Fox of Par started a letter to William Pawley as follows: 'Thy proud imperious & afronting letter came this day to my hand but to answer in an agreeable style is out of my way', and ends it 'also no one is more ready to answer a Civill Question than him who thou dost so much abuse'. We are not told the details of poor Mr Pawley's crime. George's son, George Croker Fox (I), wrote in October 1770 'I hate wrangling as much as any man but certainly where a man is ill used he has a right to complain'. The following year, for example, he became very cross about a quantity of damaged hemp, 'indisputably spoil'd' in a 'futil little vessel'. It is in this way always very reassuring, that a benign attitude did not prevent the partners from recognising the truth about a trading situation – or indeed a person, such as a scoundrel, or 'dirty fellow' as they liked to say, when they came across one: Robert Barclay Fox (I) must be admired for his almost Dickensian turn of phrase:

'I found him to be the sole clerk in the office of Tripp the share broker. The first glance was enough – a black-looking hook-nosed shabby genteel, smelling strong of spirits and altogether a creature whom I should instinctively avoid – He blew his own trumpet pretty loud – knowledge of accounts, epistolary, accomplishments etc. So I soon wished him Good Morning and said if we could not do better he should hear from us but we wanted one accustomed to a Foundry.'

The gentle spirit of a Quaker did not necessarily mean he was a man of straw. In 1795, George Croker Fox (II), writing to the newspapers about 'an eventful voyage', ended it quite forcefully: 'We shall continue to consider ourselves the victims of about as cold blooded a piece of inhumanity as ever disgraced the annals of British seamanship'. Equally forthright was the way in which George Henry Fox married theological teaching with pragmatism: on one occasion a drunken seaman (not uncommon in the life of a ship agent) attempted to swipe him on the cheek, but missed his target. Another aspect of the title of this book is that Quakers, like so many Christians, are often 'driven to the brink'; and so George, having offered him his other cheek, with the words 'have another go' (this also failed) is reputed to have said 'I have now done as I am bid by my maker; and will now proceed to kick thee down the steps'. As with so many things in their lives – most notably family letters and wills – acknowledgement, and often gratitude to God came first, but was often swiftly followed by appropriate practical action.

There is another story about an old Falmouth sea captain of the eighteenth century. Again a committed Quaker, he found himself in an unfortunate predicament when his vessel was overtaken by a French privateer. He therefore decided to abandon the steering of his ship and handed it over, with temporary command, to his chief officer. For a while the captain then paced up and down the decks, before he returned to the officer and said: 'My friend thou knowest I am a man of peace and not of war, but if thou would'st sink the ship, then port thy helm, friend! Port thy helm!'

This successful advice, incidentally, was the traditional way of saying 'Go to starboard', for vessels using a tiller, or as in the case of the *Titanic*, *as if* they were using a tiller. If this did not cause massive confusion on that tragic occasion, it must have done so in the early 1930s when the British Merchant Navy was brought into line with the rest of the world so that all orders were given as wheel orders, and 'hard a starboard' meant 'turn right'.

Except for some early models which incorporated a tiller, it has always been mercifully simpler with motor cars.

In the Preface to this book, mention is made of my reluctance to plod down the well-trodden roads of all that the Internet has to say about the Fox family; and as it happens Quakers, like the Jews, were indeed a world wide web. An example of this is the following account. One of the banking Backhouses learnt that his enemy the Earl of Darlington was planning a run on the bank. Jonathan Backhouse galloped to London, and back, in order to obtain all the gold he needed from his Quaker acquaintances and, what is more, had pleasure in telling Lord

Darlington's agent the next day that he still had enough to buy the entire Raby estates.[16]

This book, about the history of a family shipping business, cannot be written without reference to another story which has been told many times, and with some variations. One of the earliest versions is recorded in the first of 20 volumes entitled *The Percy Anecdotes*[17], published in 1823, which I reproduce here in full:

PRIVATEERING

During the war with France in 1780, Mr Fox, a merchant of Falmouth, had a share in a ship, which the other owners determined to fit out as a letter of marque, very much against the wishes of Mr. Fox, who was a Quaker. The ship had the good fortune to take two French merchantmen, and the share of

16   It was reported that on the return journey from London to Darlington, one of the fore wheels came off the chaise in which Jonathan Backhouse was carrying the supply of bullion. Rather than wait to have the wheel replaced, the banker piled the gold at the back part of the chaise, so 'balancing the cash' and driving into Darlington upon three wheels. With characteristic brevity, it is recorded in the Bank's books for 1819 as follows: '6th month, 25th day. To Bank and Cash to London: £32,000.' In the '7th month, 31st day' there was a debit of '£2.3.0: wheel demolished'.

17   *The Percy Anecdotes. Original and Select*, by Sholto and Reuben Percy, Brothers of the Benedictine Monastery, Mont Benger. Volume 1, from which this extract is taken, is sub-titled 'Humanity:–Beneficence' and is aptly dedicated to William Wilberforce, MP, in recognition of his contribution to the abolition of slavery.

the prize money which fell to Mr. Fox, was £1500. At the close of the war, Mr. Fox sent his son (who was soon afterwards elected physician to the Bristol Infirmary,) to Paris, with the £1500, which he faithfully refunded to the owners of the vessels captured. The young gentleman, to discover the owners, was obliged to advertize for them in the Paris papers. In consequence of this advertisement, he received a letter from a small village near Nismes [*sic*], in the province of Languedoc, acquainting him that a society of Quakers was established in that remote part of France, consisting of about one hundred families; that they were so much struck with this rare instance of generosity in one of their sect, that they were desirous to open a correspondence with him in England; which immediately commenced.

The 'Mr. Fox' in question was Joseph Fox, brother to the George Croker Fox (I) who was the founder of the ship agency in Falmouth.

Joseph was a surgeon in the town and because, as his son so neatly puts it,

'in country situations the practice of this art furnishes but slender opportunity for much emolument…he was always forward to embrace any lawful means of advancing his circumstance.'

There is nothing wrong in that, and for many in Cornwall the same truth still stands today. So, 'according to his pecuniary ability he took small shares in mines, he held one or two with his brother in merchant vessels, and he was part owner in a Lisbon packet for several years.'

He also had a quarter part in two luggers or cutters which were used to protect the Revenue against smugglers along the Cornish coast.

The trouble started in 1778 when during the War of American Independence France declared war in support of the colonists, and English revenue cutters, armed for privateering, proved very effective in capturing prizes from the French. Interestingly in a deed dated 30 September in the same year, George Croker Fox was appointed agent at Penryn for 'taking care of…all such Prisoners of war…at that place'; and going back to the 1750s there are, equally, letters which show concern for English prisoners of war in France.

Not surprisingly Joseph, being a Quaker,

'remonstrated against…withdrawing the vessels from a lucrative and lawful occupation, to employ them in one which was hazardous, expensive and dangerous but above all, so contrary to his religious opinions.'

He even suggested that his non-Quaker fellow shareholders should buy him out,

'but this was rejected, and the plea of the minority being bound by the will of the majority, compelled him to submit to all the risk without the pleasing anticipations which others less scrupulous do not fail to allow themselves.'

At this stage we should pause and observe two points. The first is the foolishness of embarking on any joint venture with partners who do not share your own religious convictions, or at any rate a higher code of ethics; and this was not the first or last time that members of the family had fallen into this trap. The Quaker attitude 'to see good in all mankind' can bring with it the penalties of naivety. The second is the dangers of compromise. Historically Quakers abhorred voting. It resulted in a majority and necessarily a minority, in their opinion both equally dangerous and tantamount to a compromise. This is ironical: there are many instances where it has been preferable to compromise than go to war. But even then, as we have witnessed with this country's politics, a compromise is not a wholly happy solution.

Naturally 'after ample success had attended this undertaking' the other shareholders most unrighteously declared that in the light of his objections he should forfeit his rewards from the venture. Again very significantly Joseph protested, arguing that 'having now become possessed of a property of another' he then thereby became 'a trustee to the original proprietors to whom he felt restitution' should be made.

Imagine the weight on his conscience. First he had jumped into bed with clearly a bunch of scoundrels. Secondly the character of the joint venture turned into one which was frowned upon by the Society of Friends, and thirdly he took the much more difficult decision to see that right should come out of wrong ... and not for himself (he was even offered a very handsome annuity) but for a scattered collection of unknown Frenchmen all living the other side of the English Channel. Not unsurprisingly he said nothing of this to his wife or family – nor would a great many husbands on even lesser issues. But in 1784 he wrote to his son Edward Long Fox, who was finishing his medical studies in Edinburgh, and asked him not to settle immediately as a physician but to go on his behalf to transact some business in Paris, in other words the restitution of between £1,200 and £1,300.

> 'I wish thee to go to Paris and Holland to transact some business for me, which would afford thee much pleasure, and more to others, who will cheerfully allow the expense of thy journey.'

The underlying message here is that there was no one else he could trust. 'Be very circumspect and cautious in thy answers to the Claimants,' he advised his son.

It also shows a rare degree of humility and closeness that he should eventually place his confidence in a member of his family. The restitution of funds was easier said than done and finally in February 1785 an advertisement had to be placed in the *Gazette de France*. In spite of his father's death at about this time, Edward plodded on with his mission, touchingly because of the foresight of the letter of instruction. He finally discharged his obligations in 1817, by establishing a fund for the relief of aged and distressed merchant seamen.

The whole mission demonstrates a refreshing measure of paternal authority being exercised in the life of a 23-year-old – and in time Edward's acceptance of the instruction shows how in turn he honoured his parent's request. It undeniably was going to give Edward and his wife the opportunity to travel, but more importantly it would give a greater abundance of pleasure to others; we are not on this planet just to please ourselves. It also suggests that Edward might have expected to receive remuneration from some of the recipients. But it must have been hard having to explain that this was the nature of his job, and not just to his believing family.

This well-known story and my less than amateur exegesis are included because it is an illustration of being 'on the brink of the world'. What looked like a fair opportunity in worldly terms (Quakers had a keen eye for making money) turned out in terms of Quaker ethics to be a non-starter. Yet again this non-conformist family was thrown up against the brink. Contrary to current practices, there was simply no way in which they wished to 'lick' the world: lick in the sense of 'conquer', lick in the sense of 'punish', and although they had high values of stewardship, lick in the sense of hedonistically squeezing out every last drop of enjoyment. Being on the brink was for a Christian the correct place to be, as is indicated in the following extract from a letter of appreciation written to Edward by the Quakers of Nîmes, dated 1 April 1785:

'The testimony which thou hast borne to France of the inviolable attachment to the true principles of Christ and of thy humane and pacific Disposition which has inclined thee to do good to thine enemies has caused the hearts of the Brethren to leap for joy…Proceed

Dear Friend with undaunted courage and incorruptible Zeal to accomplish the good work which thou hast begun, let not the numberless Vices of a corrupt Metropolis taint the purity of thy Faith…may'st thou escape victoriously all the mares which many will lay for thy Integrity. Consider that in the midst of a depraved multitude who narrowly scrutinize all thy actions with design to invalidate that eminent principle which gave birth to thy good deeds and to cast a shade on the Lustre which has dazzled the eyes of Mankind, that thou canst do nothing unseen by the supreme being and that as thy actions will undergo the strict scrutiny and close investigation of Slander, they will impress beholders with profound Respect or Sovereign contempt for our Religious principles…'

and so on, for four pages of foolscap. This act of redressing the balance was good training for Edward Long Fox: he was one of the first doctors to treat the insane humanely. Formerly it had been the practice to fetter those who were termed lunatics, but his asylum, opened in 1790, held a more enlightened and loving approach; and this was maintained by his descendants at Brislington House near Bristol until 1947.

Years later Alfred Fox had cause to refer to this famous story, as recorded by his son George:

'Our father was always delighted to tell us of the great honour and trust conferred on him after the peace in 1815 when he chaperoned 6 young ladies through Belgium to Paris & home. They were posted with 4 horses throughout – visited the field of Waterloo with the greatest interest – His charges spent so freely in buying souvenirs – that when they reached Paris he found he had not money enough to bring them home. He went to a Paris Banker one of Fox & Co.'s Correspondents & told the Banker exactly how he was situated – The Banker was extremely polite but said they had a rule [*which*] was never broken [*and which*] was never to advance money without personal identification. Our father sd in that case they must wait in Paris until he cd get money from Falmouth. He then had a vy pleasant talk with the Banker & casually mentioned that one of the Fox family who owned a share in a vessel that made prizes of French vessels going to war had after the peace gone to France to distribute his share of the prize money amongst the French owners of the vessels and the vessels' captains. The Banker said That is sufficient introducing. You shall – I know all abt it – You shall have the money.'

Little did he know that he was talking to someone who was closely related to both the Barclay and Lloyd banking families, and who, more to the point, was totally scrupulous when it came to money matters, both personal and business. In the absence of a legitimate arrangement, the habit of paying one's debts seems to die hard and even today a member of the family will be respected rather than ridiculed for returning just a few pence to its rightful owner. In fact, the principles of honesty are such that there is generally more insistency about paying debts than retrieving them; although there was one occasion when my father bounded downstairs and out of the building into the street to apprehend a mystified port official secretary who thought that 'borrowing' the use of the photocopier at Fox's cost nothing.

On the subject of banks, G. C. Fox & Co. did not have their own bank but, like so many companies, it certainly issued its own promissory notes. Fox, Fowler and Co., the Wellington Foxes' bank with branches in Launceston and Bude, was the last private English bank to issue its own notes, and to be taken over by Lloyds in 1921; and, as another indication of the trust placed in these Quaker businesses, when the pound plummeted or the national currency was in short supply, the public had more faith in what was known as a 'Fox' than in a 'Bank of England'.

If there is one aspect of the business which brings out the strong Christian character of the partners more than any other, it is in their treatment of the staff. One of the benefits of pre-computer days was that working out the salaries each month meant that one spent a few minutes thinking about each member of staff. A side benefit was that it exercised the brain: some of us resorted to rather a noisy thing called a calculating machine but my father used his head, and his fingers, with the result that as a child I enjoyed inventing complicated multiplications for him to solve, which he did with ease.

But retaining a Christian attitude and at the same time being disciplinary must at times have been difficult, and remains difficult. There are numerous references in the Partners' Minutes to the problems which arise from too much alcohol:

'We told him that we would rather sacrifice business than obtain it through anyone in our employ frequenting public houses' and 'recommended him to look out for something more likely to promote his welfare and more free from temptation.'

Everyone knew the story of the wreck of the *Queen* Transport in 1814, which is referred to in Chapter 5, and how many of the crew were intoxicated: in a little book called *A Panorama of Falmouth*, published in 1827, it mournfully records

'It will remain a lesson for all Mariners, never to be off their watch nor unprepared for storms, for thus in the safest harbour the Vessel and so many lives were lost, when with sobriety and common care no danger could ensue'.

In 1958, it is minuted that one member of staff had been 'sufficiently frightened' by my grandfather 'to mend his ways'. In 1969 my father wrote in a report that two staff had resigned, a manager and a secretary. As a true Quaker who prefers to see the good in people, he wrote 'There is quite a story to this but not worthy of inclusion in these minutes'. Previous partners were in the custom of referring to an 'unfortunate affair' without ever tarnishing the Minutes Books with the sordid detail. The tragedy of the company's records as a whole, and of this literary effort, is that in this way the really interesting details are disappointingly omitted from the primary sources. To the chagrin of some readers, there are also a few stories which I, in my turn, have decided to omit.

Again in 1969, this time talking more understandably about a 16-year-old boy, he wrote that the new employee had previously been working for a firm of well-known solicitors, but 'was fired by them for using a four-lettered word'. My father was good at giving people a second chance, especially in the world of shipping, where swearing and other misdemeanours were commonplace. Many years ago, a foreigner on a ship heard one particular word used so frequently in Falmouth Docks that he asked what it meant and was told it was the English equivalent of *Ça va*, or *Va bene*.

He did not practise it for long.

There was also embezzlement and fraud, causing not just loss of funds but major headaches when the crime had been revealed and the accounts had to be investigated, often by a partner. Never a word is recorded in judgement, but just the stark facts: 'He is deficient in smartness, accuracy and diligence' and sometimes a line which says more by its brevity, such as 'He sailed for Philadelphia early in March'.

Long and loyal service was cherished and recognised: John Downing was given a fluted silver bowl in 1907 in appreciation of the association he and his father had enjoyed with the firm. But the partners also expected dedicated service: in 1878 it was minuted that Howard Fox would

'arrange with the parents of one of the unmarried clerks and with the youth himself to sleep in the office in the room lately occupied by E. Trerice who is married.'

This was still going on, the minutes for the Falmouth Towage Company record, in 1914, should someone be 'called out during the night to get tugs away'.

This office/bedroom, as it might today be called, was a mere slip of a room, later to become 'the switchboard room' – spatially lacking in generosity for such a large house. 48 Arwenack Street has a labyrinth of cellars, attics, and, in those days, often empty rooms; and for a Quaker establishment it is a building in which, surprisingly, some very murky things have happened. Having spent many nights there working on my own into the early hours of the morning, I can vouch that it is not the happiest of experiences, let alone listening to the cheerful neighbouring sounds of broken glass, street brawls, vomiting, and worse.

What is strange in view of this particular requirement for unmarried clerks, is how the partners would put themselves out to accommodate employees who were having a difficult time. There are many examples of this, and of old-fashioned paternalism. When in July 1911 Captain Foss steered the *Dragon* on to the Blackhead at 12.30 a.m., on the way home from fishing in Mount's Bay, and caused some calculable damage to the tug, it was considered a minor aberration and he was reinstated. When the Union-Castle agency came to an end in 1913 'Walton – who conducted this Uni-Castle work very diligently', was given a present of £50 and the promise of future commissions. When in May 1916 Mr Reader went to join the Forces, the partners agreed to 'pay his wife £1 a week to enable her to keep their house'. That is about £60 today, but no doubt it would have bought more in those days than it does today. When in June 1930

Mr Daniell died after nearly 60 years' employment, his widow was given £200. When members of staff were ill, their families would be subsidized. Even with instances of misdemeanour they were generous: when an employee 'left suddenly after receiving his salary leaving debts behind', the Partners 'paid his landlady half what he owed her £7 -10/-'. They tried to resist the pressures of the outside world; and when other businessmen would have cut back and economised, they stretched out to their staff, and their dependants, and lavished care and affection. In June 1917 it was agreed to raise the salaries. It was also minuted: 'All our clerks have had handsome war bonuses in addition in view of their devoted service under exceptional pressure'.

In my time we would sometimes help with medical expenses; and we made loans, not all of which have been repaid.

During the First World War, several enemy ships were captured and brought into Falmouth. The landing of aliens was a delicate operation, often involving passengers, both first class and steerage, as with the *Kronprinzessen Cecilie*, a very classy liner with a Jugendstil interior[18]. Many Falmothians felt their town was being treated like a 'dumping ground for aliens', in the words of Robert Barclay Fox (II), a Harbour Commissioner at

---

18   The term 'Jugendstil' (from the German 'Youth Style') refers to the German form of Art Nouveau, the movement of decorative art popular from the late nineteenth century up to the First World War.

the time.[19] But how much worse it must have been for the aliens: jettisoned from what Thomas Hardy, in his poem *The Convergence of the Twain: Lines on the Loss of the 'Titanic'* (1912), described as 'vaingloriousness'. The crew, one website narrates, 'were transferred to various local workhouses' with, perhaps written rather despairingly, 'some being sent to Redruth'. The *Kronprinzessen Cecilie* and the attendant *Prinz Adalbert* were apprehended and brought into Falmouth Harbour just after the outbreak of war in August 1914. The passengers (by then referred to as 'aliens') and crew were disembarked before both ships were taken to London in charge of the Admiralty. Falmouth would have been swarming with troops, and of course with Germans and other foreigners awaiting extradition or voluntary return to their own countries. On 14 August 1914 the Austrian Ambassador, Count Mensdorff, with a retinue of two hundred people, arrived from London on the fastest express train ever run, and embarked on the *Aaro* for Genoa, as diplomatically as one would expect.

About this time, the family was arranging its own Quaker meetings for peace and also campaigning against anti-German propaganda (apparently 'women shouted all kinds of nasty expressions'). Members of the family did this by writing letters to the press and giving talks. At least one of my great-aunts came to work in the office as

---

19   Pamela Richardson, 'A Quaker Record of Maritime Falmouth in World War One', *Troze* (the Online Journal of the National Maritime Museum Cornwall www.nmmc.co.uk), Vol. 1, No. 2, December 2008, p. 6.

a clerk, and another found herself a modest job in Lloyds Bank, which shows both her complete lack of pride, and disregard for the fact that coincidentally this bank was founded by her grandmother's family. Another aunt, Erica, who had joined the firm in 1915 and did bookkeeping and typing (a remarkable change in role for a young middle class Quakeress of that time), kept a journal. On the front of this, the title reads 'Notes & memos of sundry events & experiences at Falmouth when war broke out 1914 & subsequently there & elsewhere – mostly kept by Erica', but nothing is mentioned of her personal thoughts about the war as a Quaker. On the back it says 'Executors of Elizabeth Fox Copy book 1849' and inside this end of the book several pages have been excised and an alphabetical index cut in order to record, in the late 1880s, the random finds of a conchologist. Such was the habit of Quakers wishing to economise on paper at the beginning of a war. One of Erica's earliest entries, in August 1914, is as follows:

'A Belgian Officer gave Cuthbert an American water melon. It is very large rose pink inside and deliciously cool and refreshing to taste.'

Quakers were endlessly in pursuit of a silver lining.

4

THE SIGNAL STATION

OCCASIONALLY, WHEN I was a boy, my father would include the family in some of his more colourful business engagements. One example was going with him in June 1958 to see Prince Philip open the Queen Elizabeth Dock in Falmouth; I remember being very disappointed that the Queen's husband was not wearing a crown, but a brown hat, and a brown suit to match, with flapping trousers. Another treat was flying to London for the day, and on the way home being allowed to sit in the cockpit, and watch England taper into its toes: Cornwall surrounded by the sea, and the sun going down over the curve of the sea's horizon.

Then one day, at the end of the summer holidays, he asked if we would like to go with him to the opening of the new Lizard lifeboat station at Kilcobben Cove. The Lizard to us in those days was the unknown territory on the other side of the river; we knew a few beaches on the North coast and had stopped for picnics on Bodmin Moor, but never the Lizard.

The odd thing was that, like helicopters at night, once again nothing was explained by my father: the role that lifeboats had to play in his work, what the Royal National

Lifeboat Institution was, what his role within it was, and what this boathouse was doing in such a strange location. I looked at the yellowing bracken and the sea birds diving around the precipitous cliffs and wanted to explore this exciting new country. Generally I preferred the company of adults, rather than my own contemporaries, but on that glorious afternoon I wanted to leave the grown-ups and all their speeches.

I had to wait another ten years before I could begin to learn what the Lizard had meant to the success of the business.

In my book *Glendurgan*, in the chapter headed 'Falmouth for Orders' (this, in other words, was the place where notification could be given of the final consignee), it says

'For an old-fashioned, family run company, which radiated centuries of stability rather than high technology, G. C. Fox & Co. always kept abreast of the times.'

There is always power in the combination of business acumen and the world of science, and with the technological advances in computers the same is as true today as it was in the nineteenth century.

The first instance of the Foxes embracing communication technology was their signal station on the Lizard. For those who are unfamiliar with the definition, this is 'a place on shore from which signals are made to ships at sea'. The free encyclopaedia might be inclined to add 'and to which ships may send signals'.

Partners' Minutes indicate that discussions about a telegraph and signal station were being held in 1870. But it was not until 1872 that, in order to obtain the first information of sailing ships passing the Lizard, the firm built a signal station: a two-storey whitewashed building with a south-east facing five-sided bay with windows on each side, and a flat roof, surrounded by a castellated parapet, with a look-out structure and a mast for flag signals.[20] It was connected by wire to the Public Telegraph Service, the overland electric telegraph having reached Falmouth in 1857. A circular dated 25 March 1872 subtly declares however that the station would be for the benefit of the ship-owner rather than the ship agent:

'Having long felt the great desirability of a Signal Station at the Lizard, whereby Merchants and Ship-owners might have prompt advice of all Vessels in which they may be interested passing that point, we have built a Signal Station house, 30 feet high with a Signal Staff adjoining the roof on the highest and most conspicuous point in the Lizard District, viz: on Beast point [*Bass Point*], about ¾ of a mile East of the Lizard Light-houses.'

20   The signal station (now a private dwelling) was listed in 1984 by English Heritage.

Lloyd's Signal Station, The Lizard

There was opposition from the Post Master General. The Partners' Minutes for 4 May 1872 state as follows:

'The Post Office Department having sent us no answer to our recent letters nor any draft agreement as promised we opened the station for signalling purposes on the 2nd April and announced the fact by issuing 1000 circulars and advertising in the shipping Gazette, New York Herald & Tribune etc.'

There was also a problem with a competing Falmouth ship agent, William Broad and Sons, who built their own signal station nearby, and who claimed access over the lane to Fox's signal station. They even had the audacity to erect a flagstaff almost in front of Fox's station. G. C. Fox & Co. bought up the surrounding fields, but even so George Henry Fox had to enlist the help of some stout local fishermen to patrol his hedges; and at one stage, he warned any likely trespassers that they would find 'every hedge and ditch lined with man and cudgel' – a belligerent threat for a supposedly peace-loving family. Strangely, another interpretation of the title of this book *On the Brink* is that 'brinkmanship' is 'the art of advancing to the very brink of war but not engaging in it.' In this instance, the situation was satisfactorily resolved when in the end it was decided that it was better if the two companies worked together rather than in opposition – and certainly considerably less confusing for passing ships wanting to signal and receive signals. A joint company was formed at the beginning of 1875 to run the station, under the name Fox, Broad & Company.

In April 1872 G. C. Fox & Co. had sent out another circular explaining the situation:

'The Post Office Department have undertaken to erect and maintain a Telegraphic Wire from the Signal Station direct to Falmouth, but pending the completion of the Wire, we purpose despatching all important messages by man and horse to the nearest Postal Telegraph Office, at Helston (about 1 hour distant) and from that place by the Public Wires'.

By June they were able to send out a refinement on the original flier, effectively a sub-lease of rooms to the Post Office:

'We beg to advise you that the Government has opened a Postal Telegraph Office in our Signal Station at the Lizard, so that we are now prepared to report by direct telegraph all vessels signalled off that point.'

The cable direct to Falmouth had been laid. In the same month they sent out another circular underlining the importance of the Signal Station to consignees – presumably it was respectively as expensive to keep ships waiting then as it is today:

> 'Our Signal Station at the Lizard (in which Government has opened a telegraph office) facilitates our giving to such Consignees as desire it the earliest notice of their cargoes being in the Channel.'

These circulars were very effective. There exists a list from May 1872 to December 1874 of about 150 ship owners, or charterers, who responded. The list paints an interesting picture of their feelings of responsibility, and also how busy the signal station must have been. Most were appreciative of this new service: 'glad' is a frequent word. Many wanted news only of specific ships or journeys, or at specific times: 'In future do not telegraph any steamers passing the Lizard except between the hours of 2.30 and 5 p.m.', and 'Any day after 5 p.m., and from Sat. 1.30 p.m. to Monday 8.30 a.m. send telegram to private address'. Another sent a message to say that they did 'not require advices about nitrate or guano cargoes'. Others who were destined for Falmouth were not so interested: 'Do not wire their steamers passing as they always head for Falmouth'. Others flatly refused the service: 'Do not have to be advised of their vessels passing', and 'Never advise them except in the event of an accident'. Others preferred to use the opposition: 'Do not telegraph them as Broads keep them advised of their vessel passing'. Most sent international code signals, but one elaborated as follows:

'Our steamers are brig rigged, funnels white with black tops standards blue with white letters. Company flag white with arms crowned eagle in red.'

Those on watch in the signal station must, by default, have become experts on recognising ships.

But no one appears to have expressed the warning, or if they did it is not recorded, that the signal station could have the unfortunate consequence of luring ships closer to a dangerous coast. One casualty in 1878 was the 734-ton iron steamer *Stromboli*, bound from Le Havre to Liverpool with general cargo and passengers. It steamed too close to the Lizard while signalling and struck the Maenheere Rock. The captain managed to steer into Mount's Bay to enable the passengers, their luggage and members of the crew to be rescued, but in worsening weather the *Stromboli* was soon submerged and most of her cargo lost.[21]

Contact with passing ships was conducted by the use of a series of recognizable flags, and at night by steam whistles, guns, rockets and probably anything else which would light up – but as can be imagined these were less reliable, hopeless in fog. Even so, the station remained open 24 hours a day and in the first nine months an impressive number of 1827 ships were recorded in one way or another (by 1877 it was noted that more than 1000

21   Richard Larn and Clive Carter, *Cornish Shipwrecks: The South Coast* (David & Charles, 1969)

vessels were using the station each month). It would seem that the company invented its own secret code, so secret as to be indecipherable: certain words, rather than letters, had to be interpreted. The evidence for this is sheets and sheets of words arranged in columns, and a few Post Office telegraphs which are dated from the early 1870s and which were half-translated with the translations superimposed. Thus 'Blue has salt toll and reaches droll soap pip' means 'Gray has left London and reaches Lizard tomorrow early'; and 'Dawn pup tool must mole heat us rooking from gin pie land' means, interestingly, 'I think government must not prevent us signalling from our private land'.

I long to see the following message decoded: 'Soot chad rook furze could not read them strap blue soak bowl roll car'. Knowing my family, I believe it is likely that as a form of mental exercise, and hilarious recreation, they actually talked in this bizarre Bletchley Park-defying language.

There was also another tenant, the Direct Spanish Telegraph Cable Company which was interested in using Bass (Beast) Point as a terminus for the submarine cable from Bilbao.[22]

In the early 1880s, Lloyd's of London (which began by

---

22   The signal station on the Lizard is not to be confused with the Eastern Telegraph Company, which owned the early submarine telegraph cables operating from Porthcurno, and which by coincidence – or maybe not – opened its cable office there also in 1872. The first submarine cable messages were sent to and from there in 1870, when G. C. Fox & Co. were first discussing opening a telegraph and signal station. Evidently Porthcurno was chosen in preference to Falmouth to minimise the risk of damage to underwater cables from ships' anchors.

specialising in maritime insurance before expanding into general insurance) announced their intention of establishing more signalling stations around the coast; and this was to have obvious potential repercussions with G. C. Fox & Co. Once again, an objective view was taken and it was decided that Lloyd's would lease part of the building from Fox, Broad & Co. for the operation of the signalling station. From 1 January 1883 the building became known as Lloyd's signal station – the telegraph continued to be operated by the Post Office. In 1889 there was a mock naval battle off the Lizard involving about 20 vessels and a great many searchlights. The start of the First World War 25 years later must have produced one of the most interesting chapters in the history of the signal station, given the increased traffic and consequent, and no doubt at times very challenging, signalling.

Lloyd's operated the signal station until 1951. It was then taken over by the coastguard service which operated it on behalf of Lloyd's until 1969, when reporting and signalling between ships and the Lizard ceased. G. C. Fox & Co. decided to sell all their property on the Lizard in 1953, except for one granite block which was inscribed with the word 'LLOYD'S' and which was removed to sit outside the offices in Falmouth.

This is the story of the Lizard signal station in essence. In reality it was considerably more complicated with a series of leases, sub-leases and lease-backs in several different directions, not just between the businesses operating from the building but also between the landowners, farmers and local residents who were all touched by the development. Equally, rights of way kept lawyers busy.

Reading through the archives, what becomes apparent is the contrast between dealing with some fairly primitive issues, and the ease with which the proponents of the scheme were able to gain access to important individuals, such as the Post Master General. This is reminiscent of the journals of Robert Barclay Fox (I): a man of tremendous vision, intelligence and energy, he was constantly having to contend with the conditions of his age, but at the same time corresponding with friends, and Friends, at high levels. In 1919 his son, whilst in London, 'called at the General Post Office and asked for the Secretary and saw a leading official...and remonstrated and pointed out the extreme importance' of the Telegraph Office being kept open for 'night works' in Falmouth.

Conversely it is flattering to see how many documents within the archives were signed by men, and women, of high rank: all the consular documents right up to current times have borne the signatures of reigning monarchs, presidents and chancellors. There is no guarantee that today a local M.P. will give a written reply, but from 1807, to give a very good example concerning a small isolated matter, there exists a note to G. C. Fox & Co., from 'the commissioners for Executing the Office of Lord High Admiral of the United Kingdom of Great Britain and Ireland by Lords of the Admiralty, Etc.' It reads, with the italics representing responses to the well-known instruction, 'Fill in as required':

'SUFFER the *Brig* called the *Falmouth* of *Falmouth* – *Mr Snow* – Master, Burthen *101* – Tons, and navigated with *Eight* Men and Boys, whereof *Anthony Fox is*

– Owner bound on a Voyage to *the River Plate* – to sail or depart from the Port of *Falmouth* – without Convoy, *provided she shall accompany the West India convoy as far as their respective courses will admit.*'

Amongst those who signed this document were Sir Richard Bickerton (later Admiral), the future Prime Minister Lord Palmerston, and the statesman, writer and promoter of exploration, Mr (later Sir) John Barrow.

That spirit of co-operation which my ancestors were able to enjoy with those in authority, in spite of considerable difficulties, would not today be considered fair trading. Together with increased form-filling, these two forces have, for many, hit the age of entrepreneurialism on the head. But it is ironic that the success of some of the great shipping companies was partly due to governmental nepotism.

In 1883, seven years after it had been invented and six after it had been demonstrated at the Polytechnic, it was for G. C. Fox & Co. a mere hop to be linked to the telephone. Theirs was the first number in Falmouth; the Falmouth Hotel and Falmouth Docks Company were respectively third and fourth. The second is unknown. A little room was appropriated for its use, to be replaced in 1919 by the first of several 'Telephone Closets', each with a vulcanite telephone. Despite these technological advancements the folding doors to the new telephone booth were, as would have been expected, made in a traditional way, with bevelled window panes, and mahogany from the company's timber business in Penryn, Fox Stanton, the subject of Chapter 9.

In 1953 a Dictaphone was installed. In 1955 a teleprinter, the first in Falmouth, joined the scene, superseded in the late 1970s by one of the first telex machines in the town; an 'answering telephone' and 'De-luxe type telephones' appeared in the early 1960s; and as for computers, the travel business was one of the first businesses to see the benefits of information technology, no doubt because of the immense detail of itineraries and the impossibly small, but crucial, small print of timetables. Fox Travel was the first to have 'Prestel' in Cornwall. In due course, but again ahead of many other firms, this was followed by the computerisation of accounts, previously done by a very efficient but noisy accounting machine. For this purpose, my brother William drove to the Midlands to collect a large computer with the memory of about half a megabyte: it cost nearly £20,000. (A good photocopier cost as much as a small car.) It was just a progression that we eventually, but ahead of many others, fell into internet banking.

In the constant pursuit of the latest methods of communications it is of small interest that in 1988 the writer was able to obtain permission to use a commercial channel on the firm's radio telephones; G. C. Fox & Co. already used a private channel. In the light of mobile telephones this proved to be an unnecessary battle, but for many years it was absurd that so much of the port's business went through one ship agency which, due to the prevalence of twentieth-century red tape, lacked this facility.

Many messages must also have gone through Land's End Radio. At Christmas, in appreciation of its assistance throughout the year, I would drive miles to the back of beyond Penzance, to a place called Skewjack, and deliver biscuits and bottles of whisky. I.T. has improved communication, but it is also answerable for the loss of personal contact.

In 1905, only a short time after the signal station had been set up, the Chairman of the Falmouth Chamber of Commerce was reported to have said the following words at its annual general meeting. They are ambiguous and not very grammatical, but the meaning is clear:

'if the custom of delivering orders to vessels off the port went on increasing the town would certainly suffer severely, because vessels when they put into the harbour, brought a good deal of business. The introduction of wireless telegraphy would enable vessels to speak the coast many miles off, and the need for coming inland for orders would thereby be lessened. Just as steam had injured Falmouth as a port so might electricity'.

But you cannot restrict progress even if it has a ricochet effect amongst those seeking employment and amongst existing businesses. In this story perhaps the greatest example is when the railway line and the train came to Falmouth in 1863, strongly endorsed by the Foxes, who were in turn encouraged by their railway-building cousins from the North of England, the Peases.[23] It might have

---

23   Several Fox relatives were involved in the expansion of the railways. The Stockton and Darlington railway, rather than a canal, was promoted by Jonathan Backhouse, who had married Ann Pease in 1774. His son Jonathan (see Chapter 3, footnote 5) succeeded him as a director of the Backhouse Bank and was treasurer of the Stockton and Darlington railway. His successor was Edmund Backhouse, who married Juliet Fox of Trebah.

done wonders for fish, but it had a detrimental effect on the trade of tall-masted sailing ships.

To take another example, magnetic mooring is efficiently practised by many countries today, but it obviates the need for mooring gangs. Nothing however can obviate the vigilance of the human eye; and today if you walk past the Lloyd's signal station, just below it there is a National Coastwatch Station, close to the most southerly point of the mainland. This is a place on the cliffs where a ground-covering plant called the Hottentot fig flourishes only to the west of the north/south dividing line. You might hear someone salute you from above, a volunteer whose task it is to scan the sea, and who is as happy to talk to you about gannets and dolphins as much as anything else which comes into view.

5

WRECKS

IT IS OFTEN assumed that the Foxes made their money solely from the business of shipwrecks, once plentiful in the south-western approaches. There is a famous apocryphal story, often quoted in jest, of their arranging lamps on a dangerous cliff in the outline of a safe harbour. Neither of these accusations is true, but there were certainly wrecks. (It is strange to think that during the Second World War decoy lights[24] were used to create a false Falmouth Docks, which was an important target for the enemy.)

When Sir John Killigrew, himself a bit of a pirate, was building his lighthouse on the Lizard early in the seventeenth century, the inhabitants complained, as is described in the following note:

---

24 An elaborate decoy system was set up at Nare Point on the south side of the entrance to the Helford River, which was designed to replicate the dim urban lighting visible from the air during 'black-out' hours. This was supplemented by a 'Starfish' decoy to mimic the effects of raging fires caused by incendiary bombing. In the event of a bombardment, coal burning braziers would be flooded with oil and ignited, thereby drawing a second wave of bombers to the decoy target. (www. historic-cornwall.org.uk/flyingpast/air.html)

'he will take away God's grace from them as they will have no more benefit from shipwrecks. They have so long lived on the calamities of others that they are idle.'

This is a revealing, and in those days possibly commonplace, interpretation of the nature of God.

A motley collection of photographs of shipwrecks would indicate that as ship agents G. C. Fox & Co. were very often on call; and photographs of ships with broken backs and discharged cargoes in Falmouth Docks are further evidence. Wrecking is the stuff of novels which have been written for children; and there is a magic woven around the subject of wrecks. But in reality nothing could be further from the truth. Wrecks were simply not the glamorised objects they have now become: they were in their time as real as any present-day travel disasters.

The imagination has to work harder with the spoken and written word than it does with anything on film; and where the imaginative powers are thus called upon, the audience is normally less passive in its appreciation. It is perhaps for this reason that I have found the archival accounts of shipping misadventures, very often written contemporaneously, so gripping. Much more than the newspaper reports, the 'notes of protest', duly notarised or certified by a solicitor and, or, by a local consul for the ship's home country, make compulsive reading. For one thing, these official accounts necessarily have to be the truth, and for another give intense detail: as much as is humanly possible is included, and often from several different but corroborating sources. Unlike press reports, hyperbole is avoided and error is shunned, for the simple reason that these unemotional reports, or depositions, are there to inform insurers, assessors, surveyors, governmental departments, and ultimately those who provide estimates for repair. A frequent remark of the reporting captain, presumably to arrest any hint of hysteria, and to deflect the finger of blame, was 'in consultation with the officers...'

What is described again and again is how, after a catalogue of destruction, the crew is surveying the extent of the damage and is thinking that the pitiful situation cannot become any worse, when at that melancholy stage along comes a monster of a wave, as if to finish the havoc it has only half-wrought. This phenomenon has its echoes in other spheres of life where things go wrong, one after another, until the final finishing blow. These are situations where those who believe continue to have faith and pray, but wonder about God, and His assurance; and those who do not believe begin to pray to a god in whom they do not believe. One thinks of those words from Psalm 107 (verses 23–24): 'They that go down to the sea in ships, that do business in great waters; these see the works of the Lord, and His wonders in the deep.' Sailors may not admit it, and may not like it, but in foul weather, or fair, those at sea have plenty of opportunity for reflection.

In 1873 a prominent American lawyer, Horatio Spafford, sent his wife and their four daughters across the Atlantic ahead of him for a holiday in England. There was a shipping collision at sea, resulting in the famous telegram from his wife: 'Saved alone'.[25] When he then travelled across the Atlantic, to be reunited with his wife, the ship passed the spot where his four daughters had been drowned. Pacing the deck, he composed the famous hymn which begins:

'When peace, like a river, attendeth my way,
When sorrows like sea billows roll;
Whatever my lot, Thou hast taught me to say,
It is well, it is well with my soul.'

Conditions in those days, by today's standards, were dreadful. According to the written reports, little on board was secure or safe; the tensile strength of ropes and, crucially, tow-ropes, was not brilliant; and words such as waterproof, water-resistant, watertight, self-righting, inflatable, non-slip, and floatable were relatively unknown.

In April 1872 the captain of the schooner *Clemence* reported to the Belgian Consul Alfred Fox, in Falmouth:

---

25   This appalling tragedy was not the end of the Spaffords' trials. Horatio's wife Anna gave birth to three more children: their only son who died at the age of four from scarlet fever and two further girls. In response to the judgement of their Presbyterian church that the loss of so many children was divine punishment, the Spaffords formed their own Messianic group and in 1881 set out for Jerusalem, where they set up a philanthropic, non-denominational Christian community which became known as 'The American Colony'. This has evolved over a period of more than a hundred years into a first class hotel of the same name, and a charity (The Spafford Children's Center), both remarkably still under the direction of the descendants of the Spafford family.

'At one p.m. the fore stay was carried away and immediately afterward the jib boom, fore mast and main
mast and the masts in falling aft on the stern broke
and shattered the stern frame and seriously wounded
the mate by breaking his left arm and five ribs [...]'

In the same month the captain of the *Louis David* similarly wrote:

'It was decided for general safety to throw overboard
the deck cargo in the after part of the ship consisting
of large pieces of wagon work – to accomplish this
the mizzen stays had to be cast adrift, and whilst so
engaged a tremendous sea broke into the mizzen,
broke the mast off close to the deck and started the
deck cargo adrift – the mast in falling aft broke the
fore and aft bridge, sky light, compasses, harness
casks, wheel, binnacles, gratings stanchions bulwarks
and rail round the stern, and the cargo by washing
about broke on the starboard and port sides main
rail stanchions, bulwarks and pin rails, also broke
and split the waterways and covering boards – the
chain plates of main and mizzen rigging were also
broken and damaged and the ship sustained various
other losses and damages which will be more particularly enumerated in the surveyors report.'

One of the most spectacular stories is from the autumn
of 1877: the loose propeller in the holds of the *Ferdinand
Van der Taelen*.

'A loud shock and noise was heard in the after hold as if something had broken adrift [...] the stern propeller and stern bush which had been well secured with ring bolts and lashed to the stanchions, had broken adrift and were rolling from side to side causing serious damage to the frames and plating, from which the ship was in imminent danger of foundering [...] the propeller had already made several holes in the side plates on the port side through which the water was rushing in in considerable volumes.'

The crew made several attempts to secure the two heavy pieces with chains, ropes and tackle but to no avail: the rolling of the ship caused the blades to cut through the ropes and into the sides again and again, and

'the sea rushed in in an alarming manner – the hawsers ropes and all available suitable articles were procured and put on the starboard side to prevent as much as possible further damage to that side where several holes through which the water was rushing in, were already visible, and it partially had the desired effect. [...] The donkey steam pump was set to work and kept constantly going – attempts were made to roll the stern bush into the lower hold and two tackles were got on the propeller and kept it steady for some minutes, but by the heavy rolling of the ship it again broke adrift and went from side to side with such tremendous force that carried away and broke all the mid-ship stanchions, pump, ventilators, sounding pipes lining boards combings of 'tween-deck hatchway iron ladder globe lamps and everything with which it came in contact was smashed to pieces, striking heavily the sides and frames and making holes therein from one to three feet in length and one foot in breadth.'

Another tackle was put on the propeller but then in a very heavy roll it came loose yet again, crashing around out of control. Fortuitously it then dropped down into a lower hold where there was a pile of coal which arrested its progress. On deck the violence of the wind had already destroyed two sails and a stay or two.

As a child I had a romantic and probably exaggerated notion, no doubt inspired by reading too many novels such as Daphne du Maurier's famous *Frenchman's Creek*, of a prosperous Falmouth packet ship captain, in an eighteenth-century frock coat and *jabot*, striding along the deck of his ship, and entering his captain's very luxurious quarters, with its windows leaning out from under the poop-deck, if indeed there was a poop-deck on a Falmouth Packet. Here he would collapse into a wig-accommodating Gainsborough chair to be served a glass of port by an over-attentive female. His cabin is festooned with richly coloured curtains and cushions.

I have since discovered that furnishings had another purpose on board: they were used to plug holes in the sides of a damaged ship. From the extensive lists of 'goods lost at sea', recurring items are often cushions and sofas. The *Ferdinand Van der Taelen* 'still continued to roll and strain in an alarming manner and the water continued to rush in on both sides and flooded the between decks – the mattresses and beds belonging to the crew the cabin sofa cushions and other available articles were all called in requisition and placed against broken plates.'

These lists tend to be much more concerned about the fixtures, fittings and essential equipment of a ship than they are about cargo. Chisels and hammers are itemised as much as lifeboats; so too are the surprisingly topical lists of groceries: tea, coffee, sugar and biscuits, etc. Perhaps cargo losses were handled by another agent – and are the subject of another book.

The detached and unemotional language of these reports is remarkable. But there is one word which occurs frequently; and because it is about the only one which is faintly loaded, or emotionally charged, it stands out, rather like a swear-word from the mouth of a man who never swears. Perhaps 'smashed' is the one verb which so accurately describes both action and destruction, and which can be used with such power both transitively and intransitively.

Selecting at random the minutes for 2 May 1907, I find they contain the details of three wrecks. Here is one, surely one of the largest rescue missions of the Royal National Lifeboat Institution:

'The White Star Liner "Suevic" 8108 Reg. From Sydney and Melbourne passengers and general cargo wool, copper, butter, tallow, carcases, etc stranded on the Clidges Rock Lizard March 17. The Liverpool Salvage Co salved most of the cargo which was brought to Falmouth Docks and shipped there by coasters and some by rail to Liverpool, London etc. The Salvage Co. cut the vessel in two and towed the after part towards Southampton 2 April where she docked 8 April. G.H.F. C.M.F. and R.B.F. and most of our staff were engaged night and day for weeks on the business.'

Remarkably, a new fore part was later added to the salvaged stern section.

SS Universal, *repaired by Cox & Co., Falmouth, 1897*
This vessel was cut in two for salvage in a similar way to the
Suevic in 1907.

This is a standard entry for an agency job involving a wreck but there are other accounts. One of the treasures within the archives is an entire album of photographs of the wreck of the SS *Minnehaha*, a 13,443-ton ocean liner of the Atlantic Transport Line, sailing from New York to Tilbury when she was

'wrecked in fog inside the "Scilly" rock forty five minutes past midnight on the night of April 17 [*i.e. the 18th*] – 1910 – Ed. Trerise for Fox & Co. went down at once – G. H. Fox left Penzance on the evening of 18th after arrival of Capt. Tubb. Supt of the Atlantic Transport Co. and Supt Engineer Mr Pottie about dusk in Eagle tug of Falmouth taking Falmouth and Penzance pilots – Thick weather stoppages etc caused them to sight the Northern lighthouse before seeing the desired Eastern light for entering St Mary's where they arrived 5 a.m. on the 19th. G. H. F. remained there till May 14 arriving Falmouth on the 15th. Cuthbert L. Fox went to Scilly soon after his father.'

Seven salvage tugs were in attendance. There was no loss of life and much of the cargo was brought ashore, including a large number of cows which were lashed alongside pilot gigs and rowed ashore on to Samson Island: it was not permissible to land livestock on an inhabited island. These cattle became the subject of a claim for remuneration by 147 boatmen of the Isles. They had taken the initiative: 'out came these islanders from watering their daffodils', but 'why should the captain have worried about bullocks worth some pounds apiece' when 'Mercedes and touring cars worth thousands of pounds were thrown overboard?'

Technically they had not had an agreement, and

therefore had no case, but in the end they received some form of compensation. The episode begs the questions: supposing the cows had drowned and been washed up on Scillonian shores, who then would have seen to their disposal, at what cost, and at whose expense?

No doubt to the delight of Scillonians, much of the cargo was also jettisoned. But, as with the cattle takers, you had to be careful with wrecks: there is an account of at least one gentleman, a boatman, who rescued 20 lbs of tobacco which he had seen floating around in the sea, and who was later found guilty of smuggling.

I have some sympathy with the impoverished animal- and tobacco-loving Scillonian daffodil grower trying to make the most of an opportunity; and I am reminded of Sir John Killigrew's lighthouse and the likelihood of it depriving the local population of their interpretation of God's grace, in the form of shipwrecks.

Elsewhere in this book I cast an envious eye on the ease with which it was possible to be enterprising over 100 years ago; and there is an interesting example from the wreck of the *Minnehaha*. 'By smart arrangements', a 'special ocean boat express' was laid on to take the rescued passengers non-stop from Penzance to Plymouth in one hour 50 minutes. (Today, admittedly with stops, the journey takes about ten minutes more than this.) At Plymouth there was a change of engines and the train continued again without a stop, arriving at Paddington at 9.30 p.m. What is more,

'excellent arrangements had been made locally by Mr Blair station master, for the comfort of the passengers on the train. A special staff had been procured for the restaurant car and the menus even had been specially printed as souvenirs.'

I know of no railway company, let alone travel agency, which could compete with that today. The *Minnehaha* was not insured. So goodness knows who paid for this pampering; most assuredly it would not have been the ship agent.

In the company's archives the story of the aftermath of this particular shipwreck is a familiar one, and seems to have been a regular occurrence. Everyone has had the experience of travel disruption, albeit more commonly with trains, planes or coaches. Apart from the inevitable cohort of complainers, and another cohort of those who have the wherewithal to make alternative arrangements, human beings are mostly prepared to be flexible, and adaptable. They gather up their belongings and wait for orders, recognizing that things go wrong even with the best modes of transport. With a shipwreck they might even be asked to jump into the sea, which could be very rough or, just as unpleasant, intentionally stilled by a heavy coating of oil. Many survived, but there are also stories of tragic losses.

Early in 1914 the German four-masted sailing ship *Hera* was *en route* to Falmouth from Pisagua in Chile when she came to grief on Gull Rock in Veryan Bay; and on a day which, in a winter of storms, was unusual for its blue skies, I attended the hundredth anniversary of the wreck of the *Hera* on 1 February 2014, marked by a Requiem Mass at the church of St Symphorian in Veryan and a re-dedication of the very long grave of those who perished. The archives of G. C. Fox & Co. from the early twentieth century include a few volumes which contain a running log of work within the ship agency, a practice which was continued in my time, when we kept an update in each file. The *Hera* is one of many entries which could perhaps be transcribed by students of palaeography or maritime history, but they would need magnifying glasses. It is amazing how in the past reporters could write so beautifully, fluently and evocatively, compared to the clumsiness of many of today's writers; here is the *Western Daily Mercury*:

'About eleven o'clock on Saturday night what was believed to be a light was discerned, but immediately after there was a cry of "Rocks ahead!" and before anything could be done the Cornish coast had claimed another victim.'

For those who do not know, it takes a long time and a long distance for a ship to turn: several miles with a super-tanker, less distance but still critical with the *Hera*. A lifeboat was launched but immediately capsized.

'It was then the case of each man fighting for his own existence [...] some managed to swim back to the ship [...] the only hope left was to clamber into the rigging. Then commenced hours of bitter torment and suspense [...] the men, in their perilous position, could see would-be rescuers in a life-boat, and yet knew that they themselves could not be seen [...] their only means of drawing attention was a whistle, which the first mate blew incessantly. He, when he felt his strength going, and just before he was sucked down by the sea, passed it up to the men above.'

The Falmouth lifeboatmen had

'worked splendidly [*and*] for hours they were search-ing round the spot where it was thought the ship had struck, and it was only the inky blackness of the night which prevented them from discharging their mission of mercy.'

Later that day, or perhaps the following day, Robert Bar-clay Fox (II), ship agent and German vice-consul, opened his notebook. It measures 15" by 9" by 2 ¼" and is covered in rust-coloured suede which, for some reason, today leaves its rust-coloured marks on anything it touches. In a precise and miniscule hand he wrote, more accurately than any journalist,

'[…] at 1.45 a.m. C. J. heard from Lelean about that vessel firing rockets off Portloe – S. W. gale – got Perran, Triton and Victor [*tugs*] away Perran picked up life-boat and towed her down – nothing to be seen but heard whistle – and life-boat picked 3rd mate and 4 men off jigger top mast only thing showing above water – vessel had struck Gull Rock between 11 p.m. & midnight come off and sunk between Gull Rock and Penare Head. 7.30 a.m. received word from Che-noweth Portscatho of wreck 19 crew including captain

drowned – Triton towed back life-boat far too risky for
Perran – wired owners fully also Consul General […]'

Because the King Harry Ferry was closed on Sundays, Barclay Fox then drove the long way round to Portloe. What
happened next fully explains the sort of thing a ship agent
has to do. He has to think on his feet. Barclay appointed
someone to represent the firm in Portloe, promising 50%
nett for anything salvaged; visited the coastguards and told
them of this arrangement; then went on to Portholland to
do the same, telling them to keep lists, and that there might
be rewards for recovery of bodies. He then informed the
owners about this. He spoke to

> 'the coroner who fixed the inquest 11 a.m. 3rd says 10
> bodies recovered 2 further along coast – authorised
> them being brought Portholland & saw 3 undertak-
> ers […]'

The notes continue in this practical vein for four pages.
The most pressing issues were salvage and reward (an
example of this has already been given from the *Minnehaha*), the importance of the inquest, and the expenses
of the burial. Dealing with these questions needs to have
the authority of the agent's principals, or at least their
ratification. The maritime law of 'general average' comes
fiercely into play: if a ship is forced to sacrifice its cargo, or
anything, to save the voyage, then all parties including the
cargo owners have to make a proportional contribution.

At the inquest Barclay Fox put in a good word for the
prompt action of the coastguard:

'their utility in saving life alone was so important that they ought to be increased rather than decreased',

a sentiment which was shared then and still is felt today.

As a footnote on the *Hera*, the *Cornish Echo* wrote on 13 February:

'The captain of a French barque, the General de Negrier, bound from Antofagasta to Falmouth for orders, related a remarkable incident when he was in port on Saturday, which may not be without its significance in regard to the disaster. He declares emphatically that he was in communication with the Hera some weeks ago, when both vessels were south of the Equator, and the lost barque signalled that she was bound for the Deadman (Dodman) for orders. He is positive he read the signal correctly.'

Wreck of the Hera *off Gull Rock, Veryan Bay, 1914*

He did; but he might have read it differently. *The British*

Channel Pilot 1859 refers to this headland being known as the 'Deadman or Dodman'.

There are customs in seafaring. There are words you should never say, in the same way as in the acting world there is a play you should never mention; and in tin mines, and on board ships, it is a human sound, paradoxically the same word as the instrument which led the lifeboat to the wreck of the *Hera*. Sailors will take care not to 'whistle up' a storm unwittingly; and many sailors would not have sailed on the *Suevic* had they known that the cargo included crates of a small cuddly herbivore with a fluffy white tail.

A friend of my father's told me about this particular superstition. He was a tug-master in Falmouth Docks. He was a very down-to-earth person and there was nothing he did not know about knots. Every summer he was an indispensable member of the crew on board my father's yacht *Quaker Girl* when it sailed across the English Channel to Brittany. One year, when we were there, he told me something else. We were walking back to the boat having had supper ashore. Along the lane were chestnut trees; and our way was guided by the stars beyond the leaves.

Once (the tug-master told me), in a severe storm at sea, the crew had to abandon ship and launch the lifeboat. Meanwhile another ship in the same area was experiencing a problem with its chart constantly being altered. No one would admit to having done this, so the captain instigated a search. A stowaway was found: a man in dripping wet clothes. He was arrested, tied up in a chair and locked in a cabin below deck, with the intention of questioning him once the storm had abated.

The ship ploughed on through the tempestuous seas, and after a while the lifeboat from the abandoned ship was sighted. It was enabled to come alongside, and the exhausted members of crew were taken on board. One of them, an old man, had sadly expired; but he was immediately recognized by one of the rescuers as the stowaway. Running to the locked cabin, the rescuer found it empty apart from the loose ropes and a pool of water.

Strange, and wonderful, things happen at sea.

A member of the Williams family, living at the nearby castle of Caerhays, had shown great personal concern at the time of the wreck of the *Hera*. The newspaper reported that at the inquest he had been the foreman of the jury but also

> 'went into the rough sea up to his shoulders, with a rope tied round his waist for safety, and brought one of the deceased to shore.'

There is also evidence of G. C. Fox & Co. having a humanitarian interest: in January 1814 George Croker Fox (III) was keen to help out with a supply of clothes for a party of shipwrecked sailors from the famous wreck of the *Queen* Transport in the Carrick Roads: the *West Briton* reported that he

> 'no sooner heard of the wreck, than he dispatched his servants to prepare the house at Trefusis, for the reception of such sufferers as might be saved [*and he himself*] hastened with several of his clerks to the

awful spot to render every assistance in his power to such as might be rescued from the wreck.'

To exacerbate matters, it had been snowing heavily.

If there should be anyone who might think otherwise, ship agency work can have its unpleasant side. Barclay Fox had had some experience of this with the *Hera* in 1914. His father, Robert Barclay Fox (I), as a 19-year-old in 1836, had become closely involved with a case of cannibalism at sea, having interviewed the captain of a stricken ship whose crew (with the exception of two who were sacrificed to keep the others alive) were rescued by the brig *Agenoria* and brought into Falmouth:

'Horrible – horrible! [*he wrote, after seeing the knife which was used to despatch the unfortunate sailors*] – a piece of human flesh, a relic of their cannibal meal!'

His cousin George Henry Fox was once

'let down over a lofty cliff on a rope to collect into sacks the dismembered remains of a shipwrecked crew, cast upon otherwise inaccessible rock.'

This has all the shades of the Revd. Robert Hawker, the mad vicar of Morwenstow in North Cornwall: he stood watching the Atlantic and at the first sight of fatal casualties he would be busy hauling bodies up the cliff for Christian committal and burial. As a ship agent, and sometimes a consul, I found that removing the incinerated remains of a ship's crew was by comparison more commonplace – 'no more than a plateful of bones, not enough for a shoe box', as a local undertaker so accurately, and rather needlessly, commented.

Nowadays, with all the modern aids and substantially less guesswork, shipwrecks are rare, but in the history of the firm one within living memory was famous, and well documented elsewhere: the *Flying Enterprise* in 1952. This made the headlines due to the captain, Kurt Carlsen, insisting that he should remain on board to the bitter end, allegedly in the interests of minimising salvage claims.[26] My grandfather Cuthbert Fox wrote, as ever, succinctly:

---

26   The still-unsolved mystery of the *Flying Enterprise*'s cargo has been the subject of speculation for over 60 years. There was a rumour that the cargo included zirconium, thought to have been intended for use in the United States' first nuclear submarine, reinforced by the fact that both before and after the *Flying Enterprise* was taken in tow by the Falmouth-based tug *Turmoil*, she was not only escorted by United States naval ships but shadowed by Russian vessels. Captain Carlsen strongly denied the suggestion that he had stayed with his stricken ship for the sake of its cargo, stating when interviewed about the episode for an exhibition at Falmouth Art Gallery in 1987 that he had taken the cargo on board at Hamburg in sealed containers without knowing its specific content, and only learnt of the rumours from Russian reporters after the event. His sole motive for remaining on board was that, in his words, it is a captain's duty to stay with his ship until all hope is lost. Captain Carlsen received a hero's welcome in Falmouth and subsequently a tickertape reception in New York City. The *Flying Enterprise*, lying at a depth of 84 metres and a distance of 57 kilometres south of the Lizard, was the subject of a salvage operation in 1960 and of diving operations in 2001 and 2005, but information regarding the exact nature of the cargo has remained confidential.

'The "Flying Enterprise" has come to our doorstep, there to become a matter of record only, in a depth of 50 fathoms of water – after being on tenterhooks for 10 days, the end was to us an anti-climax only a shade less dramatic than the climax her success in reaching port would have been.'

He went on to say that part of his job was to arrange civic receptions and press conferences but otherwise keep the – even in those days – 'rude, merciless and obnoxious' press at bay. Eventually having been pursued to the Red Lion and also the Nansidwell Hotel, both in Mawnan Smith, Captain Carlsen and members of his family, who had come across from Denmark, went to stay with my grandparents at Glendurgan. As my grandfather, in yet another attempt to foil the press, drove him out of the back drive, Captain Carlsen observed 'It's a poor fox that has only one entrance to his earth'.

This was an astute observation: the ability, unintentional or not, for the Foxes to enter one business, or exit from another, has always been crucial to the company's success.

Captain Kurt Carlsen of the Flying Enterprise

*Captain Carlsen greeted by cheering crowds as he leaves the
office of G. C. Fox & Co., January 1952 (Philip Fox behind him)*

6

HANDLING PRIVILEGE

MEETING FAMOUS PERSONAGES in the course of the ship agency business was not unusual. G. C. Fox & Co. enjoyed the visits of Her Majesty's Yacht *Britannia*; and my father enjoyed *his* visits to the Royal Yacht. It is to my own lasting regret that I was never was among the privileged few (and happily for them they were regular guests) to go on board, although I have subsequently made up for this by visiting the ship at its permanent berth at Leith in Scotland, where one is able to view very much more than just the state rooms. Its hull is like the surface of a car; in fact, the Falmouth pilot boat was once asked 'not to touch the side of the Royal Yacht'. Through the Royal Cornwall Yacht Club, and in other spheres, my father Philip already had some contact with the Duke of Edinburgh; he also had plenty of contact with many local boatmen, who on seeing both of them afloat and enjoying Falmouth Regatta, had shouted at my father in strong Cornish accents, 'All right then Philip?'

Not only did my father send the Queen a copy of the firm's potted history, which according to a thank-you letter was read 'with interest'. But on another occasion, in spite of surely knowing that arrangements for ships of the Royal Navy were made directly through the local authorities and naval area commanders, he offered the firm's services as a ship agent, a service which was politely declined: 'neither appropriate nor customary'. This did not however stop the company from taking an interest in the royal visits, and when on one occasion the Queen Mother came to Falmouth, the ship agency closed its front door, boarded the German salvage tug *Caribic* and went out into Falmouth Bay to greet *Britannia* with a display of water power from her fire monitors. After a little while, through the fog a diminutive figure appeared on a top deck, and gave that immortal wave, followed soon after by a radio message thanking us for our 'friendly display'. The local gossip, which such royal visits provoke, was also enjoyable: a guest on board *Britannia* dropped her bag over the gangway, whereupon a member of the crew 'dove', as Americans would say, over the side and retrieved it from the murky waters of Falmouth Docks, a display, if ever there was one, of water sports. One story involved a local mayor explaining to the Queen that one of the basic ingredients of a Cornish pasty was a 'nice bit of skirt', a flat cut of beef. On meeting the same man later (it is not known whether it was the result of a long day, or merely the royal sense of humour) she mistakenly, but with some merriment, addressed him as 'Mr Skirt'.

As regards the royal diet, I was also amused to hear someone in the crowds quipping about Falmouth's excellent Harbour Master, who was looking suitably resplendent:

'Well, she won't see you and your gold braid: she has gold braid for breakfast.'[27]

In the age of the Falmouth Packets a great diversity of distinguished people passed through the port. One of the most exotic was the Begum of Oudh, who had lived for a year in London where her husband was Ambassador and was leaving England for a pilgrimage to Mecca. For several days before embarking from Falmouth in December 1836, the Begum stayed at Pearce's Hotel, where she was visited by both Caroline Fox and her brother Barclay.[28] Not one for mincing her words and yet with customary humour, Caroline noted that the Begum's face was

> 'one of quick sagacity but extreme ugliness…and she had a silver ring on her great toe which lay in no obscurity before her.'

At the end of the same month, the Begum's husband also visited, on his way to Bombay 'per *Atlanta* steamer'. Barclay Fox's anecdote about the Ambassador illustrates the lengths a ship agent was required to go to assist travellers.

> 'He…came to the office with a remarkably odd story that he had £50 wrapt up in a handkerchief in his

---

27 This comment may have been inspired by the fact that within the Forces (especially the Royal Navy) 'scrambled eggs' is a slang term for gold braid.
28 *Barclay Fox's Journal*, 12th Month, 1836; *The Journals of Caroline Fox*, December 2–5, 1836

coat pocket & that in pulling out his duplicate hand-kerchief for use he supposes he forked out the former therewith, money & all, so that he is here penniless. We advanced him enough for his expenses, much to his satisfaction.'

A failure to impress, or to be impressed, would have suited very well our Quaker ancestors, about whom it is written in the *Glendurgan* book as follows:

'Of Quaker stock, the Foxes were very much *vin ordinaire*, and as is so common with non-conform-ists, from the purple of commerce, and little versed in courtly observances. Yet they remained unfazed at having to mingle with the grandees of society – what is touching is that The Queen of Portugal had objected to being decked out for the occasion, know-ing she was going to visit a family where plainness of dress was the norm. Queen Victoria, who came to Falmouth in 1846, may have been briefed in advance that she was going to meet a man, whose religious beliefs would prevent him from removing his hat, in spite of being a loyal and, as recorded by the Queen herself, gift-bearing subject [*the gift was a grape-fruit*]. The Quaker belief was that because all men are equal in the eyes of God, honour had to be given to Him alone, and therefore special distinctions, in the instance of a mere queen, ought not to be recog-nized. Fortunately the day turned out to be so hot he "simply could not keep it on"'.

As an aside comment it was, in the seventeenth century at any rate, common practice for men to keep their hats on when in a place of worship, but again probably for entirely pragmatic reasons, this was to do with a lack, rather than an abundance of heat. As it says in a notice from a quarterly meeting in 1750, Quakers would

> 'as much as possible…avoid all Superfluity in their Apparel, and unnecessary Shew and Expence on Account of Marriage-Dinners, and publick Entertainments; these Things being inconsistent with the Simplicity and Moderation [*they*] profess, injurious to the Circumstances of some, and even in such as can afford it, but an ill Example to those of less Ability.'

This may appear stuffy to some, but it is refreshingly unlike those who conform to the pressures of fashion, and etiquette.

There was another incident, similar to Queen Victoria's visit, in 1839 when Alfred Fox was awarded a Belgian honour. He had to explain that 'La Société religieuse des amis n'approuve pas les ornaments personnels extérieurs'[29] and that he would prefer 'un souvenir quelconque qui ne doit pas une decoration.'[30] There must be many others who would be happy to be rewarded with gold snuff boxes. At a later date another member of the

---

29 'The religious Society of Friends does not approve of external personal adornments.'
30 'A souvenir that does not need to be a decoration.'

family refused to receive a Belgian order – but on that occasion it was because of the Belgian oppression in the Congo. Whether he too received a gold snuff box history does not relate. In any event, to put these excitements into perspective, the one-foot long array of mounted honours and decorations my father received for a lifetime of consular duties would seem to indicate that these awards were doled out in a fairly arbitrary manner – even if they were fun to wear.

Should anyone think that Quakers were too proud when it came to this kind of morality, by the same token a complete disregard for social etiquette could also occur in an opposite direction: in 1915 George Henry Fox's daughter Annette was employed by the firm. 'She attended to [*her brother*] Cuthbert's consular work and kept the 'Sums Receivable Books' and the 'Captains Ledger'. She also went on to be highly efficacious, during the First World War, in looking after the firm's signal station on the Lizard.

Looking back through the archives there is no doubt that members of the family applied themselves to their work, but it is also interesting to see how they played hard as much as they worked hard, and if this came about because of a business connection, such as the firm's outing on the *Caribic*, so much the better.

On the third page of a commonplace book kept by George Croker Fox (III) there is an explanation of what the book is: 'a Register, or orderly collection of things, which occur worthy to be noted and retained in the course of a man's study' such as, it goes on to say, the useful subjects amongst others of 'Criticism', 'Logic and Metaphysics', 'Geography and Chronology', and 'Philosophy, Moral Political and Experimental'. He records that in August 1815, the year of the Battle of Waterloo, he and his wife Lucy, Alfred Fox, and 'several others in the barge Industry' sailed, as did many others, 'to see Napoleon in Plymouth Sound', on board Sir George Cockburn's flagship, the *Bellerophon*. The spectators 'on Friday morning the 4th caught a sight of him in the gangway' and then again in the cabin window: enough time for George Croker Fox to execute a sketch. Unlike the famous painting by Charles Eastlake, it shows Napoleon's remarkable profile, a profile which no doubt would have later exacted some very insightful comments by Caroline Fox, a keen but amateur student of both phrenology and physiognomy; it has the same bullishness of Mussolini.

A sketch of Napoleon Bonaparte on board the Bellerophon *in Plymouth Sound, August 1815. By George Croker Fox (III). Drawn from the barge* Industry

For no other reason than its being just over 200 years ago that this excursion took place, the following extract from George Croker Fox's commonplace book is being included:

'The Bellerophon having been visited by Lord Keith to our surprise got under weigh about one o'clock and was warped slowly out of the sound…A lady in a boat followed him and waved her handkerchief we were afterwards told she said she had come 100 miles to see him and that he made his appearance and bowed – He was to be put on board the Northumberland Sir George Cockburn off the Start and to be conveyed to St Helena. We were politely invited aboard the…Corvette Cap. Napier that we might have a better chance – did not however benefit much by the change – we were told it was reported there he had made an attempt to escape the night before - This is incredible – Madame Bertrand[31] actually it was said attempted to drown herself

---

31   Comtesse Fanny Bertrand was the wife of one of Napoleon's most loyal aides-de-camp, General Henri-Gatien Bertrand, who was amongst those who chose to accompany Napoleon into exile. George Croker Fox's observations confirm the story that Fanny tried to persuade Napoleon not to accept her husband's offer to go with him to the island of St. Helena. When she realised that her pleading would do no good, Fanny attempted to jump overboard from the *Bellerophon*. 'Is she not mad?' exclaimed Napoleon, as her husband restrained her. In due time she became more accepting of her fate and she and her husband remained on St. Helena with Napoleon until his death in 1821.

Nap. having said he would not quit England alive &
knowing her husband was determined to share his
fate – we had seen papers torn and thrown out at
the cabin window shortly before the Bellerophon
weighed – These an officer informed us came from
Napoleon's apartment and that one large paper was
thrown out which he did not venture to pick up –
Myself & Lucy remained in Plymouth till Tuesday
– on Monday visited Mount Edgecumbe. It being a
public day did not see the gardens – Returned in the
mail – Lucy's first trip in that vehicle. Read the life
of Nap. to the passengers – This man the subject of
general conversation & wonder is now believed to be
off Falmouth in the Northumberland accompanied
by the Eurotus frigate & sloops of war & two or three
transports – I saw her first about half past 7 – she
telegraphed the signal post at St Anthony's ….the
frigate & other ships seemed to close round her as
the night approached – The wind extremely brave –
the evening charming.'

The soul of Napoleon obviously held a fascination for
Quakers, as much as for Madame Bertrand. They were
supposedly unimpressed by either fame or lack of fame.
What is interesting is that Napoleon, this man who was
busy rearranging the map of Europe, was a very ambiguous character: for some he was little short of Satanic
and for others little short of Messianic. Ellen Crewdson,
writing about her childhood at Perran, wrote that her
father, George Fox (1746–1816) of Tredrea, had also paid
a visit: he 'came back surprising us by his modified dis-

117

like of the genial-looking conqueror of Europe, and with strange tidings, that he was not like the stern ferocity of our play-room'.

It is odd that throughout history there have been characters who, by their infamous deeds, have become famous and often admired. There were, and are, quite a few in Cornwall, perhaps the most renowned being Michael An Gof, who rebelled against a tax levy. But that such ambivalence sits uneasily with Quakers is borne out by George Croker Fox's notes on Napoleon:

'This man who for the last 15 years has played so conspicuous a part and who for 10 years of that period astonished the world and overran Europe – the conqueror of Marengo, of Friedland, of Austerlitz, of Wagram and of Jena may now have had the last sight of the shores of Europe – strange that his last looks should be fixed on that coast which he has so often threatened to invade and to overwhelm! And yet more strange that the resources of his mind and extent of his genius should be so great as to render it impossible to fix his prison anywhere within the confines of his former theatre of action! *Urit enim fulgore suo* [32] – When his virtue of life [*is*] doubtful here he might surely be said to possess all the req-

---

32   An extract from Horace, *Epistle II, Poem I*. The full sentence, of which George Croker Fox quotes only the opening clause, translates as 'The one who weighs down the merits of those beneath him blinds them by his very splendour; but when his light is extinguished, he will be admired.'

uisites to greatness – are the allies not at war with the spirit of the age and will an enlightened nation ever submit to have a governor imposed by foreigners and did we not oppose the Stuarts on the same principles as the French now oppose the Bourbons – are we burdened by taxes and debts to find our only security in depressing the spirit of enterprise of our neighbour – by incapacitating him as a rival in peace and an enemy in war?'

George Croker Fox also expanded his thoughts about the fall of Napoleon into a poem, from which the following is an extract.

'Master so late of half the subject world
Thy giant strength the other half enfurled
Now all is lost – thy second cast has failed
Britannia's sword smote home and twice prevailed
Yet thou art stately unbroken still
Subjecting feeling to thy mightier will –
The Macedonian wept that all was won
And that no world remained to be undone –
Thou weepest not for a world twice won & lost
But seems to think the prize not worth the cost...'

From Falmouth and around, and no less from the terraces of their now famous gardens, the Foxes would have looked out on an expanse of sea, and, as the *West Briton* so agreeably puts it, they would also have observed 'the fleets of France and Spain, combined for invasion, and heard the warning strains of their bands'. Bands evidently were not just for high days and holidays, or at least not for the vulnerable English; and to underline the real concern that the Cornish had in case the French should invade in the early 1800s, it is worth including Rachel Tuckett's note about the foresight of Robert Were Fox (I):

'In anticipating the arrival of the French fleet, my grandfather kept his horses ready harnessed for several days, in case they might have to take a speedy departure. Happily this did not become necessary, for though some ships were sighted in the bay, circumstances took them in another direction'.

To their delight, Robert Were Fox

'provided his young sons with knapsacks "ready for a tramp inland". He also took the precaution of sending money bills to Thomas [*his cousin at Wellington*] to be exchanged for cash in case he should have need of it.'

Meanwhile Edward Fox of Wadebridge had

'constructed a spring cart specially adapted for fast travel over rough roads, and had a chest made with a double bottom, where money could be hidden.'

Rachel's brother Howard wrote that the family was sent to live at Roscrow and 'on the first appearance of the enemy' it was planned that it 'should immediately post to Exeter', whilst their grandfather remained at their house, Bank, in Falmouth, to look after the business.

Less exciting and less thought-provoking, but to bring us back to the everyday activities of a small ship agency in Falmouth, on 31 July 1857 the *West Briton* describes an excursion by tug, the *Sydney*, from Truro to Durgan:

'The party numbered about eighty, besides ten of the Royal Miners' Artillery band, whose services were engaged by permission of Captain Ward. The party, after greatly enjoying the picnic were very kindly conducted by Mr Fox over his grounds, which for picturesque beauty of hill and dale and wooded scenery and sea views, can scarcely be excelled. The band performed in the grounds some excellent music and the company, after endeavouring to thread the mazes of the "labyrinth" etc were accompanied by Mr Fox to the beach, when they embarked and steamed back to Trefusis, where under the shady trees, they spread their tea cloths and after tea the band performed and the ladies and their partners were gratified with several dances.'

7

FISHING

VIOLET HODGKIN IS not a person you would associate with conger eel fishing. She was a Quaker cousin, an author of what second-hand book shops call 'spiritual' books, an academic, and a close friend of a scholar, whose first and second names no one ever seems to know: Alfred Leslie Rowse. With a name like Violet you would think she would shrink from anything as challenging as 'hunting the conger'. Yet in August 1919 that was the title of the piece she wrote for *The Times*:

> '"Congering" is a tricky sport [*she says*], only to be indulged in after dark, when time, tide and season are all exactly right.'

The fact that for so many, the eel, or equally the snake, is an object of fascination is possibly because it is unnerving to see something which should have legs, move around leglessly. The evidence for this is that in many snakes there are vestigial legs. Furthermore, the implication of the famous curse is that pre-curse, pre-Fall, the serpent did indeed have legs; it is frightening to see the effects that the word of God can carry. It is also a challenge to think that this is where creationist and evolutionist might meet.

The poets Ogden Nash and Stevie Smith could well have written 'The conger eel has nerves of steel'. It does. A friend in a boat on a fishing excursion once had her thumb bitten by the decapitated head of a conger eel, and when her husband tried to beat it off with a piece of wood, the fish head increased its grip. Not as painful, but perhaps more alarming was at two o'clock one night when my father was driving home with a cousin after a successful bout of congering. Their beheaded trophy lay in a tea chest in the boot of the car. But it was not properly closed: coming past Falmouth Hospital they heard a thud, and on stopping the car and getting out, they saw the half-severed body wriggling down the road, seawards bound.

This was much to the consternation of a nurse, who happened to be walking home after completing her night shift.

Violet and her companions were unsuccessful. She ends her article:

'and so back into the safety of the shadowy valley. The blue lamps of hydrangea shine by their own light till long after dusk, but even they are extinguished in this midnight gloom, up which we grope our way, disturbing the velvety owls by our emphatic whispers that we must catch these congers next time. And then we will go seining, and see the night through from the other end.'

Anyhow, as bottom feeders go, congers, with their lethal

eating habits, do not make that funny gerund, 'good eating'.

During the long summer holidays we, as children, would occasionally be invited to join a seining party, or to 'shoot' a seine, and inevitably we went. I have a memory of rather grim inhospitable beaches, a thin watery sun, and grown-ups wandering around in weird-looking clothes, shouting at each other. It was difficult to know what was going on until finally, with much heaving at two ends of a net, a few fish and a lot of seaweed flopped up on to the beach. This was my first introduction to what was probably one of the last old-fashioned seine nets, salvaged from the days of the fishing industry, and at a time when launching fees and fishing regulations were minimal, and when many Cornish coves were still untouched by the clutter of water sports, moorings, and brightly-coloured buoys.

Seine netting at Porthleven

At the very beginning of the seventeenth century, in the last years of Queen Elizabeth's reign, Richard Carew's in-depth *Survey of Cornwall* was published. There are some delightful notes on the subject of fishing, in particular the ancient practice of 'hewing', and the 'hewer',

> 'who standeth on the cliff side, & from thence best discerneth the quantity & course of the pilchards, according whereunto he cundeth (as they call it) the master of each boat (who hath his eye still fixed upon him) by crying with a loud voice, whistling through his fingers & wheezing certain diversified & significant signs with a bush which he holdeth in his hand.'

As a very informative article in the *Western Daily Mercury* in 1874 later states:

> 'a silvery gleam, indicating that a "school" of pilchards is coming in to the shore, is observed, and the inhabitants know that now is their time to gather in their harvest while they may. "Hev'ah, hev'ah!" is the magic cry. Every fisherman hurries to his boat, which is speedily manned, and in a few minutes more, deeply laden with heavy seine, it works slowly out to sea, followed by its two tenders, the captain watching from the bow where the gleaming pilchards can be best encircled.'

A rather solid cake known as 'heavy' cake, takes its name from the hewer's cry, which means 'a shoaling place'. The little criss-cross lines on top signify the nets, and the currants within represent all the trapped fish. Cavemen sketched on the walls of their caves prophetic pictures of their intended quarry. But whether 'heavy cake' was consumed for the same reason, in advance of a fishing expedition, or on triumphant return, or perhaps just at sea, is unknown.

In any event it was not, in our family, the most popular tea-time recipe.

In 1867 there was a meeting of the owners of the Cadgwith and Lizard Seans [*sic*]

'for the purpose of considering the propriety of adopting some better Rules for the carrying on of the Pilchard Fishery in that bay'

and again the subject of hewing, (or 'huing', as it is sometimes spelt), is mentioned:

'It was resolved [*amongst other things*] that the Hewers belonging to each sean [*sic*], shall not, whilst under pay, leave their hills together to get their breakfasts, and that they also be required to take their dinners on the hills, as heretofore.'

No doubt the working practices of the nineteenth-century hewer were on a par with today's equivalent: the coffee-break-conscious unionist. What differs dramatically however are today's fishing techniques. A modern fishing boat has shoal-detecting devices, can suck up a shoal in seconds, and has nets the size of football pitches; and it is doubtful that the modern net has a name such as the 'Zealous' seine, from Gorran Haven, or the 'Friendship' seine from Coverack.

It would be interesting to know if the hewer was, at times, the same person who sat on a hedge with his telescope, as described in Chapter 2, looking out to sea for potential ship agency work; and it would also be interesting to know if clairvoyants were employed, as happened in ancient times when the Venetians scanned the horizon for the first signs of a trading ship.

The early letter books of G. C. Fox & Co. overflow with references to fish and fish-oil. They seem to represent the bulk of their trade as merchants. But apart from the availability of fish, and its low cost, it seems a questionable business with worrying fluctuations and constantly open to abuse. George Croker Fox (I) wrote on 24 January 1771 to Messrs Wills and Leigh as follows, one of hundreds of letters which dwell on fish size and condition:

'I note your remark about the quality of the pilchards and am very sensible of the propriety thereof but I believe I have before hinted to you that the fish are always abundantly smaller in such years of scarcity [...] and there is no such thing as making the fishermen alter the package [...] it has been their custom time out of mind to put the larger fish upon the top of the smaller ones in the middle [...] you'll therefore observe for your future government that this is not owing to the villainy of the fishermen with respect to the size but arises entirely from the nature of the fish unless indeed when they mix summer with autumn which some rogues may be wicked enough to do but when we have large shoals and plenty then the fish are good enough throughout and well coated

[…] my endeavours shall always be […] to get them manufactured with as much care as possible.'

From 1760 to 1936, the company was actively involved in the fishing business, not just as merchants, but as shippers, agents and curers, and up until the late 1870s as part-owners in fishing boats all around the Cornish coast. They issued annual Pilchard Circulars, at first laboriously handwritten but by the late 1840s they were being hand-printed. Those in receipt of these valuable circulars would then send back further data on imports and exports, market prices and prospects. The company owned or leased fish cellars all along the coast of Cornwall and the partners were not averse to inspecting them. In 1871 Robert Fox from Newquay wrote

'Fish very much same size throughout as packers get the castaway fish they are careful to exclude all soft poor or small fish and others. Samples generally fair but some soft and others without scales […] several rather bloody.'

In the summer of 1872 George Henry Fox records rather nonchalantly that he 'walked to White Hart St Austell in 72 minutes' from their cellars in Mevagissey. No doubt he needed the services of a pub by then, not unlike his first cousin Barclay who also records 'trudging' long distances. Howard Fox, talking about his father Alfred, records his

'examining the pilchards curing in the fish cellars at Gillan and Porthallow. [*They*] then drove by Coverack and Cadgwith to the Lizard examining fish cellars at each place and returned to Falmouth the same day'.

Apparently 'whenever a messenger arrived at the office announcing a seine in water with pilchards enclosed,' Alfred 'would go at once in a carriage & pair to inspect & give advice'. He gained much respect for his dedication to the fishing industry, and when one day he was at Whitby in the far north-east of England, Cornish fishermen there engaged in the herring industry 'swarmed' off their boats to shake his hand. This is all the more impressive when it is remembered how apprehensive the Cornish were of the North Sea merchants. To the disappointment of East Coast smacks which dredged for oysters in the River Helford, Alfred had been one of several prominent men to help the local oystermen succeed in banning dredging out of season in 1846.

An important part of the Foxes' fishing business was that several members of the family became actively and personally involved. Alfred had given valuable evidence on the pilchard fishery to the Parliamentary Select Committee on British Channel Fisheries; and both Howard and later on his nephew Cuthbert had produced papers on the state of the pilchard fishery business. In fact, there is abundant evidence of the Foxes' knowledge of ichthyology, fishing technologies and technicalities, political fishing issues, and an ability to lecture on crabs, mackerel, herring, etc. They could talk volubly on such knotty subjects as 'What is a sardine?' and the tax implications of exporting pilchards to the Mediterranean. In 1846 Alfred even presided over the drawing of a seine net at Swanpool for the pleasure of

Prince Albert. As Alfred's nephew Barclay recorded, rather more poetically than in the royal diaries:

> 'the fish however, were shy of majesty and not one was caught.'[33]

In 1874 the company, researching a market for undersized fish, opened in Mevagissey a fish-canning factory, which in the following year became known as the Cornish Sardine Co. (Ltd). Its purpose was

> 'the preparation of Sardines in oil on the most approved system adopted in France.'

An opportunity, the circular goes on to announce, was

> 'thus given to the public of supporting a native industry instead of depending upon a foreign market for this delicacy [...] a new field of food supply [...] hitherto unworked.'

This presumably is a reference to the fact that the new business was all about *small* pilchards, which up to then had been considered to have no value and, as an inconvenience to fishermen, would be returned to the sea; the new company used nets with smaller meshes. Among a host of appraisals from the press, *The Field* said

---

33 *Barclay Fox's Journal*, 30 September 1846 (Cornwall Editions reprint, 2008). Queen Victoria also kept a journal in which this event was recorded: 'When it was drawn there was not one fish!'

'We have tested a box, and we can conscientiously aver that we never ate better'

and *The Liverpool Mail* thought that they were

'Capital sardines'.

Best of all, and a beautiful piece of writing, was an article in the *Western Daily Mercury* in 1874, already referred to. It sets the scene, for setting a seine:

'Lovely beyond compare is that vast impressionable mirror of water, that sheet of shimmering light spread beneath the sun, dappled with green and blue, gold and purple, ever changing, never resting, covering remorseless purpose with dimpling smiles',

then continues, with reference to the new company:

'The enterprising gentlemen of the firm named have found that Cornish pilchards can be properly cured in oil and rendered quite as excellent and nutritious an article of food as the so-called French sardines which are imported into England.'

I sometimes stand and look at the price of sardines or mackerel in local fish shops and wonder how money can ever be made out of such a fish. But it is the volume of fish which drives the price, and in this context the article is very enlightening:

'There are a hundred and sixty boats attached to Mevagissey, and of these sixty one are employed in drift and twelve in seine fishing [...] The Mevagissey seines are the largest in Cornwall, being sixteen fathoms in depth, and about two hundred and ten fathoms in length [...] Every morning from forty to fifty carts arrive at Mevagissey quay, and each cart carries away from a thousand to three thousand fish.'

It is no surprise that the author writes:

'Mevagissey has an ancient and fish like smell [...] Well-nigh every man and woman you meet looks fishy, and you feel that even the donkeys as they ecstatically wag their tails at the drinking troughs are redolent of pilchards and salt water.'

(These donkeys were used to bear away the fish; at the end of each week stray donkeys at the comparatively small fishing hamlet of Durgan were rounded up and put into a 'Pound house' – very much part of the history of Glendurgan. The owners of the donkeys could then come and pay for their retrieval.)

Sometimes people will talk about a subject, or write a book about a subject, without actually describing the detail of it. If someone tells me about a delicious dish which has taken a long time and involves a complicated process to prepare, I want to know the recipe. Because the pilchard business was for over 150 years such an important part of G. C. Fox & Co's history, here follows surely one of the most accurate records we have from that time of the process of

133

manufacture, by the same masterly journalist of 1874. He starts by announcing that it

'is interesting and simple and may be briefly told'

and then continues at length and in a way which is full of the reality of the fish processing business: the smell, the oil, the blood and guts.

'Under several long sheds a number of zinc-covered benches are erected, upon which fish are lying in various stages of progress, and busy scenes may be witnessed when the women employed are hurrying with trays of pilchards to and from different parts of the establishment. The first thing to be done when the fish are brought in fresh from the sea is to separate the large from small pilchards, the latter being the most valuable for the purposes of the curers. They are then washed and deprived of the head and the gut and washed again. Tightly packed among salt in barrels, they remain in that condition for two or three hours, according to their size, this being the great secret of the brilliancy of the fish in the tin boxes when we open them; and when taken out of the barrels they are washed and dried in the sun for three hours or longer, according to the heat of the sun. The pilchard after it leaves its native waters is metamorphosed in various ways before it reaches the dining-room. Being sufficiently dried through exposure to the sun, the fish are gathered together, placed in rows on wire frames and boiled in Lucca oil for a certain time in large vats.

They are then baked in small tin boxes, the tails being trimmed off with scissors, and oil poured in till full, after which the boxes are left open for not less than six hours, when oil is again poured in, and they are carefully soldered to exclude the air. The box to be soldered is placed on a rotating disc, which is worked by foot, and the workman seating himself at the bench, turns round the disc, and with a hot iron quickly runs the solder round the edges of the lid. In this way a good workman can solder from 500 to 600 boxes a day. The oil being wiped off the boxes, they are boiled in water, cooled, and subsequently packed in cases ready for the market. Each box contains from ten to sixteen fish, and weighs about eighteen ounces, being sold at a shilling, which is considerably cheaper than the French sardines. The foreman who superintends the works has been brought over from one of the largest sardine factories in France, so that the process is conducted on the same methods as that adopted by the French manufacturers. The sardines thus cured are every whit as good as those imported from France.'

This report on the Foxes' new enterprise is full of fascinating detail, but as stated at the beginning of this book it is not intended to go too much into technicalities. It is enough to finish with the author's closing sentences:

'[…] the effort now being made to render pilchards saleable in England is being hailed everywhere with the greatest satisfaction. Let us hope that the effort will be successful.'

The Cornish Sardine Co. (Ltd) was sold to a private group the following year, but with members of the Fox family still owning some of the shares.

The Foxes were now leaders in brine 'tanking' rather than bulk-curing, and in 1875 a second plant was opened in Newlyn, just beyond Penzance. This must have been grievous news, no doubt, for the Bolitho family which held equally serious fishing interests in the far south-west of the county, and with whom there was a tacit understanding about areas of trade. As it happened, by 1878 the company had gone into liquidation and in any event by the early 1890s the Bolithos had pulled out of fishing.

Stencil design for pilchard barrel

A final comment on the success of this little business comes from the First World War. A soldier on the battlefield bent to pick up something glittering on the ground: a gold metal label from the Cornish Sardine Company, possibly one which had been soldered on to a tin in

Portscatho. He later wrote in a letter of gratitude to the company:

'Whilst so doing, a shell burst, and had it not been for my stooping attitude, it would have found a victim in me.'

Obviously the sardines had life-saving properties as much as many other worthy qualities,

'much appreciated [*he continued to state rather drily*] to be found so near the firing line – where only the most essential things are carried, viz: food and munitions.'

'The Returns made by the Fishery Inspector of the Cornish Fisheries 1898' include not just the well-known fishing ports but also hamlets such as Portloe, Durgan, Penberth, and Porthgwarra. For the busier ports it also goes into details such as curing houses, barking places, boat-builders, sailmakers, rope-spinners, oilskin-makers, net-makers, crab-pot makers, fish hawkers, drift nets, pilchard seines, mackerel seines, ground seines, trawl and crab, trawl and long line, trawl and drift, trawl and seine, long line and seine, drift and seine, trawl, drift and long lines, oyster dredges, trammels, pollock nets, mullet nets, long liners, and crabbers. Such was the diversity, and such were the industries which many would like to see continued even today. They do not, as will be revealed in future chapters, make good tenants.

In April 1899, following a serious gale, an appeal was sent

out by the Mayor of Penzance. A fund of at least £24,000 (over £2 million in today's money) was required. The importance of the industry and the urgency of the letter are more than evident from the economy of vocabulary:

'Men who follow a most dangerous occupation lost in a night the fruit of years of industry, and are face to face with want. This following a succession of unremunerative seasons intensifies the suffering, and if help is not afforded, these poor men will be irretrievably ruined [...] The fishermen are a most deserving class, their life is hard and hazardous under the most favourable of conditions, and when robbed of the means of pursuing their perilous calling their position becomes pathetic in its helplessness. The cause appeals to the popular imagination, and it is hoped that the whole of the community, interested as it must be in this large industry, will befriend these hardy toilers of the sea, who not only face danger in pursuit of their calling, but also render noble service in the saving of lives and property at sea and manning of lifeboats.'

An additional curse to the fishing business, and to the Fox family whose Quaker members did not attend church, was the business of fish tithes and tithing, customary payments and only enforceable by common law. In 1830–31 the drift fishermen of Mousehole and Newlyn had successfully warred against the collection of tithes[34],

---

34   Tony Pawlyn, *The Falmouth Packets* (Truran Books Ltd, 2003).

but for seine fishermen it was another matter, possibly because the proprietors were more identifiable, and more able to pay. Unfortunately the Foxes fell into this category.

Since the very beginnings of Quakerism, members of the Society of Friends – or simply 'friends', as they became known – had suffered for their non-conformist ways. Much of this, shamefully, was at the hands of the clergy as the following extract shows:

'George Hawkin and others

'William Pike preist off ye parish off Stoake: on ye 26th day off ye 5th month: 1666 Came with his son Jo: Pike & several other ungodly men: & tooke away by force upon ye high way ye Corne yt [*that*] George Hawkins & his son & others were Carryinge home to there house: & did alsoe fetch there Corne out off there mowhay: & some Corne they threw over ye hedges: & after fetcht it away: And ye preist & his son: with ye rest off his Crew did beate George Hawkin very much & struck him to ye grounde & drew his bloode: & they had almost strangled his Son: And ye preist & his Company did take ffrom George Hawkin about ye fourth parte off his wheate And on ye 6[th] day of ye 6[th] mo[n]th & yeere aforesd ye preist Came againe with his wicked Crew & Carryed away neere ye fifth parte off all his oates: & ye preist & his son did againe Cruelly beate George Hawkyn [*sic*] & his son with there staves and there

139

bodyes were soe much bruised thereby: yt [*that*] they
Coulde not worke ffor several days after:'[35]

This record does not make pleasant reading and as well as
beatings, culprits regularly had their legs 'sett in ye stocks'.
It is an irony of some cruelty that for those who believed
so much in the equality of the sexes there was no discrimination when it came to these disciplines: maltreatment
was meted out to both Quakers and Quakeresses.

As far back as 1663 in Richard Farnsworth's *The Quakers' Plea with the Bishops*, the Quakers had argued that
they should not be persecuted for avoiding attendance at
church:

> 'Christ so loved the church, that he gave himself
> for it, that he might sanctify and cleanse it [...] but
> where is it written that cathedrals and parish-meet-
> ing-places (commonly called Parish-churches) are
> the body of Christ, or that Christ is the Head of
> them, or that Christ laid down his life for them, or
> that they are nourished and cherished by the Lord?'

Although Quakers and other dissenting Christian
denominations were welcomed in Falmouth, and made a
contribution both economically and socially, in much the
same ways as the Jews, there must have been some who

---

35   From *Record of the Sufferings of Quakers in Cornwall*, tran-
      scribed and edited by Norman Penney with an introduction
      by Lucy Violet Hodgkin, published by the Friends Historical
      Society 1928, page 64.

resented them. In 1667, admittedly before the arrival of the Fox family, Thomas Holden wrote from Falmouth to James Hickes saying, in a way which would be not tolerated today by any religious group, that

> 'the Quakers of these parts grow so impudent that they are building a house purposely to meet in.'

Apart from anything else this is an unintelligent remark: the evidence is that the focal importance of trade has always been *uniting*, with the result that centres of trade then become *inviting*. Where people unite in the face of a common foe, or in fear of being ostracised, that can be to their advantage. It is strengthening; and the Society of Friends was an example of this.

Quakers believed fervently in the true Church but the business of paying tithes to a man-made organisation was, in their opinion, not Biblical and an imposition. Alfred Fox

> 'refused consistently to pay Rector's Rate Tithes, Fish Tithes and Wodehouse Place was repeatedly stripped of furniture and silver to meet [*the*] same.'

Consider the paradox, and any perceived indignity, of an eminent businessman and respected employer of many, having his chattels 'seized' from Wodehouse Place[36] on 12 January 1898 and sold by auction at the Town Hall a week later. At Glendurgan, which inconveniently for his

---

36   Alfred Fox's town house in Woodlane, Falmouth.

son George Henry Fox straddled two parishes (Mawnan Smith and Constantine), his sister and tenant Rachel Tuckett records

> 'Each year something to meet [*the tithe*] was taken – hay – a cart – a pig – a cow – they would take much more then they ought to have done and keep the extra money – Papa would not interfere and let them take what they liked.'

It was the habit of Quaker families to look on silently and without objection as their chattels, often more valuable than the tithe, were appropriated. As a side observation, what is interesting is that occasionally there was restitution, but not necessarily of the things that were taken, which perhaps explains why some established Quaker homes are adorned with items of an ecclesiastical but not necessarily aesthetic nature. A cousin recalled, with typical Quaker absence of malice, but to my hardened mind a degree of naivety:

> 'We had a yearly excitement in the coming of the church rate collector. He always went into the pantry and helped himself to silver spoons, no doubt a hateful job to the good man; and much delighted he was to come in one day when the money for all the outdoor wages was ranged on the table, and to help himself. We suffered much from the fear that our special spoons would be taken, but mine is still quite safe.'

It is recorded that one of the Wellington cousins, Thomas Fox, 'insisted on the formality of a legal warrant'. He wrote

'I have a real objection to paying tithe, and I cannot consent to any collusive mode of doing it.'

As in Falmouth, 'the family looked on silently and without protest as their beasts were driven away'.[37]

In an undated reminiscence George Henry Fox wrote that

'Fish tithes at Mevagissey and elsewhere were peculiarly unjust and obnoxious, and the cause of much heart burning.'

He then continued with a story about a friend of his father's, a Falmouth shoemaker who

'objected to pay the Rector's rate & the Rector called on him, and argued the matter, and said seats were available for the Shoe maker and his family in the church – & the Shoe maker said he did not want the seats, and the Rector replied "but you might have them". The Rector ordered a pair of boots and at the end the year the S'maker sent a bill for two pairs of boots and the Rector called on him & said he had

---

37   From *Quaker Homespun: The Life of Thomas Fox of Wellington / Serge Maker and Banker / 1747–1821*, by Hubert Fox (George Allen and Unwin Ltd, 1958).

not had two pairs. The Shoe maker replied "True, but you might have had them." '

More than once Alfred and his brother Robert Were Fox were summoned to appear before the justices of peace at St Austell's town hall, on account of outstanding tithes being owed to the Reverend Henry Algernon Baumgartner, vicar of the parish church of Mevagissey. In an account 'furnished' by the vicar's solicitors in 1870, recoverable costs include 'levying distress', as well as auctioneers' charges and advertisements. Clearly the vicar had no idea of the distress, or 'great oppression' he and others caused to seiners (G. C. Fox & Co. had shares in seining companies round the coast). In an interesting letter dated 15 March 1870 to a brother-in-law, Sir Joseph Pease, George Henry Fox puts forward the fishermen's plight:

'I write to you as an MP to ask if there is any probability of so small (though well deserving) a matter being taken notice of and their prayers answered [...] it is a matter [...] in which we are much interested, both directly and from sympathy with the poor men who can ill pay such a tax.'

He goes on to imply that the taxes are especially unfair as

'there is no statute law to support in any way such tithes – they are claimed on prescriptive right.'

Worse is to follow:

'the seine owners pay £1/13s/4d per seine per annum whether the fish are taken or not, so that of late years the vicar has been making a steady profit off our and other people's seines, whilst the owners of seines there have been making heavy losses.'

George concludes with a beautifully apt and emotive metaphor (many of the family were keen conchologists):

'It will be a great blessing if we can relieve these three unfortunate spots [*Portloe, Gorran and Mevagissey*] from such an abominable tax – I will send you copies of the petitions when ready, and hope your grand measures now before the House won't swamp out our worthy cockle shell.'

It should be noted that tithes were opposed not just by Quakers. Pilchard drivers in general fought against their collection and were particularly incensed when the tithes went to mere impropriators, as at Paul, in the far west.

To digress for a minute, but in order to cast a wider perspective on the subject of tithes, if you go to one of the most meritorious of museums in Cornwall, Penlee House Gallery and Museum in Penzance, you will be simultaneously engaged and educated by its collection of Newlyn School paintings. A large percentage of these focus on the business of fish. Pilchard circulars and reports kept by G. C. Fox & Co. provide valuable statistics; and no doubt the Newlyn School painters might have liked to have known that the Foxes' pilchard records were bound in leather which was a surprising shade of spinach green, with gold tooling. But the paintings have another more powerful purpose. There is, for example, a cruel irony to the drama of the painting by Percy Robert Craft entitled '*Hevva*'. A man walking down the sunlit part of the street is waving a 'puff', a sort of calico balloon made with withies, to signify the location of the shoaling and 'token' the boats; this must have been a refinement on the 'bush' mentioned in Richard Carew's *Survey of Cornwall*. There is an air of excitement. But to the two women selling vegetables in the foreground it must also have been an omen of tragedy, as much as income. Despite all the scenes of breathtaking beauty, these masterpieces portray again and again the theme of early widowhood caused by 'loss at sea': the fatherless children, the young mothers who struggle on their own, and the elderly mothers whose lined faces and melancholy eyes respectively tell of their own battles, and of their complete empathy for others who have similarly been bereaved, or even more tragically, are about to be bereaved. 'For those in peril on the sea' are the words that come to mind, swiftly followed by my own (with too many words in the line to scan): 'and those who are left behind struggling to make ends meet'. If the smell of fish was, as Ellen Crewdson opined, 'unutterable', so too was the grief of the average fishing family.

For one reason or another, the harshness of being a fisherman does not seem to have been used as a weapon against the tithe-takers. But writing now, and looking back at life as described by those Newlyn School artists, who would have known all about the impoverished plight of the parishioners of Paul, the injustices of the 'fat-cat' vicar in his pretty vicarage must have been hard to bear, let alone understand.

An advertisement for at least one rectory included, persuasively, the words 'subject to tithe of fish' in much the same way as it might say 'with productive orchards'. At someone else's cost, this could bestow benefits on the rector, especially when the high tide was particularly productive, and when it became known as 'the parson's tide'.

As much as anyone might wish that fishing boats and fishing trips should be blessed, and as much as the fishing community was aware of those who cared for its spiritual welfare, the uninvited presence of vicars has not always augured well in fishing communities.

Fishermen at Looe, 1900
Photograph, inscribed verso: 'Taken at Looe 1900 – and facing the sea – Joseph Warne Age 70 – Thomas Toms Age 82 – Samuel Organ Age 62 – John Clements Age 85 – Richard Solt Age 65 – John Davey Age 76 – Harry Toms Age 15 – Robert Prynn Age 56 – William Prynn Age 70 – Benjamin Menhenick Age 73 – James Toms Age 61 – William Southern Age 68 – From Geo W Prynn Shutta Lane Looe'

As is usual in the fishing business, success rates are dependent on shoaling, and in 1907 G. C. Fox & Co. felt led by the obliging fish, along with a number of other curers, to set up premises in Falmouth. In 1910 they started a curing store at Portscatho. Cuthbert Fox, George Henry's son and my grandfather, with his eye of an engineer, took an active part in its construction, recording everything in meticulous detail. For this purpose, he sailed over in his yacht *Syrinx* and lived on board; probably writing up the day's events was a pleasant way of filling in the summer evenings, and an unnecessarily large logbook. Names of boats were diverse: *Pet*, *Rufus*, *Chips*, *Olive*, *Alvina*, *Grace Darling*, *Deerhound*, *Providence* and *Little Maid* being a random sample. (One of them, the *Edith*, ended up, by a strange quirk of fate, having a re-fit years later in our Penryn boatyard.)

My grandfather's logbook is full of dry statistical records, and there is only one narrative entry, presumably made because of the remarkable catch:

'1912 October 12th

[…] During the night of the 12th 28,000 fish taken out of inmost seine – mainly by men standing up to waist in water tucking fish in baskets into seine boats. Some were picked out of pools – some dead off rocks. Delivered to our store by 7 a.m. – in good condition but J. Hunkin reports ¼ hundred and every 2 hundred scaleless – firm broad good fish otherwise […]'

(Once, in Mylor, I witnessed that experience of shoaling, of standing in shallow seawater which was turbulent with fish. I lowered one bucket after another into its boiling mass; and was pleased to be 'tucking' grey mullet rather than pilchards. Red would have been ideal.)

Then came the First World War. Fishermen were called up, and the Falmouth venture flopped. In the minutes of July 1916 it states

'the fishery was a complete failure last year East of the Lizard. None were cured at either Looe Polperro Mevagissey or Falmouth Stores and only 4¼ casks at Portscatho. In Mounts Bay the fishery was the worst on record.'

It is recorded that the total export in 1918 was 'only about 3000 casks', and that not one fish was cured in the Falmouth stores for the four years between 1915 and 1918. However with some signs of improvement in 1919 they bought a cellar in St Ives, and also

'a motor lorry to assist Josiah Hunkin to start a fresh-fish business at Portscatho.'

This must have been rather a waste of money: there is in the notebook a page headed in very optimistic writing

'Portscatho 1920–21'

and then underneath, disappointingly,

'No pilchards caught.'

On 20 March 1920, the company bought Colonel Paynter's[38] freehold fish store in Newlyn for £880 – to be sold in 1945 for £1,400. The property in Portscatho was to follow in 1951 when it was sold for £750.

As my grandfather Cuthbert went on to record, the business was neglected during the years of both the First and the Second World Wars. He tried to resuscitate it and there was a flash of activity with the USA and also Italy. But looking back over the history of the business it is easy to see that the writing was on the wall, and at the end of the 1935–36 season, G. C. Fox & Co. pulled out of the trade.

Interior of a fish processing factory, probably at Portscatho, c. 1930

---

38 Colonel Camborne Paynter (1849–1964) was the colourful owner of Boskenna in West Cornwall, famous before the First World War as a rendezvous for many of the Lamorna Cove artists (including Alfred Munnings and Laura Knight) and later as the setting for some of Mary Wesley's novels. Guglielmo Marconi (1874–1937), popularly credited as the inventor of radio, grew to know the Paynters when he was experimenting with transatlantic wireless transmission from Poldhu Cove in 1901. Over 20 years later, he became involved with Colonel Paynter's only daughter Betty; there were unconfirmed reports of their engagement in 1925 when Betty turned 18, but the relationship soon fizzled out.

This chapter on fishing ends with some personal recollections from more recent times. When I decided to join the business in 1976 my father, knowing that I had nothing to contribute, suggested that I should go back to college and gain some kind of qualification. Against all the odds I acquired a Distinction in Business Studies. Part of this involved producing a thesis, the title of which, in a fairly casual moment, was given to me by one of the lecturers. I gulped: what on earth did I know about 'The effects of the fishing regulations of the European Economic Community on the South West of Britain'? But as is so often the case, when you become immersed in a subject which appears to be boring, it can turn out to be deeply fascinating; presumably it was the same for all my ancestors who ended up writing treatises, theses, lectures and reports on pilchards, sardines, crabs, lobsters, oysters and mackerel and ichthyologic sciences in general; and this was as well as the endless petitions they wrote to M.P.s about the injustices of the industry. I became completely absorbed and a minor, but no doubt tedious, expert on mesh sizes and quotas.

On joining the firm I was initially apprenticed to our paint storeman in the Docks[39], but increasingly I was weaned away from him in order to help out with the ship agency business. By the late 1970s and early 1980s the common mackerel, *Scomber scombrus*, was shoaling,

39   A lucrative part of the business for many years was the agency it held for International Paint Marine Coatings; at one time the store even had its own siding for the delivery of paint by rail, extending from Falmouth Docks Railway Station.

very advantageously for us, in the Celtic waters. This meant that Falmouth Bay was full of fish factory ships and also 'mother' ships, mostly from the Soviet Union or Soviet satellite states, plus a few ships from Egypt. The office was a hive of activity, and not just from 9 a.m. until 5 p.m. It became a round-the-clock business, and as agents for owners or charterers who had to submit to the local demands of the Harbour Office, Custom House, Immigration, and Port Health, G. C. Fox & Co's boarding clerks were expected to be the first on board, even if this was in the small hours of the night. If they were not the first on board, it was not competing agents but local ship chandlers who would be found in the captain's cabin, drinking vodka with him and his officers.

Completing Customs declarations and other paper-work in the captain's cabin may have been complicated due to language problems, but this was nothing compared to the difficulties to be witnessed of monitoring and recording fishing activities. Because of my studies I was interested in this, and it very quickly became apparent that those who had dreamed up the regulations had little idea of the realities: often highly dangerous conditions caused by wind and rain, with scant regard for health and safety, or efficient equipment, never mind a whey-faced fishing inspector with his clipboard and measure. Slipped statistics were as common as 'slipped catches' – fish which, although often valuable, were thrown overboard because it was not part of the fishing policy for a particu-lar fishing fleet. (This was nothing new: there had always been issues over fish which had mysteriously disappeared, between catcher and trans-shipment and trans-shipment and curer, etc., but perhaps not so much overboard.) But what is more, and in spite of the 'boxes' inside which you were allowed to fish, and in spite of the quotas, it seemed almost impossible to farm fish in the effective way in which, for example, you can farm mussels or salmon in the comparative tranquillity of a loch or estuary.

Sometimes unwanted fish could be to the advantage of the ship agent, or indeed any other visitor to a fishing boat. Once we were given a huge box of frozen Canadian halibut. The office hammer was produced and applied with the office chisel, to no avail. So I took the box to the top floor of the building and threw it down onto the concrete floor of the back yard; and that evening we all went home with glassy chunks of this most delicious of fishes.

That was an age when there were in Cornwall only about three restaurants where you could eat superbly well, and when the variety of fish being served today was unknown. Now, writing with hindsight, I ponder on the effects of four things which were scarcely born in the late 1970s: the dramatic hike in fuel prices, the advances in technological fishing equipment, our carbon imprint on the world (quite high in fish-farming), and lastly our mania for fish, its effects and its cause: a plethora of Cornish fish restaurants.[40]

---

40   My father liked eating fish. Once he went to try out a new fish restaurant in Falmouth. The management knew he was coming and had made a big effort. My father looked at the extensive menu with its mouth-watering fish dishes, and chose. I learnt after the event that a waiter had run from one end of Falmouth to the other in order to provide him with fillet steak.

8

MINING AND THE AGE OF THE ENTREPRENEUR

POKING AROUND IN the forbidden places of the unexplained geography of our childhood, my elder brother, Robert, and I would occasionally resort to our grandparents' garage. It did not score very highly on points of interest, but at the back, behind the Humber, there were two heavy crates containing a collection of rather strange and beautiful rocks, resting in wood shavings. We later came to learn that they were crystals. What became of these forgotten treasures no one seems to know: sold, loaned, or given, they are probably now languishing, unlabelled, in the basement of some geological museum, along with the collections of many other Cornish dynasties. Little did I realise, but this was my earliest introduction to a mining ancestry.

Until 1857 the family held large and mainly speculative shares in the mining industry. They were very quick to realise that it was the added values of mining which could be really beneficial, e.g. building ports, importing and exporting. Copper, for example, was exported to South Wales for smelting.

George Fox (1746–1816), the son of Edward Fox (I) (born 1719) of Gonvena, Wadebridge, had moved to Penryn in the late 1760s and gone into business with William Phillips, a Quaker, who was a dealer in coal and timber, both of which were, in time to come, to make significant contributions to the profits of G. C. Fox & Co. A subsidiary business was set up at Perranarworthal: Perran Wharf had already been in use for the export of copper from the Gwennap mines. By 1785 there was a partnership called Fox Phillips & Fox with, amongst others as partners, Mary Fox, George Croker Fox, Robert Were Fox, Richard Phillips, George Fox of Perran, and Edward Fox from Wadebridge.

George negotiated leases from the Basset family of Tehidy. These were for properties on the north side of the river; and in due course he had drawn up a lease for some wasteland in the parish of Mylor, effectively the south side of the River Kennall, giving him

> 'power to construct within two years messuages, warehouses, kilns, quays, dams, wharves, docks and ponds or other buildings or works as to him may seem fit.'

George's half-uncle was George Croker Fox (I) from Falmouth and the two of them must have been a powerful combination. George Croker in his Foreign Copy Book writes in 1771 that he had

> 'a concern in a considerable business at the head of the river where there was an opportunity of supplying the miners to more advantage than from some other places.'

But in 1791 it was George Croker Fox's two sons, another George Croker (II) and Robert Were (I), who were to invest in the engineering business and establish an iron foundry at Perranarworthal. Perran Foundry, as it became known, was more convenient for the Gwennap mines than the one at Hayle, much further to the west; it was also at the head of a deep water estuary. Charcoal was imported to be used in the process of smelting tin, and pig iron from Sweden was used for making pure iron. Timber from Norway and the Baltic, and later Quebec and the West coast of America was used in the manufacture of pit-props, and other essential mining structures, much of it being floated up the river, and left in log ponds to be 'pickled' until ready for use. Up to thirty ships lying off Restronguet, and awaiting berths, was not an uncommon sight. In the same deep water powerful lifting gear was available to lift heavy machinery brought down by barges from the foundry, and to tranship it onto sea-going vessels. The Redruth and Chasewater Railway Company, in which the Foxes were later to hold shares purchased from the Williamses of Scorrier, owned a tug called the *Sydney* which was used to assist ships which had become becalmed; it was also used for the occasional excursion, as described in Chapter 6.

To the delight of those who worked in the family business, mining was inextricably linked with both timber and shipping.

In 1792 the Foxes bought the Neath Abbey Iron Foundry in South Wales. This too was a neat move: it eliminated the competition, and brought to the business both technology and new resources for raw materials. They also bought in expertise: Peter Price, a Quaker foundry man trained by Abram Darby from the largest iron foundry in Scotland, and William Wood, an ironmaster from Swansea.

The investment of capital for these two foundries, between the years of 1790 to 1795, has been calculated in twenty-first century values to be £6 million; and almost all of this was raised from Quakers in Cornwall. At one time the Perran Foundry employed over 150 people and according to a present day archaeologist, it was in its time, both in terms of expertise and capital investment, the equivalent of a rocket station today: at the cutting edge of technology in the first quarter of the nineteenth century. There was nothing in terms of engines, pumps, boilers, etc. that they could not manufacture, and to customers from all over the world. Wilson Fox records that

'the two largest pumping engines in the world at that time were made by the Perran Foundry Co owned by the Foxes and Prices and Williams and by the Hayle Foundry owned by the Harveys, for draining the Lake of Haarlem.'

There were in fact three steam-driven pumping stations built to drain the Harlemmermeer dry, which was achieved in three years after the pumps started work in 1850. One of them, the Cruquius engine, built in Hayle, survives to this day as a museum and landmark on the European Route of Industrial Heritage, near to the fort Cruquius which is itself a World Heritage Site.

(Writing this in recent years, with much of England periodically flooded, I wish that both the foundry and its pumps were still in operation.)

In due course, they progressed at Perran Foundry to producing cylinders up to 100 inches in diameter, and in

1815 a beam of 28 tons was cast in two parts at a cost of £400.

But it was not such a completely mechanised age: Ellen Crewdson, whose father managed the foundry, recalls one of the casts for mine machinery requiring 24 horses to drag it up Cove Hill past the entrance to Tredrea, where her family lived. In 1843, 19 of the total work force of 110 were aged between 13 and 18 years and two were below the age of 13; mining was not about the romantic clifftop ruins which walkers flock to see today. Moreover, all this industrialisation was happening when there was scant regard for safety: visitors to the foundry stood afar from the furnaces but watched with admiration as the stokers, stripped to the waist, ran in relays to refuel.[41] But refreshingly there was also an absence of bureaucracy, which was to the considerable advantage of entrepreneurs.

In 1802 the Foxes had turned the foundry into a partnership with the Williams family.

It is a remarkable declaration of trust that the initiation of one of the most dynamic joint ventures of the Industrial Revolution is signed, sealed, and dated on one side of

---

41   Caroline Fox visited Perran Foundry on 13 February 1840 'to see them cast fourteen tons of iron for the beam of a steam engine.' She continued, 'This beam was the largest they had ever cast, and its fame had attracted almost the whole population of Perran, who looked highly picturesque by the light of the liquid iron. My regretting that we had not chestnuts to employ so much heat which was now running to waste induced a very interesting discourse from [John] Sterling, first, on the difference between utilitarianism and utility, then on the sympathy of great minds with each other, however different may be the tracks they select.' (*The Journals of Caroline Fox*, February 13, 1840)

a piece of paper which is no larger in size than two-thirds of what is today known as A4. In its context, but not content, it is hard to imagine anything less significant. Maybe it was merely a letter of intent; and in some far-off archive there may exist a subsequent pile of relevant deeds. But for two families to trust each other over such a massive investment, maybe it could also be conjectured that this scrap of paper was all that was necessary for business to commence: lengthy pre-nuptial, or even post-nuptial, agreements do not resound with feelings of commitment but more with elements of potential mistrust.

Other documents involving third parties, however, are significantly much more complicated, covering every eventuality in the customary litigious way. For example, in 1822 there is a bond to William Paul of Truro, signed and sealed by three Foxes and two Williamses, and witnessed by Richard Tregaskis; and in 1831, there is a deed about the transfer of a ship called 'the Alchymist with all and singular the Masts Sails Sail Yards Anchor Cables Ropes Cords Tackle Apparel Boats Oars and Appurtenances whatsoever to the said ship'. It goes on to give all the statistical details and finally, lest there should be any shadow of doubt, adds 'no Galleries and no figurehead'. It was clearly not a ship, on the face of its description, to merit a sheet of paper of almost A1 size, signed and sealed by three Foxes and one Williams, and again witnessed.

Together the two families were responsible for establishing the tram-road which took minerals to Portreath on the north coast. Eventually the tram-road was to extend to the south coast, where at Point there was a Customs House: between 1827 and 1877 1,500,000 tons of minerals went down the river at Devoran, which became a very busy port. Locomotives, with names such as 'Miner', 'Smelter' and 'Spitfire' were used, but the section above Carharrack and the section from Devoran to Point remained horse-drawn; and the Portreath tram-road was always a horse-drawn plateway. Even so, these tram-roads were a significant improvement on using solely a multitude of mules, which had been the previous, noisy-with-hoofbeat, mode of transport for moving 200,000 tons of copper per annum – let alone any other minerals. (The Cornwall copper boom lasted from 1830 to 1850.) It is said that one of the Fox family, presumably for the benefit both of mules and of those on horseback, was responsible for installing granite horse-marker posts to mark the river bank at Perranarworthal in the event of flooding. Some of these my grandfather just remembered before they became buried in road widening schemes.

Lord de Dunstanville – a member of the Basset family – who owned Portreath, and whose family made more money out of mining in Cornwall than any other, had already heavily invested in the port; he then leased it to members of the Fox family who created the inner basin and who improved the access roads from the mines to the quay.

Perran Foundry produced and exported work all over the world. A major scheme, well documented on the internet but in which the role of the foundry is relatively unrecognized, was one in which Fox and Williams were the main contractors for the Plymouth Breakwater. In 1814 Robert Were Fox (I) wrote to his son

'Thou shalt also have the sixty fourth of 5/6ths in the Breakwater contract which contract in the present year will I hope produce about ten thousand pounds profit. Mr Williams made a collection of cost from the adventurers in this concern'

and in 1830 Charles Fox wrote from Perran to the Commissioners of the Navy

'I beg leave to offer myself as a security to the amount of twenty thousand pounds, for the due fulfilment of Alfred Fox and John Williams of a contract for the completion of the Plymouth Breakwater on the terms at which they now offer to undertake it, having myself no interest in the contract or the Profit or Loss.'

Charles's writing is large, fluent, generous, easy to read, wise and communicative. It gives the impression of a man who thinks before he acts or writes, but then does so with great deliberation and clarity. It slopes optimistically forward and has all the confidence of a great statesman.

The enterprise at Perran was first directed by Edward Fox's son, George (I). It was he who built Tredrea House, overlooking the foundry, and who lived there until his death in 1816; and it was his son, yet another George, who continued to run the business until the early 1820s when his half-cousin Charles took over both the business and the house. Meanwhile George Croker Fox (II), who had established himself at Grove Hill House in Falmouth, died in 1807 and his son, a third George Croker (1788–1850), then became the head of that branch of the family.

As if the business were not enough to occupy him,

this particular Fox was by all accounts something of an intellectual, a classicist and a mathematician, both of some distinction: he produced two commonplace books, which, excepting the account of Napoleon in Chapter 6, are more full of academic treatises, algebraic equations, and sentimental poems than anything of relevance to our history. Here are some lines from one of several odes he wrote to his wife Lucy:

> 'Tell me my love, my mistress and my wife
> Whence spring the magic charm of wedded life…
> I grant the swain was not a matchless wight
> Linked by unequal fates to Beauty bright.'

What is significant is that because in 1815 a Quaker would not have been permitted to enter university, the likelihood is that his studies of the classics were largely self-taught. Perhaps that is why so many members of the family were in the habit of throwing themselves at the feet of the lions of literature – and art. Not directly connected to our story, this is amply described in the *Journals* of Barclay Fox and his sister Caroline; and it continued into the twentieth century with friendships on the peripheries of the Bloomsbury set, as much as of the Pre-Raphaelites, and aesthetes such as Roger Fry, who was related. The Falmouth artist Henry Scott Tuke, also from a Quaker family and as happy in a boat as he was at a canvas, was another close friend, especially of Charles Masson Fox (Howard Fox's elder son, who was a partner in the Falmouth firm from 1901 onwards and Consul to Russia and Sweden). In this context it is curious that the

Victorian art critic, artist, writer and philosopher, John Ruskin, who had so much in common with the Foxes and their sense of wonder, should state over several pages of the most eloquent prose that to him the most wonderful thing in the world was the bow of a boat.[42] Again conjecturing, possibly this preoccupation, this passion for exercising the mind, and for searching the aesthetic, is something else which kept the Foxes on another type of brink: the brink of hard-headed commercialism and sharp practice.

George Croker Fox (III)'s uncle, Robert Were, had married Elizabeth Tregelles of Penryn, and from that marriage stemmed three remarkable men: the aforementioned Charles, and his brothers Alfred and Robert Were (II). Often overlooked, when talking about these three brothers is the fact that they were from a family of ten children and one of these siblings, although not involved directly with the business, also needs to be mentioned: his name was Joshua. He was delightful in so many ways, totally at one with nature, and more in the next world than this; in fact, one could say he was probably not 'on', but 'beyond' the brink. In spite of being a shareholder in the business, he never seemed to have any money, and what is worse, seemed to have difficulty in receiving it. His letters of refusal, and the letters of entreaty from

---

42 Coincidentally, in her diary Caroline Fox quoted her friend John Stuart Mill: 'A ship in full sail he declared the only work of man that under all circumstances harmonises with nature, the reason being that it is adapted purely to natural requirements.' (*The Journals of Caroline Fox*, March 20, 1840)

his brothers are very endearing; both must have been a hidden burden to the firm. Here is one in response to his niece, Rachel Tuckett, who had begged 'him not to over-run his quarterly allowances too freely':

'My dear Niece,

Thanks for thy two letters, received but not read by me. Like the little limpet on the Lizard rocks which draws only the closer to its protecting friend when it hears the roaring of its native element, so I, when I hear surging without me the waves of this troublesome world, withdraw into my shell and am at peace'.

This is a burying-one's-head-in-the-sand attitude with which many of us are familiar. But the letter also tells us something about Joshua's character. He was imaginative and poetic in his prose. He was clearly an observer of nature. He was stubborn, and like all Foxes, at home in a maritime or, at any rate, littoral world.

As regards the other brothers, the following extract from the *Western Morning News* on 22 April 1878, describes them well:

'The Cornish Foxes were always distinguished by their business capacity, their unflinching integrity, and their deep interest in all philanthropic work.'

Although there had been previous, and were to be subsequent, generations to possess these fine qualities, somehow it seems that the Victorian era was the age when prosperity and philanthropy met, when men would give their names as much as their money and their time to an endless list of worthy projects. It was the age of exploration and documentation, which just fed into the Victorian way of life, like an overdose of nectar to the bee; and people were hungry. Lastly, as has been described, there was a refreshing absence of unnecessary paperwork, and of official and unofficial persons pontificating about what was permissible and what was not. It was an ideal climate for men such as Robert, Alfred and Charles Fox. The study of geology was fashionable, and they became keen mineralogists.

Robert Were Fox II (1789–1877), the eldest son, was a natural philosopher and an 'experimentalist', or what today is called a scientist.[43] He was a Fellow of the Royal Society and was interested in thermodynamics, electro-magnetism and heat flows within the earth's crust: he developed the first dipping needle which could be used at sea and measured the angle between the magnetic field and the horizon. His less well-known inventions included a hydrostatic safety chamber, shown at the Polytechnic, and allegedly installed in the offices of 48 Arwenack Street. His knowledge on these matters was encyclopaedic and must have been invaluable to the family's mining interests, as well as to the business at Perran Foundry. He married advantageously into the banking family of Barclay.

---

43   The word 'scientist' was coined in the 1830s.

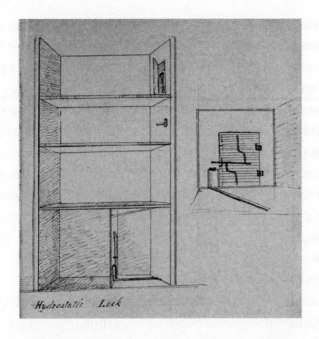

Hydrostatic Lock

A MODEL OF A HYDROSTATIC SAFETY CHAMBER was also exhibited, which the committee, on account of its practical utility, think it proper to describe. It represents a vault or chamber, containing treasure; with an iron door secured on the inside by heavy bars. A cylinder and piston are placed by the side of the frame work of the door, and a small tube communicating with the bottom of the cylinder, is carried through the wall, to one on the upper apartments of the building: an opening being made in the tube, in which a cock is inserted, so as to allow the water to flow into some vessel in an intermediate apartment, and create an alarm. In order to open the door, the cock in the intermediate apartment must first be closed, and a small quantity of water poured into the tube from the upper room, which descending into the cylinder in the vault, and acting under the piston, causes it to rise, and lift the lever connected with the bars. Thus the lower chamber cannot be opened, unless the two upper apartments are first entered, to stop the cock and pour in the water. The persons lodging there would consequently be alarmed, and the greatest degree of security from depredation is thereby obtained.

167

There has seldom been a true Quaker without an eye for a good business deal, but the next brother Alfred was the born administrator. He was still working into his very old age, not just because his nephew and young partner Robert Barclay Fox (I) had died prematurely, but also because, quite simply, he had an excellent brain. Like his brother Robert Were, Alfred also married advantageously, into the banking and steel manufacturing family of Lloyd. To give the full flavour of the Victorian Quaker businessman about his ship agency work, no one can improve on the memories of his son (my great-grandfather) George Henry:

'His snuff boxes impressed me, especially a silver one which he carried in his pocket, and which he needed to tap on the cover before opening it to take a pinch. His waistcoat was not always free from traces of snuff. He used to carry more than one large bright coloured cotton handkerchief in his pocket. He wore a broad rimmed hat [on] Sundays, and [on] week-days a straight collared black cloth coat, and stand up white collar and black stock. He could surprise people [with] the date when his various hats were bought, having entered the date inside the lining of each; and he would produce a large gold watch bought at a second hand shop, and enlarge on the wonderfully good time it kept, and say he had not altered the hands a minute for the last five years (but he took care not to say that no one [else] had altered the hands). Father was often late for meals in coming from the office, and dinner did not come till he was in and rang the bell, so we got to depend on its being half an hour or more late. In the sixties I used to walk up from the office about two or two thirty with him, and as he walked slowly then, he would say "Thee can go on George and ring the bell". He was fond of chatting with captains, at the office, and last words often delayed him.'

This was when he was not on his horse: he liked to ride whenever he could and once galloped in 25 minutes at 6 a.m. from Glendurgan to Falmouth in order to catch the paddle steamer *Sir Francis Drake* bound for Plymouth. On another occasion he rode to Mevagissey before breakfast. In his younger days, according to George's brother Howard 'it took him 20 minutes to walk from Green Bank Hotel to Wodehouse Place Gate when not interrupted by social claims'. He was obviously very attractive, charming and easily charmed:

'He often walked to Badger's cellars where Fox & Co. had stores for their merchandise of cargoes and was so sociable and fond of ladies that he was not always punctual'.

Alfred 'avoided controversy and was bright and cheery and submissive even to bad treatment'. There exists one particular letter he wrote in pencil:

'In imprisonment Bodmin 28.3.52

My Dear Sarah will pity me with the rest of the jury after a night's confinement without fire, or even chair enough – or anything to eat or drink – but I had a good breakfast at 8 a.m. which so far has stood by me nicely – we are told that we shall not be liberated – but I hope we shall be, after spending 24 hours more here without food or fire – 3 Jury men stand out against the others – we enjoy ourselves as well as we can and are cheerful in spite of our disappointment & annoyance. I long to be at home and know not when that happiness may be mine – farewell dearest in bright hope thine very affectionately Alfred Fox'.

The nature of his alleged offence is unknown, but is most likely to have been the non-payment of tithes, although it could have had something to do with the rights of oyster dredgers.

Charles Fox (1797–1878) was also a scientist and authority on mining. In 1836 he offered a prize for the best machinery for raising miners up the shaft, and in 1837 he offered £100 for the first mine to adopt it. This was an improvement on sometimes two thousand feet of ladders to descend and ascend. He helped to found the Miners Association of Cornwall and Devon, being president from 1861 to 1863. As has been said, for some time he was the resident partner at the foundry after his cousin George left in 1822 and until the Foxes extricated themselves in 1848. Sarah his wife, in some recollections of his life, wrote revealingly

'It so happened that the first time we appeared together out of our own premises, after he had been superseded in the position of manager of the works at Perran, was for a drive alone to Truro in a little pony chaise. On ascending the long hill out of the Perran valley we saw before us a line of wagons dragging some large heavy machinery from the Foundry, with parties of 5 or more men, and from 16 to 20 horses with each wagon, at long intervals apart. As we approached the men with the nearest wagon I noticed that they stopped the horses and drew up in a line, then they all took off their hats and remained uncovered until we passed them. *Really* respectful as the Cornish are in feeling and conduct, they are anything but deferential in manner, and will rarely touch their hats even to a lady: and at first I supposed the proceeding to be accidental. But as we reached the second detachment the same stopping and uncovering their heads, with an almost reverential manner towards us was enacted, and so on with each party to the top of the hill; and then it burst upon me that it was a silent expression from these honest faithful hearts, of gratitude and respect to my husband, who had for so many years been not only their master but their friend and benefactor in weal or woe, and they thus testified that they looked up to him for his worth alone. Neither of us could speak, and his emotion was as great as mine.'

This extract is also doubly touching, if not humbling, for another reason. Because part of the Quaker attitude was that every man should be equal in the sight of the Lord, the doffing of hats was not therefore in Quaker eyes seen to be a sign of respect, or good manners; so much for religiosities. Moreover, in those days throughout all privately owned industries there was often a vast disparity between those at the top and those at the bottom; how to handle this, and any potential resentment, displays a mark of genius.

The Foxes earned respect, not just for their integrity, but because they were employers who by their entrepreneurial spirit created jobs for the masses, and a wealth of ancillary jobs which fed into their varied industries.

Charles Fox was also an aesthete, with a learned appreciation of both literature and the fine arts. He had a strong interest in all things Middle Eastern and, as a Biblical scholar, travelled extensively in the Holy Land. He was also a sinologist. He was in a word, a polymath; and unlike his great-great-great nephew, another Charles Fox, and author of this book, 'profitless conversation never took place'.

The Foxes came out of the foundry business in 1858. Alfred records in an unusually discriminate vein that 'owing to deaths about two thirds of the Perran Co. fell into the hands of ladies who could do nothing to promote its prosperity and they sold their shares', together with Alfred's, to the Williams family of Scorrier. The foundry finally closed in 1879, but even today I receive letters from all over the world, enclosing photographs of, and asking questions about, bits of machinery bearing the stamp of the Perran Foundry.

A connection which often seems to be overlooked is the fact that the Royal Cornwall Polytechnic Society partly owes its origins to Perran Foundry. Models, inventions and mechanical improvements were often presented to Robert Were Fox, whose daughter Anna Maria, together with her sister Caroline, realised that this represented an opportunity both for further education and also for exhibitions.

On a headland just outside Falmouth there were once two chimney stacks, 'Anna Maria' and 'Caroline', so called because they were tall and conspicuous, like the sisters' unfashionably narrow but impeccably Quaker skirts. Because they were also emblematic of mining days, it is a shame they are no longer standing, as monuments to two remarkable women who achieved so much in the name of education, and charity, and from the fortunes of a mining family.

As intimated in the Introduction to this book, the Polytechnic Society has a history in its own right. But in relation to the family business it was very much like a charitable trust set up by a business, or a family, to run almost in tandem with the business. Barclay Fox, brother to these two sterling sisters, had confessed in his *Journals* that, at a very early age, his income was sufficient for him never to have any anxieties. With a deeply philanthropic background, and Quaker ancestry, it would have been almost expected that the Foxes should plough back some of their prosperity into the community. To put things into perspective this was not unusual in Victorian England: many of the country's banking families, Quaker or not, were acting in the same vein. What was unique about the Polytechnic was firstly that its founders and their relations took a hands-on approach to the enterprise, giving many of the lectures and prizes; and secondly that, in surprising contrast to this, the Society had royal patronage and was presided over by all the great and good of the county. Whether the family's subsequent involvement with educational establishments was a ripple effect, or whether again this would have happened in any event, is debatable. But the influence of the Polytechnic on the town was immense, particularly in an age when many were deprived; and others, so it is said, were not.

*Mining stack chimney at Pennance Point, Falmouth
Photograph, inscribed verso: 'G. H. Fox, Jan 13, 1921.
Chimney on Pennance Point. The first that was built to take
arsenic fumes from smelting works…called the stack, alias Anna
Maria. The second one built later on top of the point being
called Caroline and was blown up/down about 1900/8 many
years after the first one was pulled down.' Both stack chimneys
are visible at the top of the inside front flap.*

Following the collapse in the price of tin, Perran Foundry fell into a period of gradual desuetude. Its decaying buildings presented a challenge to any developer. They are listed, next to a river, bounded by conservation woods, and by two types of conservation marshes; they are also bordered to the north by one of the busiest main roads in Cornwall. They lie in the coldest valley, the old coachmen used to say, between London and Land's End.

For about twenty years of my life I lived in Perranarworthal, first in a conversion of what had been the stables, and second in a conversion of what had been a barn, both at Tredrea, originally the home of George Fox (I) (1746–1816). I came to know the area and its history intimately, and was shown some treasures, such as the Foundry office, with its original safe *in situ*, and a window pane inscribed by one of my ancestors. What I was not told challenged my imagination: the little beach at the foot of Cove Hill before the main road from Falmouth was extended in an easterly direction along the side of the estuary, the hill up which one of the older residents of the village remembers one of the Tremayne family being transported back to Carclew from the station by a cart and two men, the deer park belonging to that noble mansion, and the Victorian diarist Francis Kilvert who stayed at Tredrea's neighbouring property of Tullimar. Before the turnpike between Perran Wharf and Carnon Downs was built in 1828, the river was navigable not just up to the Foundry but also up to Bissoe, and for vessels of considerable size. This was achieved in the following way: at high tide a body of water was retained behind closed dock gates, which were then opened at low tide, with the effect of sluicing out the river.

I must have witnessed at least two launches to a programme of restoration for the old foundry buildings, but it was not until the last few years that finally they had new life breathed into them in the form of a comprehensive residential development by the Perran Foundry Company. As we shall see with G. C. Fox & Co.'s properties in Penryn, it is demonstrated that the best, and most viable, way to preserve industrial buildings is to turn them into homes. What is ironic is that the bodies who seek to preserve such buildings are also those who would today vehemently oppose the idea of industrial development in such a beautiful area. They would not have approved of the involvement the Foxes had in mining arsenic higher up the valley above Ponsanooth, in the Kennall Vale. This today is one of Cornwall's most beautiful walks, at its best when the bluebells are flowering, and the beech tree leaves are new. Perhaps in another age, rather like the Luxulyan Valley before the construction of the Treffry Viaduct, it was not so wooded, and not so picturesque. Nonetheless the mere idea of 'expense magazines'[44] in such an area would have raised the eyebrows of preservationists had they been around at that time. As an extension to this it could be asserted, facetiously, that there would probably have not been any mining at all in Cornwall, and thereby, to the archaeologist's dismay, no tin-mining histories or buildings. It is an interesting but understandable case of *volte-face* that, undaunted by the fact that it was his family which had been partly responsible for the indus-

---

44   Stores, often attached to forts, for holding shells and other ammunition in Victorian times.

trialisation of this valley, my grandfather, in the 1960s, vociferously opposed the same site being used for the permanent exhibition of Barbara Hepworth sculptures. Pleasing decay, it would seem, is only pleasing when left untouched by the hand of modern artists. The fact remains: the archaeologically interesting ruins which now litter this valley were originally built by individuals hailed to be men of progress, industry, power, and employment. To give another more well-known example, the pillboxes which were built during the Second World War and which today create interest on many Cornish headlands, were built with another definitive vision: that of defence.

The Kennall Vale Factory was a subsidiary of Perran Foundry; and licences for the manufacture of gunpowder (never to be used as ammunition) were granted in 1811. The business ran successfully until the late nineteenth century, when it was sold to one of the country's largest explosives companies. A matter of incidental detail is that, utilising the River Kennall, the Foxes created what the Cornish call a 'leat', a small stream, much like a Roman irrigation channel, to bring the plentiful supply of water to Perranarworthal at a higher level and then to drop it down to provide power for the water wheels in the Foundry – an extension, perhaps, of the hydrostatic lock.

Such was the husbandry and ingenuity of the industrialists.

9

TIMBER

IN THE 1950S you would sometimes see going in and out of Eastwood Road, in Penryn, rather strange-looking lorries: they had only half a cab, which enabled them to carry extra-long lengths of wood. These planks extended precariously from the very back of the truck to beyond the place where a passenger might have sat. I did not know then how much these vehicles must have appealed to the Quaker sense of economy; nor did I know that they were the property of Fox Stanton.

From the late 1760s, when the family had formed a partnership with William Phillips, a coal and timber merchant in Penryn, and for over the next two hundred years, the timber business made a major contribution towards the prosperity of the company. Other Fox cousins similarly had established Fox Elliott, a timber business in Plymouth. There is a letter dated 'October 9th 1757' and addressed to George Fox 'Deal Merchant' at Fowey; and along with fish and grain, many types of timber are a frequently mentioned commodity. When in 1759 his family moved further west, the business was based in Penryn in an area either side of the river, and above the bridge, now known as the Inner Harbour Area. In 1872, following a serious fire in which the Penryn Sawmills were burnt down, the timber business was offered for sale, first to Harvey and Co. at Hayle and then 'on their declining to treat' to the Williams Foundry at Perranarworthal, and finally to the related timber company Fox Elliott in Plymouth. All declined, and the partners must have decided to keep the business: records show that the firm was renting property on the Penryn waterside in 1877, and in 1882 and 1883 land referred to as Penryn Sawmills was purchased from the Ecclesiastical Commissioners.

This must have been part of Glasney College and the Bishop's Palace, land acquired and built on in the thirteenth century as a result of a vision given to Bishop Bronescombe in a dream: three times he dreamed of a willow tree and a swarm of bees at the head of a creek, marking the location for the college. Glasney was an important collegiate church until the Dissolution, when chunks of dismembered granite found their way all over Penryn, into the neighbouring estate of Enys, and even as far as the Scilly Isles.

Also purchased by the firm was 'the foreshore in front of all our premises as far as the centre of the channel'. This was done without any forethought of the effect that the 'meandering' of the channel might have when it came to selling the property about a hundred years later. There were further depots in Truro, on the river, more or less where Tesco now is, and also in Falmouth Docks, where 'a sawmill, timber shed, and office were built at the expense of the Dock Company'. In 1909 another depot was opened at Grampound Road, and in 1927 another at Portscatho. In the same way that today articulated lorries prefer industrial sites and tailgate entry, the Foxes always looked for access either by water, or as in the case of Grampound Road, by rail; as has been mentioned, even the shed in Falmouth Docks at one time had its own siding.

When Robert Were Fox (II) was the American Consul in Falmouth he was asked in 1854 to complete a lengthy questionnaire. Unfortunately only the answers are extant, and frustratingly very often just a simple 'yes' or 'no', but we can more or less safely guess they refer to ship building within his area. They give a good idea of how important timber was in those days:

'the frame is of English Oak – Planks sometimes English Oak, and sometimes Canadian Red Pine – Decks are chiefly of Quebec Yellow Pine, sometimes Red Pine. The Oak is obtained from the Tamar River, Plymouth, Salcombe, Teignmouth, Exeter, Southampton, and Bristol Channel etc. It is brought to this district by large Barges or Lighters…Masts of 17 inches diameter and under generally of Canadian Red Pine and those of greater diameter Canadian Yellow Pine…standing rigging –rope made in most cases of Russian Hemp…Canvas (British manufacture) made of flax.'

It is mystifying to think how in pre-computer days the completed questionnaires were analysed to produce some kind of profile of the state of ship building.

There is not a wealth of archives relating to the timber business, which must have been a lively and valuable diversification, but readers might like to reflect on two particular wooden constructions dating from the second part of the nineteenth century, which would have undoubtedly called upon the company's resources.

One was when Charles Fox had bought Trebah estate, and was planning the garden. He had an intellectual interest in geomancy or what is now called Feng Shui, and accordingly used this to determine planting positions: giant wooden towers were constructed and under his direction shunted around by the gardeners to simulate the effect that trees might have on reaching maturity.

The other was when Anna Maria Fox died in the autumn of 1897: her popularity, the respect for existing graves, and awareness of the effects of wet grass, were such that the family had the foresight to cover the entire Quaker burial ground with a raised platform, with just an aperture left for the lowering of her coffin. (This was a curious reflection of something that happened in her lifetime. At Penjerrick there was in the conservatory a Norfolk Island Pine which grew so tall that it was hitting the roof. Various friends, as ever keen to offer advice, started to suggest she either cut it down or have it transplanted. Anna Maria simply had a hole cut in the glazed panels and thereby raised the ceiling. Unlike her grave, however, it proved to be a temporary solution and the tree eventually had to be felled.)

It was not until a Mr Stanton announced he wished to leave the business that in 1909 a private company was set up under the style of Fox Stanton & Company, Timber Importers, Merchants and Sawmillers. He finally retired at the end of 1911 and died a year later in Melbourne, Australia; but the name remained.

Minutes from the time of the First World War are limited: they begin by being written in a spindly hand, like wisps of hair strewn across the page, and entries are brief and random. One has a picture of a rather relaxed type of business, compared to what was going on in Falmouth. A 'sawyer' was engaged, a motor cycle was purchased, then a 'motor wagon', and then something that looked like a black and gold sewing machine but which was in fact a Mignon typewriter. Someone cut three of his fingers and a man called 'Bettison met with an accident…by tumbling into the creek from the bridge'. Someone else lost his job because he refused to undergo an operation for varicose veins. The inconvenience of war, as is common throughout the Fox archives, is mentioned without comment, almost as if, being Quakers, the partners did not wish to give it the credibility such evils might seek or attract:

> 'The Russian Govt. have notified the British Govt. that owing to their being at war with Germany traffic with Finland has been closed. We have therefore to forego our Kotka cargo.'

But they were happy to make money where they could out of the war:

> '6th October 1914
> A contract has been made with the Army Services for firewood from 4th October for 6 months to supply

100 tons a month (more or less) to be delivered to Place Quay, St Anthony.'[45]

More work from the War Office was to follow in 1916 in the form of contracts to supply initially 200 and then 300 butchers' chopping blocks. For good Quakers and potential conscientious objectors a line does not seem to have been drawn when in August 1916 it is minuted that they accepted a contract 'with the Ministry of Munitions for 10,000 Ammunition Boxes'. Some of these may have found their way to the rifle ranges at Pennance Point, Rosemullion Head, St Anthony and the Roseland Peninsula. Clearly onto a good thing, in 1917, quoting for half this number of boxes, they increased the price from 4/- to 5/- a box.

They also supplied posts for fences. Their distant Quaker cousins in Wellington (see Chapter 1) meanwhile were churning out miles and miles of material to be made into 70,000 pairs of puttees for the British Army. For the high moralising pacifist it is hard for him to know, either visibly or invisibly, how his day-to-day activities feed into concerns of which he expresses disapproval, any more than today it is possible for the environmentalist to monitor his true carbon imprint; and inevitably, as ship agents, we must have handled many ships which, unbeknownst to us, carried questionable cargoes. Again, during the war there was no compunction about making

---

45   Pamela Richardson, 'A Quaker Record of Maritime Falmouth in World War One', *Troze* (The Online Journal of the National Maritime Museum Cornwall www.nmmc.co.uk), Vol. 1, No. 2, December 2008, p. 8.

inroads into the woods of various local estates: Carclew, Tredrea, and Trewarthenick, where they actually set up heavy duty machinery on site. It is only latterly that it has become apparent how few trees were planted during the wars, never mind how many were felled. Control of tree growth was an important part of the management of garden estates such as Glendurgan, but it is clear from this entry in George Henry Fox's diary that, in peacetime, it was not something to be taken lightly, even though he would profit from the sale of the timber.

'Feb 22 [1926] Cut down a big spruce in bottom below Manderson's Hill & Quarry – which has been getting more & more of a pyramid filling up the view – also opening up a big piece of the river – but losing 3 ornamental healthy trees which it went to my heart as well as theirs to cut down. Fox Stanton & Co will take the ash & elm: the spruce is on such a steep slope & below the road it is not worth the labour horse hire etc involved to sell it.'

Digressing for a moment, but still on this topic of conscience, in 1815 Robert Were Fox (II) wrote to his father about a possible transhipment of gunpowder, as ammunition to 'wage war on each other and sell the Portuguese their prisoners as slaves'. He continued

'however this may be the ultimate destination of this gunpowder does not appear to me to be doubtful: I confess under these circumstances I do not feel doubtful how to act with respect to the propriety of our being agents or in any degree promoting so shocking a purpose which has been so much and so justly decried in the House of Commons. But I need not I am sure enlarge upon it, thou wilt see how improper it is for us to have anything to do with it (a hundred times worse than prize goods)'.

He was reminding his father of Joseph Fox's unfortunate involvement with privateers, the story already told in Chapter 3.

Timber came mostly from Fredrikstad in Norway, in the form of spars, poles, deals, battens, boards, lathes, and floorings. There seems to have been a roaring trade in egg boxes, 'made from home grown fir' during the Second World War. I have a distant memory of having seen some of these being loaded at Truro railway station, each box with metal handles and a padlock, and able to carry six dozen eggs, probably in wood shavings, if not otherwise protected by cardboard dividers. I certainly remember chicks in boxes, each bird cheeping like mad, as if it were they, not me, catching that hateful train back to school. In 1940 broccoli crates were purchased and also flower boxes, which were sold mostly to the Scillies where the company had 22 customers. I remember too the stencilled boxes containing cut foliage such as *Pittosporum*, being delivered to the station mostly by spinsters. They drove Black Marias with forward-opening doors and divided front windscreens, and hardly any windscreen at the back; they touch-parked.

But in those days there were not many cars parked in front of the station.

The timber business must have originated not just because of boat and ship building, but also because of the manufacture of pit-props for the mines. Much of this happened at the foundry in Perranarworthal; and there is evidence of log ponds being used to store logs once they had been unloaded at Devoran and then floated up the creek to be turned into pit-props. Some of the timber was imported from Norway; hence the inn of that name. The premises at Penryn were used for the storage of timber, for planing and sawing and for retail sales. It must have been a rewarding business: the partners in 1900 met twice a week, on Monday and Tuesday evenings, to discuss the activities of the timber department. During the First World War 'ordinary trade fell off badly, but demands for pickets firewood, etc. in connection with the war and naval departments' kept the company busy. During the Second World War there was an increased demand for home-grown timber. It was used, amongst other things, in the construction of Mosquito bombers and rifle butts; and from September 1939 until March 1945 a total of just over 1,000 tons of soft wood timber was drawn in regular horse loads from Enys down to the Penryn depot.

During the war, ports and dockyards were an obvious enemy target. It can hardly be the case that the upper reaches of the Penryn River represented much of a threat. But in 1941 the town was hit twice. Once again without emotion or comment, it is recorded that the cashier and most of his family were killed and the company's various properties suffered damage to roofs and windows. The way in which disaster seems to have been accepted by the partners of the firm is another indication of their spiritual walk.

After the war, a shortage of housing helped to promote the popularity of the timber-frame building. But in 1957, having valiantly tried to keep up with the new fashion for timber-clad buildings, decking and panelling, the business was merged with Harvey and Company, Hayle. Harveys had been friendly rivals since the eighteenth century and both companies had respectively been proprietors of the Hayle and Perran foundries. It was a decision which has been echoed so often in the history of G. C. Fox & Co., and in many other companies: you either expand or sell. With tanalised wood beginning to make its impact, and on an impressive scale changing the face of farm buildings in particular, it made sense.

In those days my father's uncle, Romney Fox, and a first cousin of my father's, Anthony Fox Laity, were partners in the firm and worked at Fox Stanton. I enjoyed visiting. 48 Arwenack Street had an air of sedateness, whereas the timber yard, by that time, had become distinctly more industrious. Tony had joined the firm in 1950 and was what is now known as 'cool' (in his early 90s, he still is): very laid-back and polite, but very go-ahead. Both he and my uncle had an inner tranquillity, and a sense of humour to match, but I particularly remember my uncle's sense of mischief. At the cost of wandering slightly from the subject, the reader needs to know that there was little of the Puritanical in the Fox family, or if there was, it did not prevent them from having fun. It was this uncle who taught me the art of creating havoc in a hotel dining room: onto a folded-out napkin on your lap, place a pat of butter and then sharply pull the napkin taut, thereby catapulting the butter up to the ceiling, where in the warmer strato-sphere, and to the dismay of the helpless restaurant manager, it will begin to drip. Vacate your chair at the earliest opportunity.

The 'S. S. Loof Lirpa' was a rather more serious dare. He sent round the port a message, commonly known as an E. T. A. or Earliest Time of Arrival, that this well-known Italian ship was coming to Falmouth, with a long list of requirements: fuel, spare parts, and ships' stores to be delivered, crew changes, planes and trains to be met, owner's representative to be accommodated, etc. A stream of orders was initiated, creating a delta of further con-sequent orders. In addition, the port officials, Harbour Office, Pilots, Customs, Immigration, Port Health etc, were notified. It was not until the ship's imminent arrival had become so fraught with complications that someone with a higher level of I. Q. suddenly realised that 'Loof Lirpa' spells April Fool backwards. It was still before 12 noon and there was the opportunity to strike back at the wicked uncle, who found himself being asked to sign a cheque for a vast sum of money to be paid in advance for a supply of coal, an order which he had initiated.

Much to the horror of my aunt, my uncle enjoyed going around corners in his car on two wheels, if he could. Like so many mild-mannered men my uncle was also very brave: as a Quaker he was in the Friends' Ambulance Unit during the war. Reading through the personal mem-oirs of George Henry Fox, Romney comes out as a star: supportive, practical, talented, energetic, communicative and the soul of a good party.[46] It is likely too that, being the youngest, he got away with blue murder. I wish I had known him better. Once he and my grandfather, as young boys, disguised themselves as an old woman in widow's weeds and a young urchin in rags, covered in smuts, and suffering from a damaged ankle. They came limping to the back door of Glendurgan one winter's evening when their mother happened to be entertaining to tea, amongst others, a local doctor. They were admitted to the servants' hall, and given some refreshment; and in due course they were taken into the drawing-room to be examined by the doctor. He naturally found nothing amiss, and then, on behalf of Mrs Fox and her other distinguished guests, who included his wife, remonstrated in a loud voice. The disguises came off and much laughter was had by all, except one presumes, the doctor; and no doubt his embarrassment was not improved by a severe lecture he received from his wife, to whom he had nothing to say, on their way home.

Fox Stanton's offices, naturally, were floored and panelled at every point, and Tony had also designed and built himself a very capacious bungalow similarly floored and panelled. There was also a huge wooden shed in which he kept chickens, on ample supplies of sawdust. At my parents' house there were parquet floors, a staircase and galleried landing, and panelled doors which probably all had their origins, just after the war, in Fox Stanton.

---

46   In George Henry Fox's private diary, he records asking Romney if he were to have the initials C. E. M. after his son's name what would they stand for; and in a flash Romney replied 'Civil, Energetic and Mirthful'.

In 1967 the business became part of the United Building Merchants Group, at which point they moved out of Fox Stanton's property, and subsequently became Jewsons. The change to be noticed in 48 Arwenack Street was the end of a typical Quaker economy: the stoves which burnt sawdust fell into demise, the flues were disconnected and most of the fireplaces were removed.

The land in Penryn had been retained and the company then embarked on a series of tenancies, which on reflection were no more than treading water. The rents received made a small contribution towards the expenses of maintaining the old and derelict buildings, and were no contribution at all towards the restoration of some of the warehouses. In fact, the company lost money. In order to obtain vacant possession of one particular building, the tenant's sail-making business was purchased; and for a time we tried to be sail-makers. I soon realised the omens for this when I visited a competitor, who was making sails in a room the size of a tennis court, with a false floor and traps, etc. In the same way it did not take long to realise that the small boatyard we had started in some of the old sheds was never going to make huge sums of money. Boat owners, who flinched at the cost of a winch, and tenants were slow to pay; and in high winds the sheds creaked and waved about in rather an alarming way, especially when (I tried not to think about it) the accumulative value of laid-up, and propped up, yachts undercover was not exactly low.

In the late 1970s, having investigated the possibilities of demolishing the buildings on either side of Eastwood Road, and replacing them with modern warehouses, it was decided to renovate and repair. Following this, a considerable amount of money was spent on clearing the river, moving the sewer pipe, sinking a concrete base for the purposes of cranes, and repairing roofs.

By the 1980s it was apparent that a major rethink was required, and an enlightened residential development scheme was therefore put together for the entire inner harbour area. This was contrary to the local structure plan whereby all this area was zoned for industrial and commercial use, but to my untutored mind it seemed that heavy goods vehicles finding their way around the narrow lanes at the head of the creek was not a practical way forward: articulated lorries prefer tailgate entry as close as possible to a main road. There seemed to be more than ample evidence that the one way to preserve and conserve ancient listed warehouses was to convert them for residential use, as was to happen with the Perran Foundry. Justice needed to be done to the quality of some of the buildings, and also to that area of Penryn where the creek flows under the bridge and the visitor has his first glimpse of the sea. Looking back at the history of the area, the trouble perhaps started in the early 1930s when the idea of a fixed bridge was re-introduced. The swing bridge which existed then operated like a level crossing, and facilitated trade, whereas a fixed bridge would be a serious impediment. The company went to battle with Cornwall County Council but was advised by its lawyers that it would be possible to claim compensation only for damage done to the freehold value of the property and not for the interference with trade. In the end £1,000 was paid in 1936 for 'injurious affection' to Fox Stanton's water rights. (About

30 years earlier we had received nothing for the imposed alteration to our front steps in Arwenack Street). The value of the Penryn properties was written down by this amount and the company 'built a ladies lavatory costing about £30 and improved the upstairs accommodation'. Later in the same year it paid £400 for Bohill Wharf and £300 for Summercourt, a property which at one stage had been the quayside home of a member of the Enys family. The company built a wooden bridge to connect these properties to its property on the south side of the river, known confusingly as North Yard.

Returning to our plans for the rejuvenation of this area with a residential development, maybe the council's officer was thinking that we would want to economise (he was right in this) but when I explained my intentions to depart from the local plan, it was astonishing that he should ask, and on site, 'You do realise that this will require the use of expensive materials such as granite and slate?' I looked at our glued-together buildings, their extensive use of corrugated roofing, the heavy-duty polythene which flapped from windows, and the tons of concrete; and I looked at the one ancient warehouse so worthy of rescue. Without wishing to sound, or wanting to be, extravagant, I replied 'That is the whole point.'

Fortunately the planning application was called in, following which, a public inquiry was held. It cost G. C. Fox & Co. nearly £100,000, at least ten box files of correspondence, and most of my time for about ten years. It was a good thing; it seemed as if every square foot was somehow touched by the complications of way leaves, consents to discharge, access, road widths, contamination, and disputed or unclaimed land ownerships, etc. Fortunately my father was still alive and able to sign several statutory declarations about wills, annuities and property transfers dating back to before the war. We had to assemble a team of experts including a solicitor and a Queen's Counsel, both with scissor-like brains, and even more expensive than them, but just as brilliant, a leading historic buildings consultant, a man also equipped with judgement. They performed an excellent demolition job, and a significant planning permission was achieved.

Then a man called Edward Kennerley came into my life. Refreshingly he was the only professional who said incisive things like, 'You can leave that to me', 'It's important that you …' 'We need to act quickly here', and 'They are being economical with the truth'. Other distinguished companies would have in small print at the bottom of their distinguished writing paper 'Whilst endeavouring to supply our clients with the best advice that we can offer, we cannot take responsibility …'

Also refreshingly, he charged only a nominal fee, saying that it had all been 'a one-off bit of fun'.

Thanks to Edward the property was finally sold – albeit another ten boxes – and then, sadly, he developed a terminal illness and died in the same year, 1996.

The Penryn Inner Harbour Area was developed as a sort of harbour village; at a later date the council's own property in this area, the Anchor Warehouse was also converted into residential units. Whether the overall resulting development of the Inner Harbour Area is pleasing or not, what has to be said is that, as with the Perran Foundry, a considered residential development will raise, rather than lower, the tone of an area, and often the level of the local economy.

Those early bishops must have prayed for the future of this area, and if as a member of the public you walk to the head of the creek and look up at the side of a building, you may notice a slate plaque engraved with bees, and the leaves of a willow tree.

10

BUNKERS AND TOWAGE

ENDLESSLY IN PURSUIT of diversification and fresh opportunities, in 1870 members of the partnership helped to form a company called 'The Falmouth Steamship Coaling Company'. It imported a diversity of coals with names such as 'Great West Coal', 'Hastings West Hartley', 'Tredegar', 'Newcastle', 'Powell's Duffryn', 'Nixons Navigation' and impressively, 'The Marquis of Londonderry's'.

They acquired what was properly, rather than derogatively called, a 'hulk' aptly named the *Gorilla*, soon to be joined by – and one cannot but think of the film *King Kong* – *Lavinia*:

> 'October 30 1871… Mr Clift reported that there were 80 tons in Lavinia & about 200 to 220 tons in the Gorilla'.

But on 20 November 1873, George Henry Fox recorded the bad news that

> '50 boys and 4 Plymouth smacks were found with coal stolen last night from the Gorilla & dead calm had prevented their sailing.'

The next day, he noted that these

> 'Plymouth men were brought before the Magistrates
> & committed for trial at Bodmin.'

By 17 April 1873 the company had a capital of £4,800.
Unlike the tugs that G. C. Fox & Co. were to own and oper-
ate, the business was insured, one presumes because of the
flammability of coal; and unlike the fishing business that
G. C. Fox & Co. were involved in, it would seem that, contrary to any Biblical doctrine, they accepted some orders
on Sundays. The company grew, and by June 1875 it owned
'six hulks always afloat'. Both Falmouth Docks and Perran
Foundry were employed to look after the hulks and supply
their every need. At a meeting held on 3 February 1876 its
successes, and the business of the port, are recorded thus:

> 'The following is the number of steamers coaled by
> the Co. during the last four years and the proportion
> they bear to the number of steamers arrived at Fal-
> mouth during those years:
>
> 1872 196 29%
> 1873 198 33%
> 1875 148 29%
> 1875 126 28%'

But in July 1877 the board felt that the venture was
becoming less and less remunerative, and that for what
the *Gorilla* cost it would be much more profitable to have
a land-based store.

No further mention is made of coal until in 1920 a new, more serious company was formed called the Falmouth Coaling Company, precipitated by the popularity of the steam ship and its requirement for coal bunkering. William Cory and Sons contributed £15,000, G. C. Fox & Co. £4,000, and Broad and Sons £1,000. But the company was undercut by a rival coal-bunkering operation and by 1922 had ceased trading; it was finally wound up in March 1963.

Falmouth Steamship Coaling Company had the advantage of owning its tugs, and in about 1882 a new company was started by the partners for towing sailing ships in and out of the port. It acquired G. C. Fox & Co's tug, the *Pendragon*, for fishery purposes, but this clashed with Fox & Co's own towage business and the two companies therefore merged, forming a single company called the Falmouth Fishery Company owning both the *Briton* and the *Pendragon*. Fishing, however, fell away and in 1893 the name of the firm was changed to the Falmouth Towage Company. Tugs such as *Triton*, *Dragon*, *Victor* and *Durgan* became known in the chief ports of western Europe, and not just for towage: the company was also very successful with salvage operations at sea. In April 1887 the Chairman of the company said

'The Triton had made more Channel towages than any other boat in the port and had made them satisfactorily. She had been south into the Bay of Biscay and north into the North Sea.'

For tug enthusiasts, details of the 'Full Power Performance of S.S. "Triton"', built in Falmouth in 1883, were as follows:

> '251 total Indicated Horse Power
> Steam pressure 80 lbs per. Sq. in.
> Vacuum 28 inches
> Revolutions from 129 to 131 per. Minute
> Cylinders 16" and 30" diameter
> Stroke 21" '

What half of this means is a mystery. But it is a certified copy of the actual card, and taken from the inside cover of a minutes book, so presumably of some value and of interest to someone.

The tugs were uninsured: the firm relied on the zeal and care of the local crews. This was of grave concern to at least one of the partners, Howard Fox, and was regularly minuted at Partners' meetings. In particular he was anxious about any towage jobs in the English Channel; they apparently represented a higher risk. This is surprising: for, as with car accidents, experience has shown that many accidents happen closer to home. For example, on 26 May 1877,

> 'Broad's boarding steamer "The Lizard" and the "Merlin" came into collision shortly after leaving their moorings...causing serious damage to both.'

The company was prepared to spend the best part of £1 million, in today's values, purchasing new tugs and relatively little money paying the crew; yet their sense of

Quaker economy meant that they baulked at the costs of insurance, even at the time of the First World War when the tugs suddenly found they had a new role.

In September 1914 the minutes of the company read as follows:

'It was reported that soon after war was declared all three tugs were requisitioned for moving troops and baggage to and from St Anthony – they were also required for attendance on liners taking off Austrian ambassador and suite and accompanying party about 210, with baggage.....also landing from liners German and Austrian subjects, and landing other aliens from steamers calling here. Many towages in and out of Harbour and Docks and up and down the Fal river were also incurred by steamers ordered here by cruisers, or sent by owners here for orders.'

In 1915

'the "Dragon" was requisitioned by the Admiralty to go to Dover to tow barges and other purposes and went to Invergordon and towed a large ship away from Stornoway to Sheerness'.

In June of 1916, the *Dragon*

'was again requisitioned and sent to Southampton to have wireless instalment and other alterations for naval purposes...the crew being taken over entirely by the Admiralty and Willie White captain of the "Perran" went as one of the crew. R. B. Fox and William Thomas went to London and conferred with the Naval Authorities who agreed to pay £2.15 a day'.

In August the *Perran*, with some resistance from the partners, was to follow, 'and payment for her was eventually arranged at 31/- a day to be returned in like good order, wear and tear only excepted'. Undeterred in the running of their own business, the *New Resolute* was hired in lieu of the *Perran*. Unfortunately, it

'was run into by the steam drifter "Dixon" and six planks below deck on the port side were cut into amidships. The owners sent her to Malpas for this and other repairs'; and she was replaced by the 'Queen of the Fal'.

Things did not improve. The partners recorded receiving instructions from the Ministry of Shipping Transport Department:

'By a letter dated Feb. 22 1918 [*it*] notified us that the Admiralty decided to requisition the "Triton" and "Victor" tugs. They took no notice of our letter remonstrating but notified verbally through the Admiral stationed at Falmouth that it would reckon from March 6. Their form and terms and charter in several respects do not seem fair to owners under present conditions and considering the excellent condition in which these tugs have always been kept up.'

In January 1919 the *Triton* and the *Dragon* were returned by the Admiralty, as was the *Perran* which was returned on 18 July. 'William Thomas engineer and surveyor on behalf of the owners met Mr Williams of Plymouth on behalf of the Admiralty and with Mr Brooks of the Admiralty surveyed her.' The tug was found to be 'in a very dirty state and engine badly needing repairs' and it was agreed that the Admiralty should 're-condition her'.

In 1919 the tug *Durgan* was bought for £7,500, about £325,000 in today's values. She was launched by my great-aunt Annette Fox – one of the Fox girls who in various ways were to have an involvement with the running of the firm. She (the tug) was 70 feet long, 16 feet in the beam, and had a draft of six feet. Her trial trip on 31 July recorded an average speed of 9.5 knots.

The towage business pottered on after the war but the future became increasingly bleak. Tugs from other parts of the world began to make their appearance, sometimes with exclusive rights to towage work. An attempt had been made in 1911 to fill the slack time with fishing but to no great avail. In 1914 George Henry Fox, as chairman, gave a frank appraisal of the company, perhaps giving us the first idea that the business was more trouble than it was worth:

'The Directors considered the [*management*] fee of £120 was inadequate in view of the increasing amount of work necessary in connection with the tugs. Whereas in former days a great deal of the tugs' work was of a routine nature & carried out locally, a large proportion of their earnings now was gained on jobs that had little or nothing to do with Falmouth: for this type of work there was of necessity much more office work. We quoted for 3 or 4 jobs for every one we obtained and when obtained there was far more in the way of accounts, & expenses to be gone into and settled, and more arrangements for carrying them out to be made, than in the class of work we used to undertake. The whole of the office of G. C. Fox & Co. worked for the good of the tugs… Mr R. Barclay Fox spent a large portion of his time about Towage Co's concerns and generally there was far more telegraphing, sending wireless messages & telephoning, which demanded prompt personal attention'.

Robert Barclay Fox (II) received in 1919 a letter from his wife's brother, Ralph Bassett, who also worked in the firm, and who evidently was busy during an absence of his brother-in-law. It offers a rare description of tug activity even if it touches on giving the impression that he was trying to paint a rosy picture:

'I have managed to keep pretty busy what with the flour and the tugs. The Sunday you left, the Dragon did quite a useful salvage job in the S. E. gale blowing then, she towing a little schooner called the "Meuse" clear of Trefusis point only just in time before she would have struck the rocks. I was forced to arrest her yesterday as we had received nothing satisfactory from Pritchards who are acting for her Owners (French), but there is a wire for the Captain today asking him if he considers our claim of £400 a right and proper one, and I have no doubt that he will agree to this, we asked bail for £650 but said we would take £400 without prejudice.....We had bad luck with the Dragon on a steamer the "M. Arnus" a Spaniard with engine room trouble wanting a tug off Mevagissey, as before the Dragon got there the steamer had taken the Gallant of Fowey but she was able to proceed under her own steam to Falmouth, we thought we were in for a good job as the report was that her rudder had gone and her engine room full of water. The Dragon is now at Queenstown waiting to tow the Birkdale to Barry for £300 as you know. The £260 from Hardie for the Killoran came today also £4000 from Pritchards to Fox & Co. re Ango, which letter I suppose will be held over for you to deal with.'

He ends the letter by thanking Robert Barclay Fox for a 'most generous present which was never worse earned by anyone'. Short of remuneration for his services there is no hint of what this might have been.[47]

The Falmouth Towage Company was liquidated in 1921 when the Docks set up their own tug and salvage company, with for many years a member of the Fox family on

---

47 Readers might be amused to hear that the rewards for an extra-mural job in the world of towage has more recently been known as a 'mini', i.e. two in the front and two in the back, which apparently means two hours in the morning and two in the afternoon.

its board. Robert Barclay Fox kept a towage book which indicates that towage jobs continued into the 1930s but by the spring of 1936 the *Durgan* had become an encumbrance. She was used infrequently, 'small craft requiring towing being very few', and had already been laid up for nearly a year. It was decided to sell her for £950 – if obtainable. 'This little tug', it is endearingly recorded, 'was sold to Peter Foster and Co. Hull on May 5th for £925.'

There is something very touching about the sight of the Falmouth tugs at work, some tugging, some holding still, some pushing and some nudging. They have all the alertness of sheep dogs, and are just as wonderful to watch, as they herd their ships into position. The tugs have all the necessary technological equipment to make their manoeuvres, but they often seem to move about intuitively. There is a spirit of co-operation in which they are at times forceful, and at other times gentle, towing and pushing, and pulling together for the success of the port as much as for the protection of their charges.

Reading through the minutes today, they convey the impression of a small family-run business, conducted with the utmost propriety and caution, the small matter of insurance notwithstanding. Yet they were dealing with fairly impressive sums as they bought, sold and ran a handful of tugs; and the modern reader should bear in mind that all this was conducted in comparatively unwieldy pounds, shillings and pence, and without the aid of calculators, or Tippex. If the significant Quaker businesses of the nineteenth century were not run by Quakers, you would expect the minutes of their meetings to be considerably more bombastic. But, certainly with G.

C. Fox & Co. and its allied or subsidiary businesses, they never were, not even in living memory. It was almost as if the partners were unaware of the company's success; and contrary to today's exhibitionist tendencies they remained modest, but nonetheless bravely adventurous, in their attitudes.

In 1929 the fact that the annual turnover of the firm ran to nearly £100,000 (over £5 million today) was recorded with as much enthusiasm as one might note down heavy rainfall; and in 1947 the fact that the cashier paid out a sum equivalent to £1 million today is again nonchalantly recorded as a mere detail. At the other end of the scale there are minutes which would indicate the very Quaker penchant for looking after the pennies:

'Feb 13 1931

G. R. F. reported that he estimated Portscatho yard brought us in about £30 per. a. after paying rent & Chenoweth's commission. It was therefore decided not to sell this.'

Even in moments of crisis Quakers resented waste. The famous story of Caroline Fox's encounter with a bull[48] comes to mind: after she had been startled by the animal (his 'autograph' next to hers on the ground) and had recovered from imagining she had met her Maker, she had the presence of mind to collect all the oranges which

---

48   *The Journals of Caroline Fox*, March 10, 1853.

had fallen out of her basket, even if she 'acted as a somnambulist, with only fitful gleams of consciousness and memory'. Oranges were in those days a luxury item.

Looking at the old accounts what is also apparent is that at any one time the partners had easy access to substantial amounts of working capital, either in cash or in the form of realizable investments. For men of an entrepreneurial spirit who wanted to start a towage business how convenient this must have been and, I cannot resist remarking, in extreme contrast to my own experience in the business.

Even in more recent times however, there were occasions when vast amounts passed briefly through our hands; and for a short time we felt rich. When crews' wages had to be collected from the bank, the company's insurance company specified that this task should be carried out by a certain number of named staff, with alarmed briefcases attached by a collar to the wrist, and capable of setting off a siren and emitting clouds of confusing blue smoke. Mercifully this never happened. The nature of our business was blatantly obvious to most of the shopkeepers in Falmouth. But they were ignorant of the potential siren accompanied by blue smoke, and unaware that often the briefcases contained hundreds of thousands of pounds. Similarly, in 1928 no one knew that under cover of darkness the *Durgan* steamed 12 miles out to sea and became involved with the transfer of £1 million of Soviet gold. This must be one of many stories told and untold about the Falmouth tugs.

In the context of the history of G. C. Fox & Co., this chapter illustrates how the company, although small, did indeed have a long reach. It became involved in ventures which were risky in themselves, but which also risked the loss of significant capital. The fact that the tugs were uninsured is perhaps another indication of how practising Quakers preferred to put their trust in the divine puppeteer rather than the ever-solicitous broker. The chapter also paints a familiar picture of juggling. The many changes within the tug companies' ownership, and the final liquidation, perhaps prefigured the way in which the firm was destined to act with its other lines of business.

11

THE HONORARY CONSUL

AS A CHILD, something I particularly enjoyed would be when a number of taxis came down our drive, and out would step anything up to a dozen naval officers, all in uniform and with clanking swords. They then formed the focal point of what used to be called a 'drinks party' which my brothers and I would witness from between the spindles of the upstairs landing banisters. To our young eyes and ears this was a strange affair; it was also my first glimpse of consular life.

Entertainment, I was to discover, is to consular or ambassadorial life as oil is to engines.

Over a period of more than 200 years, and in different parts of the United Kingdom, various members of the Fox family served as honorary consuls for three dozen different countries. In the last 50 years these appointments diminished solely to European countries: Norway, Holland, France, Germany, Spain and Greece. Prior to that they had included other European countries and states such as Sweden, Finland, Denmark, Belgium, the German Empire, Prussia, Oldenburg, Mecklenburg, Portugal, Sardinia, Tuscany, Parma and Italy. There were also appointments from more exotic countries such as Mexico, Brazil, Colombia,

Argentina, Peru, Bolivia, Costa Rica, New Granada, Venezuela, Ecuador, Honduras, Russia, and Turkey.

Perhaps most distinguished, and certainly the most accurately documented, was the American Consulate. Edward Long Fox (1761–1835) received his appointment from President George Washington in 1793, but perhaps because of his particular destiny described in Chapter 3, held it for only a year. Robert Were Fox (I) was appointed American Consul on 30 May 1794, his commission also being signed by the President. His consular district included the West of England, and it was not until 1810 or thereabouts that a separate office was established in Plymouth. He held the appointment from 1794 to 1812 and again from 1815 to 1818, this second commission being signed by President Madison. The break in service was occasioned by the 1812–14 War between the United States and Britain, when the consulate was closed and the consulship dissolved.

Robert Were Fox died on 2 November 1818 from eating a 'high mutton chop' at the White Hart Hotel, Cullompton, and was buried at the Quaker Cemetery at Spiceland, east of the village of Uffculme in Devon. His son, another Robert Were (II), succeeded him, his commission being signed in 1819 by President Madison. He served until 1854 when Augustus Scharit of Missouri, an American citizen, was appointed. Under the administration of President Pierce, this was in accordance with a policy which supplanted honorary consuls who were not American citizens, replacing them with political appointees who were American citizens. Robert Were Fox (II) wrote pointedly to the Secretary of State in Washington, but with a degree of grace:

'It is gratifying to find that the manner in which I have discharged my official duties has had the approbation of the Department, and I am obliged by the very full manner in which thou hast conveyed this information to me. I have always highly appreciated the confidence and kindness which has for the last thirty five years, during which I have been entrusted with the Consulship, been manifested towards me by the Government, and also to my Father for the twenty five preceding years, he having been appointed to the office by General Washington in 1793 [*actually 1794*].'

Robert Were Fox (II) died in 1877 and was buried in the Friends' Burial Ground at Budock, just outside Falmouth. He, and his daughter Anna Maria, did much to cultivate friendly relations between Great Britain and America, especially over issues such as the slave trade; and it is highly likely that the hand of friendship was warmly extended to the new consul. In spite of this, and perhaps partly because of this, Scharit must have felt superfluous. The loyalty, efficiency and long service of members of the Fox family to America was more than evident. Scharit became homesick, and in 1855 the Consulate was turned over to Alfred Fox, the Vice Consul and brother to Robert Were Fox (II). Alfred's petition to become Consul was finally granted in 1863 in recognition of valuable information supplied by him and which had resulted in the capture of sundry blockade runners during the American Civil War. On 2 April 1863 he, like his brother before him, wrote to the Department:

'It has afforded me much gratification to learn that my appointment as Consul has been so readily recommended to President Lincoln and especially to find that the official conduct of my family and myself, during the very long period we have had the honour of representing United States interests, is so highly appreciated by the Department. Allow me to express my sincere thanks for this mark of confidence and to add that I shall continue to do my best to discharge with zeal and efficiency, the honourable and important duties of the trust confided to my care.'

Alfred was born in 1794 and had six sons. The eldest, Alfred Lloyd Fox, served as Vice Consul for a number of years, and the third son, Howard, served as Vice and Deputy Consul for 11 years, Consul from 1875 to 1906, and Agent from 1906 to 1908 when the Falmouth office was closed. Another brother, George Henry, served as Vice and Deputy Consul from 1875 to 1900 when he was succeeded by Robert Barclay Fox (II), a great-grandson of the second Robert Were Fox, and he also continued until the office was closed.

Thus ended 115 years of service to the United States.

Old Quaker habits of economy die hard: all my notebooks have started life as discarded address books, diaries, laundry books, and even one notebook priced 3d. In another example of a book being taken over, one volume which bears the title 'PORTSCATHO FISH STORE' on its spine also contains an account of the American consular office from 1833 to 1854. All consuls were required to give an up-to-date three-monthly report of what was going on in their areas. One wonders if Robert Were Fox (II) had to scratch his head every three months to find something suitable to say, or if he was asked to concentrate on specific subjects. However, farming and mining are the two subjects on which he writes in depth, and with typical Victorian eloquence, for example in July 1836:

> 'The prospects relative to the harvest are said to be not very promising in some parts of England, and more especially in Ireland – in this area I do not hear of any complaint on this head. The mining interest in this county is in a very thriving state and so it is generally throughout the nation and there is a difficulty to get an adequate supply of men to carry on the extended mining operations.'

Prices for tin and copper are given regularly, and early in 1838 he writes

> 'It seems by a return which I have seen that the mines of this county have produced 142,089 tons of copper ore in 1837 producing 11,209 tons of copper and the mines received for the ores £822,516.'

As for crops, an example from 1842 reads

> 'The price of wheat and flour has been falling for some weeks and is expected under existing circumstances to go lower – the present price is 58/- to 62/- per quarter according to quality and flour 45/- a sack of 280 pounds.'

It is strange to think of the United States of America, with all its rich resources and golden prairies, wanting to hear news from Cornwall. But this was the case with all the American consuls, not just because of Cornwall's international reputation for mining, and for the area around St Day, to be precise, being allegedly 'the richest square mile to be found anywhere on earth'.

What Robert Were Fox's reports do substantiate very strongly is the vital importance of farming, of subsistence, and of employment in an age which had not encountered subsidies, deep freezers and the welfare state; and nowhere else in the archives have I come across any other member of the family having such a delightful awareness of crops, and the effects which weather may have on them. With a little imagination the English countryside can be seen as it was before the advent of the telegraph pole and the car – or tractor: stooks, or shocks of corn-sheaves in the fields, staddle stones, farmers in smocks and wide-brimmed hats and with scythes and sickles in their hands, and horses in harness; and as they harvested into the dusk there would be a moon overhead, to complete the bucolic vision. Mining stacks and chimneys were an intrusion, and unsurprisingly are seldom depicted in Arcadian scenes.

In 1843 mining must have been going well: Robert Were Fox (II) sent a small box of Cornish minerals to the Secretary of State in Washington. But in 1848 there is another convoluted message:

'Commercial affairs in these parts partake of a dullness which so intensively prevails in this kingdom and the foreign corn in warehouses here is in but little demand [...] the mining interest is also depressed and wages low averaging I believe little more than 13/- a week for the men – some of them have emigrated to Australia to work the copper mines which have been discovered there and said to be rich.'

Then in 1851 things were looking up again:

'The mining interest is in a thriving state & the investments in mines seem to be much on the increase.'

Later in the same year he writes as follows:

'The labourers are generally well and pauperism has evidently been on the decrease during the present year.'

How edifying all this must have been to the Secretary of State in Washington, we can only guess.

What does an honorary consul do today? Few countries can afford the cost of career officers at every consular post and the corps of career officials is therefore supplemented by honorary officers, usually residents engaged in trade or professions in the locality. The honorary consul is a public officer, authorised by the state whose commission he carries, with the approval of his own government in the form of an exequatur, to protect and foster the commercial affairs of its subjects in the foreign country in which he resides. He is also there to carry out any duties specified in his commission, and finally he is there to answer the needs of anyone who is in his area and who has come from the country he represents. Although this includes residents as well as travellers, the consular appointments within G. C. Fox & Co. were most relevant when Falmouth was one of the busiest ports in the Northern Hemisphere. It was in this way inextricably connected to the ship agency business, and often the ship agent and the honorary consul were the same person, much to the annoyance of the disgruntled sailor. Quite often a dissatisfied captain with a grievance would come into the office to see his agent, and on getting nowhere would then demand to see the consul. The agent would then have to walk out of the room and then come in again wearing a different hat, his consular hat.

Perhaps this function is best described in the original words of one of many letters and documents supporting the consular appointments.

This one dated 1803 is from the 'Commissary of the Royal Armies of His Catholic Majesty, His Chargé d'affaires at the Court of London, Consul & Agent General of Spain in the United Kingdom of Great Britain and Spain':

'Whereas it is very convenient for the service of his Catholic Majesty and for the Protection and Convenience of the Commercial Navigation carried on by the Spaniards in these Kingdoms, that a Vice Consul of Spain should be appointed in the port of Falmouth, who may assist either himself or by his deputies, all the individuals of the Spanish

Ships which may arrive at the said Port, as well as the vessels which may be driven or shipwrecked on those Coasts; and likewise those that may require any favour or assistance; in as much therefore, as are found in Don George Carlos[49] [*sic*] Fox in the neighbourhood of that Port, the quality requisite for the discharge of this appointment, in virtue of the Powers granted to my appointment by my Sovereign to name the Vice Consuls whom I may judge necessary, I do by these presents, name the said Don George Carlos Fox for my Vice-Consul of Spain in the said Port of Falmouth and I do pray the mighty King of the United Kingdoms of Great Britain and Ireland and his ministers to permit the said Don Carlos Fox freely and placably to exercise his Vice-Consulship, giving orders that no one shall interrupt him in the free discharge of his Commissions, and that they will give him all the assistance he may stand need of: for which end I deliver to him this present appointment, signed with my hand sealed with the arms of his Catholic Majesty.'

The honorary consul's stamp and signature are useful in the following circumstances: crew changes and repatriation, the certification of death, and the certification of life certificates enabling foreign residents to obtain their

---

49 This is an error in the document, which clearly refers to George Croker (not Charles or 'Carlos') Fox (II), demonstrating that in all the pomposity and formality of these documents, mistakes were occasionally made.

pensions. His duties include attending to those who have landed themselves in trouble, whether wilfully or not: criminal behaviour, loss of passports and/or identity, loss of money, etc.

The honorary consul is often the last resort for a host of general enquiries; one particular correspondent was convinced that she was the object of 'torture – illegal gases and elements known to cause disease' and sought political asylum in every country we represented. Someone else, acting on behalf of a granddaughter, 'admired the girls with long hair in Germany, Austria and Switzerland' and wanted to know more about hair styles that resemble 'a diadem, and on each side of the head looking like a macaroon'. An illustration of the desired style was included.

In my time, with the six countries I was fortunate enough to serve, we derived a good deal of fun from of our consular appointments which, in view of the absence of fees, was perhaps just as well, or certainly a compensatory factor. Rather like going on board foreign ships, entering an embassy is also like stepping aboard, and abroad. Ships tend to be utilitarian, but the embassies or consulates I visited were almost parodies of themselves in terms of their being full of individual character. Given the expense and organisation that consular conferences must necessitate, this might appear lacking in gratitude, but what I appreciated most was the way in which one could be transported: to the Tundra by Norwegian panelling, log fires and stuffed caribou; to a Spanish Parador by tapestries, Goyas and gold leaf; or to the Greek islands by marble, leather, and cigar smoke. On consular conferences, again the character of each country was marked by incidental detail. In Germany, it was the imperial efficiency with which our aeroplane on arrival was immediately surrounded by a fleet of outriders and Mercedes Benz limousines. In France, it was the opening remark of the Frenchman sitting next to me at a lunch party: 'did you know that *pâté de foie gras* is the only food with which you can drink red or white wine, Rosé, champagne or sherry?'

On one occasion in Munich we were taken to the opera house, which makes the Royal Albert Hall look something like a thimble. A fellow consul had a ticket for seat number 1 and on the grounds that this was bound to be the best seat in the house and that he thought he knew nothing about music, but that I did, he was keen to effect a swap for my ticket, number 117. I argued vociferously that if this were the case, maybe here was an opportunity for him to learn something. But this was to no avail, and in due course I found myself going round and round the gilded corridors looking for seat number 1. Eventually an attendant, who was fully attired in eighteenth-century costume, was able to help: 'This is royal box,' he said, conducting me up a flight of steps to some gilded double doors. I entered, unprepared for the sea of faces which turned to inspect me; and having realised that this was probably the only time in my entire life that I would ever be so privileged, I then went out and came in again (just like the ship agent who puts on his consular hat) but made this second entry as if it were a regular occurrence – and yet with some aplomb.

At one of these consular conferences I was told the story of an ambassador who had been at a grand dinner, where some of the cutlery was made of gold. He noticed a man at another table stealthily pick up a knife and secrete it down his sleeve. He picked up his own knife to examine it and by mistake it glanced against his glass and made that noise which is spelt 'Ting ting', and which usually heralds a speech. Everyone fell silent and the poor ambassador with a gold knife in his hand was lost for words. 'My lords, ladies and gentlemen,' he finally declared, 'I was going to make a speech, but on reflection I thought I would show you a conjuring trick.' With some deftness he gave the impression of throwing the knife, and then calmly walking around the tables he went and retrieved what appeared to be the same knife from the sleeve of the thief, who thus suddenly came to fame as an accomplice in conjuring.

Before the Iron Curtain came down we were agents for a number of East German ships; and on one horrible winter's day there was a defection. As part of our commitment to the ship owner we had to alert the police, who in due course caught the fugitive running across some fields near Mylor. Had we been consuls for West Germany at the same time there would have been a diplomatic incident. Fortunately that appointment had lapsed at the time of the Second World War, when my grandfather refused to sign a document which contained such conditions as:

'1 I am the son of George Henry Fox late of Falmouth aforesaid and neither myself or my Father or our respective wives are of Jewish origin or descent or connected by Jewish descent in any way whatsoever.

'2 I have resided in Falmouth all my life and my family for several generations have lived in and around Falmouth and have not intermarried with or been connected with any Jewish family in any way.'

Interestingly, after our appointment for the Federal Republic had been resurrected in 1982, I learned that it was part of the honorary consul's job to be at least *civil* to all Germans, both from the East and the West.

I had a favourite consular client. She came to see me annually in order to have her life certificate stamped, so that she could continue receiving her pension from Germany. She telephoned in advance of her visits and would arrive by taxi, with a large collection of dogs, mostly poodles, all of which were inseparable from her. There was a bitch called Coco who bit: 'Oh she's a naughty boy,' her mistress said.

I grew to admire this indomitable person, and when finally she became too old and ill to make the journey into Falmouth, I used to go and see her in her home the other side of Helston. She had clearly fallen on hard times, living in a neglected and seemingly unoccupied bungalow with peeling paint and surrounded by long grass and weeds. But, as was evident from her photograph albums, she had been accustomed to a privileged childhood living in a large house with a park, horses, plenty of poodles, and that most noble of dogs, a much-loved Weimaraner. She had married an oil magnate and spent much of her adult life entertaining and being entertained on board cruise ships and in hotels and restaurants.

She became interested in retrieving her family's property, which had been confiscated, in East Germany. We pursued her claim, one of millions, the Embassy said, which were waiting to be processed and were housed in hundreds of hangars. I refused to accept any payment or petrol money from her, and when one day she protested I suggested 'Look, when and if you get your property back you can take me out to dinner.'

'Mr Fox,' she replied, 'let us hope it is not a fish and chip shop.'

She became so obsessed with retrieving her property that I was curious to see a picture of her old home. She extracted from her wallet a tatty photograph of a busy main street, stretching into the distance, with houses either side, four or five storeys high, and linked by heavily-laden washing lines. When I asked her if she had a shop or a flat in this street, she looked at me in astonishment and said 'Mr Fox, it was the entire street.'

She never lived to see the return of her property portfolio. I was sad when she died, and not just because we had to forgo the dinner.

There are three observations from my appointment as German honorary consul. One was that – talking of dinners – as a guest of the German Government, the food was of the best. Another was that Germans do have a sense of humour, often dry. An ambassador giving a speech at a consular conference apologised for his delay, saying that he had just been to see the Queen. He explained how he had enlightened her on the value of the European Community, extolling the English for their cuisine, the French for their humility, the Italians for their organisational skills, the Dutch for their imagination, and the Germans (no doubt, for a moment he was appealing to Her Majesty's Hanoverian ancestry) for their sense of humour. The only other instances of April Fool jokes which did not originate from within G. C. Fox & Co. came from the German Chamber of Commerce. They had already sent us details of a BMW which had a sunroof that could stay open even during the heaviest downpour: a tunnel of wind was produced to blow across the aperture with such force that it kept the car's occupants entirely dry. The next year we received a newsletter about a new type of mineral water called 'Kick'. It was not until halfway through reading it that we realised it was a joke:

> 'to ease the problem of transporting a heavy and bulky product over long distances "Kick" will also be marketed in solid form, in sweets looking rather like the sugar almonds. This is intended especially to appeal to eastern countries, all the more useful where it is not right for a woman to be seen drinking.'

The third observation was that within the Embassy they are very aware of negative images of Germany and would do anything to dispel them. On these lines I was touched to hear that a friend of mine each year takes a wreath of flowers to the Embassy on the anniversary of the bombing of Dresden by the Allied forces in February 1945, which resulted in terrible devastation. The Embassy set a spy on him, with the unexpected result that he and his wife were invited to tea by the Ambassador to express appreciation for his gesture.

Another story which showed the arm of reconciliation

at work involved a young German lorry driver. He was one day driving east down the long hill into Lostwithiel when his brakes failed. He swerved to avoid some children and crashed, killing himself. Neither his family nor his employers wanted to take any responsibility, with the result that the people of Lostwithiel arranged and paid for his funeral. I went to the service, and during a moment of silence an elderly man stepped forward and, screwing his cap in his hands, said that he had been brought up in London during the war and taught to take a certain attitude towards the Germans. Then, as he spoke through his tears, he said 'But my feelings today are just feelings of forgiveness and compassion'.

Finally, German people are full of the most delightful surprises: at an ostensibly rather dull banquet it was a relief to find myself sitting next to a man – a member of the Embassy staff – who turned out to share with me an enthusiasm for plant-hunting.

Some of my work, such as pension renewals, could be planned, but every now and again there would be, out of the blue, an apparent emergency – often at 5.30 p.m. on a Friday afternoon when I was going away for the weekend. Sometimes it was on returning home, after a weekend away, and finding messages on the answerphone. Some of these alarm calls turned out to be more diplomatic, for example, one particular message we picked up at 1 o'clock in the morning: it was about three Germans who had been on a ship that sank. On investigation it transpired that one had died, one was in hospital and the other had been flown home. In each case, everything that needed to be done had been done; and because, at that late hour of the night, there was nothing more that could be achieved, I went to bed.

Every day quantities of consular post, mostly newsletters, arrived in the office. This was so unlike the nineteenth century, when the boot was on the other foot and Robert Were Fox (II), the American Consul in Falmouth at that time, was sending his three-monthly reports to the Secretary of State in Washington. As an example of the vast amount of paperwork which embassies and consulates must generate, I was unlikely, for example, to attend the memorial mass in 2000 for H. R. H. Doña María de las Mercedes de Borbón, Countess of Barcelona, mother of H. M. King Juan Carlos I of Spain. Although it was nice to be invited.

In my case, and despite this deluge of mail, the level of consular clerical work had, paradoxically and dramatically, declined in the previous 20 years, much of this due to the plastic card and technological advances in the world of communications, which now of course include email. The implication was that there were, and presumably still are, many other honorary consuls in similar situations, where they have outlived their need, and are little short of anachronisms, accumulatively representing considerable cost to the countries they represent. Nearly 100 years ago my great-great-uncle found himself in a similar situation, when his appointment as American Consul came to an end:

'This in no way through dissatisfaction with Howard Fox but by way of reducing the Consular appointments in Europe and hardly any consular work done here, American shipping calling here having fallen very low. Full thanks were given to Howard Fox for his services.' [Partners' minutes]

Although, as has been intimated, there was an element of fun (the skid pad testing ground for Mercedes Benz was terrific) as much as reward to the consular conferences, there were also plenty of moments which I did not enjoy so much. I felt pretentious, after devouring a huge and delicious lunch, to be sitting in an airless room and having to listen to some poor official who had obviously been commandeered to talk for two hours about, for example, the socio-political economic situation in South-West Bavaria. Question time, when the consuls would tend to ask self-gratifying questions, was just as tedious. I would gaze out of ambassadorial windows onto ambassadorial lawns, and long to be outside, either in the sun or under an ambassadorial plane tree; and instead of taking notes on the acres of paper provided, I sketched, with distinctly unambassadorial results.

Throughout the whole history of the consular business, the Entente Cordiale has always been very gratifying and there is a nostalgia for phrases such as 'by order of the Emperor', let alone his signature. So when in 2001 I resigned from my consular appointments, it felt as if I had taken a saw and felled a living tree which, in spite of an increasing eclipse of emperors, kings and queens, had been growing for a long time. It was noticeable however that there were no complaints from any of the countries I represented. When I was taken out to a farewell lunch, and given leaving presents by some of the Dutch consular staff from London, I asked them about this, the fact that there had been so little opposition to my resignation. They gently reminded me that an honorary consular appointment is the gift of a monarch, or president; and because of this it is not the place of anyone else to terminate it. Neither is it the habit of monarchs or presidents to terminate appointments. The exception, of course, is when a Ministry of Foreign Affairs decides to close a consulate, as often happens, and the consul's appointment accordingly ceases.

Nonetheless a recipient can resign, and in many cases this can be to the economic advantage of the country he, or she, represents, although on the whole the appointments are unpaid. In industrial centres such as Birmingham, some honorary consuls are so busy they have a consular secretary. Indeed numerous applications for the post of consular clerk would suggest that this was certainly the case in Falmouth before 1900. Some of the documents for applications, appointments and deeds of restriction existed for men who were taken on because of their linguistic abilities. It must have jollied things along in the office to have had a healthy mixture of Latinate staff, with names such as Zuppelli, Figaro, Becherini, Vassallo and Angelo Repetto, and others of Teutonic blood: Altaber, Ludwig, Berg, Fehlmann, Kugge, Daner and Christian Karsvig. With wars raging on the Continent and immediate antagonism to anyone who represented our islands' foes, life in the pubs and streets must have had its moments too.

But away from the hurly-burly of the waterfront was another side of consular life. In a letter to a cousin in 1857, Alfred Fox writes,

'Aunt Charles has made acquaintance with the Queen of Bavaria[50] [*and*] the Prince Adalbert who was here last year with the Prussian Man of War – most of the officers spent the day with us at Glendurgan.'

Again in 1871:

'on 1 Feby Robert Fox as Northern German Vice Consul invited all the German Captains in port to dine with him at the Falmouth Hotel.'

This amounted to nearly 20 and the party also included two German clerks, who were presumably within the firm's employment. In a commonplace book it is recorded that, on seeing lines of footwear lined up in the hall at Wodehouse Place,

'two Ottoman captains left their boots in the ante-room as a sign of respect as they do in the East [...] A late comer shook hands with the full dress white-tied hired waiter thinking he was the host who had risen to welcome him'.

In case anyone should consider that the hiring of uniformed staff was an instance of *folie de grandeur* perhaps it should be added there must have been several occasions when male members of my family were mistaken for the gardener.

---

50   This probably refers to Marie of Prussia, who was married to Max-imilian II of Bavaria, who became King of Bavaria after his father abdicated in 1848. Adalbert was Maximilian's younger brother.

George Henry Fox's appointment as Ottoman Vice Consul, 1875

With official visits, one of our duties as honorary consuls was the organisation of official entertainment. This
came in two forms. There would be a visit of the captain
and officers, all in uniform and with swords (they are
not designed for taxis), to the Mayor's Parlour, followed
by a reciprocal visit to the ship in question. Then in
the evening, on board, there would be a cocktail party
which we had to arrange. I have the fondest memories of
those occasions, either during the summer on deck, just
catching the last of the sun as it sank behind the town,
or sometimes during the winter, snugly underwater in
a submarine. Often as we left these parties at about 8.30
p.m. we would see coming towards us what might be
called the *alternative* party, not arranged by the honorary consul; and it would be no surprise that on Monday
mornings, taxis, being all things to all people, would have

to be dispatched to collect those seamen who had failed to return to their ships. On one such morning, my wife and I were watching a mine-sweeping squadron depart, finally, with all the crew lined up on the decks. They looked magnificent in the spring sunshine, every sailor saluting Falmouth Docks. There was much hooting from the ships, and flag-waving from the quay. As the ships ploughed powerfully out to sea, my wife said, 'Think of all those broken hearts and promises to be neglected.' So much for what is officially, and euphemistically, called 'R & R', short for 'Rest and Recuperation'.

By far the most enjoyable aspect of these visits for me would be taking the captain and a few officers away from the civic receptions and mayors' parlours, and showing them parts of Cornwall they would not ordinarily see. I was happy to do this, walking, cycling, and sometimes sailing. Members of a Dutch crew once so enjoyed the three-hour walk into Falmouth, after lunch at the Ferry Boat Inn on the River Helford, that in the evening they walked back out to the pub and then back again by moonlight. This was much like my ancestors, who considered moonlight a great benefit to the economy of one's day.

Just outside Penryn lies the ancient estate of Enys, until recently relatively unknown and undisturbed. During the Second World War it was occupied by members of the Dutch navy; and as Vice Consul for Holland I occasionally had the good fortune to accompany some of the officers on commemorative visits, and into the house as well as the garden. They had fond memories and not just of the place. They were by all accounts both charming and well-behaved which must have made them doubly romantic in the eyes of the eligible Misses Enys.

If I could be asked what I enjoyed most from those consular days, it would be the warm feelings from having helped individuals in distress; this could range from someone who had lost his passport or wallet, to someone who had lost a relative.

Some of my work involved the restitution of graves. In the churchyard of St Winwaloe, Gunwalloe, stands a gravestone inscribed with the names of sixteen Norwegians who perished when the steamship *Heidrun* was wrecked in Mount's Bay just after Christmas 1915. This was the work of the Revd. Peter Long, who for years had wanted to replace the long-lost wooden crosses with something more substantial. The Embassy rose to the challenge and helped with the funding, and on 4 June 1996 the Norwegian Consul flew down for the day from London, changed into her country's national costume, appropriately in the Norway Inn at Perranarworthal, and attended a service of committal. I combed Cornwall for Norwegians, with the result that a sizeable number gathered to worship in their native tongue.

Another involvement I had as Norwegian Consul was the story of Mrs Shilling (re-told here with her approval). She had discovered that the man she had thought was her father was not her real father, who turned out to be a Norwegian who had been injured during the Second World War and admitted to Falmouth Hospital, where her mother had been a nurse. Mrs Shilling had been able to find his entry in the admissions book. She then came to me in my capacity as a ship agent, wanting to look for a record of her father's ship in our registers; little did she know that I could help her much more in my capacity as an honorary consul. Within a very short time the Embassy was able to establish that her real father had eventually gone back to Norway where, before he ever came to Falmouth, he had already produced his own family. He had died, but in due course and much to Mrs Shilling's credit as a person with both determination and a spirit of adventure, she then went to Norway to find all her half-relations; and subsequently they all became close friends as well as half-relatives. This was an emotional time for Mrs Shilling and speaking on the telephone her gratitude was boundless, in spite of my protestations that I was just a cog in the system. So one day I said to her 'Why don't you just find some nice quiet place where you can say thank you to the person you believe in and the person who likes to see untied threads tied up?' to which she replied through her tears, 'Well, I cannot be in a better place to do this because I am the secretary to the Clerk of Works at the cathedral.'

12

TRAVEL

AS LITTLE AS two hundred years ago there were Cornish-men who crept up out of their valleys and regarded the surrounding landscape as abroad. Unlike Iron Age man, the Romans, or any nomadic tribe, they decided not to visit. One such person, an old woman living all her life in St Ives, went to the top of a nearby hill, called Trencrom, to hear a Methodist preacher give a sermon, and said, 'I never knawed the world so big before'. She thought that some distant hills 'must be in France or Spain, or possibly one of those far off countries' she had heard of in the Bible. This reminds me of a conversation I once had with a Cornish friend, who lived at the bottom of one particular valley. I was trying to justify a neat little beard which I had started to grow, and said 'Well, all the Apostles had them.' She replied 'Oh yes, so did they,' and then as she leant over the half-door of her cottage and gazed out to sea: 'Mind, I has only ever seenum in the fotograffs.'

For many, both geographical and chronological history merged, in much the same way as at secondary schools today, where pupils leap with apparent ease from studying the Egyptians to looking at the Victorians, or Marxism. But perhaps this was what it was like to live in Cornwall, and the broadening of one's mind by travel was not the prerogative of all.

To give an idea of transport in the nineteenth century, here are some of Howard Fox's memories:

'My earliest recollection of our parents was being carried in the arms of a servant to the back door of Wodehouse Place and seeing them drive off in a Coburg to Redruth on their way to Birmingham. From Redruth they travelled on a primitive Railway to Hayle. One hill was surmounted by a double line of rails on a steep incline: the passenger train was hauled up by a train of loaded trucks descending the adjoining rails. On the return journey the descending passenger train & engine hauled up the train of loaded trucks. A large grooved wheel at the top took the cable. At Hayle a small evil-smelling paddle steamer took passengers to Bristol whence they proceeded by coach or in later years by rail.'

Quite easy really; one wonders if, at any stage of negotiating the steep hill, passengers were asked to dismount, and perhaps even push.

The blueprint of today's package holiday had its origins many years ago. The following letter to the directors of the Union Steamship Company is the nineteenth-century equivalent of a mail-shot which might have gone out in the 1970s. In the first paragraph it talks of discounted fares due to an agency agreement; in the second paragraph it describes the advantages of having in-house facilities; and finally it adds that the company has the very latest technology, a signal station which can give the Earliest Time of Arrival for ships passing the most southerly point of Great Britain. The reader cannot fail to perceive that here is a company which in today's parlance 'has a man on the spot', a representative, and the basics of the modern package tour.

'Falmouth 25 March 1873

Gentlemen

When your R. M. S. Saxon was obliged to put into this port on the fifteenth inst owing to the very strong Easterly gale prevailing in the Channel we had pleasure in meeting Captain Diver as soon as the tender brought him with the mails and some of the passengers to the Docks and we hastened to procure the immediate attendance of the postmaster, thus succeeding in getting the Mails dispatched by that afternoon's mail train. Notwithstanding the storm of wind and rain several other passengers wished to land here so the writer went off in the tender for them brought the Examining Officer down to the landing place, it being out of Custom House hours, saw all the passengers comfortably housed at the Hotel and furnished them with Ocean passengers passes by which they were enabled to travel up the line at about half the ordinary rates without expense to your Company. This is owing to an arrangement we have with the Associated Railway Companies.

As part owners of the certificated steam tender "Pendragon" we can command her services when required a most important matter in efficiently attending to mail steamers.

We have established a signal station at the Lizard and steamers coming to Falmouth signalling there can have a tender awaiting them outside the harbour into which to tranship mails and passengers without anchoring and proceed on their voyage after but twenty minutes detention or even less.

You will thus easily understand that we possess special facilities for such business and as we have had more experience in this line than any other firm in the port we trust whenever your boats again call here or you have any other affairs in this district in which our services can be of use we may have the pleasure of continuing to act for you and we shall much value your special appointment.'[51]

In September 1912 it was minuted that agencies for the Union-Castle Line, as it became known, were being unified, and that Devon and Cornwall were to be put entirely into the hands of Warings of Plymouth. This was a blow to G. C. Fox & Co. To add insult to injury Barclay Fox (and this was after having been given lunch by the almost-General Manager of the line, on board a mail boat) had been told that Union-Castle was prepared to

---

51   Another later example was in 1928 when George Henry Fox noted in his diary that his daughter Annette had booked her passage to New Zealand through the family business.

give the company '£150 per annum as a retainer not to represent rival lines'. This was not the first time that this sort of treatment was to be meted out by principals to their loyal and long-standing agents, both in the travel and the ship agencies, and often in spite of winsome assurances to the contrary.

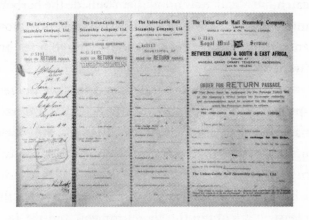

The Union-Castle Mail Steamship Company booking form, 1909

Although the firm had continued to make travel arrangements in conjunction with its ship agency business, it was not until the late 1950s that a travel agency, as we know it today, was opened. There are records of taking over a Falmouth-based company called 'Travelways', and also of many visits that my father made to companies in London in his determination for the firm to be 'appointed agents for International Air Travel Association' – now known as the International Air Transport Association or, more widely, IATA. Amusingly there are also records of another partner, a very switched-on first cousin, taking interest in

'Display' exhibitions: another novel, but very necessary, subject for the firm.

In the 1960s my father had the idea of the specialist holiday. Fuelled, one suspects, by his own passion for the sport of golf, the newly-formed subsidiary, 'G. C. Fox & Co. the House of Travel', started a series of package holidays to Portugal, Spain, and the West Indies. Unfortunately, this was not something he could secure by patent; and since those early days the world has seen the birth of specialist tours for every subject under the sun. Fox Travel, as it became known, went on, however, to market its own series of mini coach tours to European cities, starting with Paris and then progressing to Amsterdam and Venice and some of the – then – more adventurous European capitals. These trips sold for £15 to £30 each and were very popular at a time when many people in Cornwall still had not travelled beyond the River Tamar. Indeed, there were some who had once crossed into Devon, and never wanted to do so again.

As travelling by air became an increasingly preferred option, the firm sent members of staff on educational days to Heathrow, so that clients who had never flown before could be given first-hand advice on how to cope with the perils, such as escalators at an international airport. There were the inevitable jokes, in this new industry, about the airlines: Better On A Camel; Try Walking Across; The Hostesses Are Inscrutable; Such A Bad Experience Never Again; and worse. We also had an interest in what was known as 'intourism'. One afternoon we were shown around a hotel which had previously been a convent. We were told that the chapel had become a conference centre and could hold 150 standing and 100 sitting, to which valuable information my brother William, who has inherited our father's dry wit, commented 'And how many kneeling?'

Fox Travel had its emulators, and no sooner had a package holiday been advertised than the almost identical holiday was to be seen being advertised by a competitor the following week. At a Managers' meeting it was sarcastically suggested that Fox Travel should promote an almost-sold-out tour to some undesirable destination. There were however some excursions which could not be copied: in 1982 Fox Travel chartered the Isles of Scilly ferry, the *Scillonian*, for a day. This, the bright idea of one the managers, was in order that the ship could sail up from Penzance to Falmouth Bay and witness with grandstand views the start of the Tall Ships' Race – a race which in previous years had not had this tourist appeal and which historically was just a race for yachting enthusiasts. Neither had it ever faced before the challenge of such an unexpected wind-hazard.

One hundred years earlier no one would have thought of using a steam ship to witness the progress of tallmasted sailing ships, generally engineless yachts some of which once were the conventional means of transporting cargo around the world. Today you would not come across an entry in the *Western Morning News* such as on 29 November 1893:

'About thirty windbound vessels left Falmouth harbour yesterday. Among them was the schooner Silver Spray, Captain Wells, with pitch, for Cardiff, and the ketch Surprise, 70 tons, Captain Thomas, of Padstow, from Plymouth to Watchet, with alum cake.'[52]

Which is not something you would wish to eat.

The bones of what was at one time the essence of G. C. Fox & Co.'s business, trading ships such as these, at a later date, became a tourist feature for a subsequent business, and additional bones: travel. In the late 1970s I once talked to an old man who, as a cabin boy, had sailed on such a boat. He had photographs of what it was like sailing against the Roaring Forties, when in a gale the sea froze as it came sloshing on board, and soaking, and then freezing, amongst other things, a consignment of pigs. He had worked for the eminent Swedish firm of Gustaf Erikson, who was in the habit of going aboard his ships as they returned from their missions. Sailing up the Atlantic, crews would start to paint the rigging in anticipation of his tour of inspection, and woe betide anyone who let even the smallest drop descend on to the deck.

Fox Travel also arranged what were known as 'educationals' to some of the more glamorous places in the world, often in conjunction with the big tour companies. The intention was that the humble travel clerk would return to his humble desk and talk persuasively and authoritatively about, for example, a safari tour. Fox Travel took all this

---

52   Over 30 years later, such vessels were still sometimes used for transporting cargo. In his diary (12 February 1927) George Henry Fox recorded being taken by car to Porthleven, where they 'saw the 3 m[asted] sch[ooner] Urda of Swedenborg towed by motor boat Energetic out of inner harbour & to sea in fresh E. winds. She had discharged salt from Cadiz.'

Pamir, one of the last commercial sailing ships
Photograph, inscribed verso: 'Presented to Philip H Fox by Capt
H Eggers 22 December 1956. Outward bound from Antwerp
for Monte Video, put back from 300 miles out with cargo of
methylated spirits in barrels shifted. His 17th voyage in Pamir'

very seriously and members of the staff were expected to write a report and also put on a promotional evening, but my personal observation of most other travel agents who enjoyed these educational trips was that they tended to treat the tours as 'freebies'. For many they were also opportunities to be upgraded, for drinking champagne, and for disreputable behaviour. On safari in Kenya one young girl was in despair because a monkey had entered her tent, stolen her contraceptives and, sitting in a tree, was in the process of eating them. At Nyali beach, on being shown into a magnificent honeymoon suite, the manager explained that all their honeymoon suites had one double bed and also a single bed, 'useful for the baby' as one of our group so resignedly commented. Men were equally expectant, and on one occasion I remember receiving rather frosty looks and comments for declining, no doubt providentially, an invitation to go to a night club run by so-called high-class Nubian princesses.

I never took advantage of these educationals. I tried to behave, but am human enough to confess readily, with the other partners of the firm, that we all enjoyed the extensive travelling incurred during the course of owning and running four retail travel agencies and one business house travel agency (the weekly worldwide destinations of Cornish businessmen were, and continue to be, astonishingly impressive). Fortuitously for us this was at a time when the world had not been completely opened up by the great tin-opener of tourism; my parents were fortunate in this respect, often being away on cruises in the 1950s and '60s. We were involved in the early days of creating fairly hefty carbon footprints, and were also guilty, then, of sending all sorts of questionable liaisons around the world. One friend of my father's came to him in confidence to explain that the holiday he had booked was not with his wife. My father told him how we prided ourselves on our discretion, which was true. But I could not help thinking about my mother, more or less at the same time, being concerned about an unmarried couple coming to rent one of her cottages: 'What might the village think?' she questioned.

Once, Falmouth was on the brink of the world. Today, there is a ship called *The World* which occasionally comes to Falmouth. We have progressed from an age of ships to an age of tourism, from an age of need to an age of indulgence. Today, Falmouth at any time of year is full of yachts from all over the world. The town is awash with restaurants; and there is an attempt at continental café society. Roundabouts are planted with palms, and roads are bordered by dracaenas, dramatically unlike indigenous scrub. The county throughout is now rich with the results of the plant hunting expeditions. Views out to sea, and beyond the brink of the horizon to distant lands, are framed by horticultural trophies from all over the globe, in ways which would have been unfamiliar in the mid-nineteenth century.

13

PROPERTY

IT IS PROBABLY true to say that many pig farmers say 'Never farm pigs'. My grandfather, Cuthbert, used to say 'Never own property', a remark which, however odd it sounded coming from him, he was well qualified to give. My experience is that while the rents continue to come in, everything is lovely in the garden. But every now and again a boiler bursts, or a roof comes off in a gale, and one has to act swiftly to resolve the problem, most of us without the back-up of a sinking fund. I used to dread returning from a holiday, or even a weekend, and bounding up the staircase to my office, with an admittedly slightly contrived sense of enthusiasm, to be greeted as follows by secretaries, who after all were only doing their jobs to the best of their abilities:

'Had a nice holiday? Just to say that there's been a burst pipe at number 16. I've been in touch with the plumber and he's sorted it for now but he wants to talk to you about replacing the whole system.'

Or sometimes:

'Just to say there's been a break-in at the boatyard and I said that you would pop along as soon as you got in.'

This, understandably, is why serious estates employ someone who acts as a buffer against such cheerful little messages; and this useful person is called *the agent*. Indeed, we had an agent but, in order to economise, I invariably cut across his bows.

As for the rents, not everyone pays a realistic rent, and not everyone pays on time. There is at least one person who still owes us money and who now runs a delightful cream tea establishment. I have not paid a visit. Other tenants were unofficial and simply occupied spaces illegally. There were several squatters, with all the paraphernalia of squatters, in our boatyard. At the back of the offices at 48 Arwenack Street there used to be an open garage and at the back of this, under its roof, there was a small lock-up shed. A vagrant man took up residence on the flat top of this shed: bedroom, kitchen, and worst of all, lavatory, all in a space of about eight feet by five feet. Another tenant – official – had an air gun and took pot shots at the back elevation of the office. The staff complained to me; I complained to him with a warning that if there was any repetition the police would be informed; he repeated his game; the police were informed; our tenant took me by the lapels of my jacket and said, 'From now on I will be your neighbour from hell'; and I thought, 'Join the crowd'.

Termination, never mind eviction, was also a miserable business; and I have on my conscience forever the lives and deaths of a few tenants with whom we had to be 'realistic'. It made it worse that some of the firm's cottages had connections with what are known as 'loyal servants'. There was a time, much mourned by local people today, when cottages could be bought for a few hundred pounds in this country; and the partners were keen on this for a couple of reasons. It meant that very often they could have a man on site; for example, in 1919 at Fox Stanton's timber yard in Grampound Road, they bought two cottages for £200 and £220 – under £10,000 each today. It also gave them more control in the area, if there were a chance for expansion, or as at Penryn, demolition and alternative access, in order to develop their business. Apparently this is also the current policy with at least one major supermarket chain: it likes to buy up surrounding properties.

In such a cottage we once had a tenant with a little dog. It had the inexplicable habit of barking in a particular passage, an area where the temperature fell by about five degrees. One day I asked if anything strange had ever happened in the property.

'Nothing, nothing that I can think of.'
'Are you sure?'
'Well there is this story that a long, long time ago there was a little girl who fell off a cliff in the back yard and was killed…but that was a very long time ago'.
'And was that the end of the story?'
'Yes … I think so … except that her mum and dad always said that it was the girl's silly fault and that they had warned her enough times not to climb around in that part of the garden; and they never forgave her.'

How sad, I thought, to die as an unforgiven person, especially by your parents. I rang up a friend who had authority in these matters and the upshot was that, with the tenant's consent, an obliging vicar was asked to come to the cottage and conduct Holy Communion and a service of committal in the tenant's front room.

Normal temperature was restored and the little dog's barking ceased.

This was one of the more rewarding aspects of being a landlord.

Returning to more regular concerns, what compounds the potential problems of letting is that nowadays everything has to be in A1 condition. The days when my mother was able to relegate every chipped tea service, broken vase, threadbare blanket, old pillow, or foxed watercolour to a holiday cottage have disappeared, as are the days when I helped her lay Fablon on the shelves of Victorian kitchen cupboards. Inventories I regard as a waste of time: whether there is an inventory or not, a fork is a small thing to be replaced, and on the other hand a missing television is immediately noticeable by its absence, but also needs to be replaced.

The buildings we used as offices were not impervious to disaster: the Truro travel agency office was flooded by an underground river two or three times. On one occasion an employee who worked there was able to realise the dream of her lifetime: a fireman's lift. As the staff migrated to an upstairs room, her opportunity appeared: a uniformed fireman on a ladder. To begin with, she froze: it was too good to be true. Apparently she finished her journey to safety by being rowed across Victoria Square in an inflatable rubber dinghy purchased from a nearby well-known store, and by ending up at a takeaway for a cup of tea.

Nosey-parkers gave us quite a bit of gyp. In our Camborne travel agency office, because we had increased our workforce by one, in order to help the unemployment situation, we were politely informed by someone from the council that we would have to have two separate lavatories. This was going to cost a disproportionately large amount of money. My father thought of the facilities on board trains, and aeroplanes; and responded by saying that he was going to dedicate the existing facilities for the use of the female staff, whilst the male staff would make their own arrangements *elsewhere*, i.e. in a nearby public convenience.

One year we decided to re-roof 48 Arwenack Street. The scaffolding had scarcely been erected before a neighbour telephoned. He politely informed me that for three years he and his wife had been monitoring the lives ('why *lives*?' many would ask) of some seagulls who lived on part of the roof: what *provision* would we be making for them, and the defenceless juveniles, in view of the building works? He might have liked to have been told about an entire morning when far too many staff had tried to rescue a seagull which had swallowed a fish hook: we managed to disentangle the line from its feathers, but then off it flew with the line trailing hopelessly out of its beak.

Health and safety had its similar irritations, such as the likelihood that staff would fall out of windows, and the urgent need to protect them from this ghastly fate. As far as records go, in a period of over 200 years this has never happened. Like hotels and many other businesses no doubt, sometimes it was enough of an effort just running a business, never mind looking after the clients; and, as should be clear by now from foregoing pages, there were always enough fires to extinguish without having extra potential ones imposed by the rules and regulations of health and safety.

So, having taken the mythology out of owning property, and leaving other properties to speak for themselves within the context of their own histories, this chapter will look one building which for over 200 years was the nucleus of the business, and which within the context of Georgian Falmouth has some pretensions: 48 Arwenack Street.

It would seem that a Dane by the name of Niels Falck built 48 Arwenack Street around 1782. By 1790 he had run out of money and the leasehold was sold, ending up with the Fox family. In 1848 there was in Falmouth a sale of property, belonging to the Wodehouse family, such as never had been seen before, or since. Number 48, or Plot 231, as it was described, was 'a spacious, substantial, detached family residence with mercantile offices, yard and garden', and at that time leased to G. C. Fox and other members of the Fox family. The presumption is that they then bought the freehold; they had also leased a warehouse in this area but it had been demolished in 1814 to make way for the Custom House.

The mid-eighteenth century building has an architecture of what aesthetes call 'pleasing simplicity'. It has a principal elevation of brick, over granite plinths with two higher string courses, a top cornice and full width parapet. The front or east elevation has two Doric entrance doors each at the head of a flight of fine granite steps. Architectural historians may be interested to note that at one time these steps were considerably finer, insofar as they extended further into the street, but at the same time 'projected a considerable way on the pathway and consequently caused a great inconvenience to people'.[53] This says something about the business of both pedestrian and presumably mostly horse-drawn traffic in the street. In the early 1900s G. C. Fox & Co. agreed with the Highway Committee that the flights could be shortened and 'the Corporation to pay for the alterations on both sets of steps'. Perhaps one day with the current enthusiasm to pedestrianise, and restore, they will be returned to their former elegance (one could say less pedestrian), appropriate for a fine portico door case and fanlight, open pediment and fluted pilasters surmounted by medallions. (At one time when the exterior of the building was being repainted it was discovered that so many layers of paint had been applied to these medallions that they had become like mere oval blobs. We were able to uncover one of the original lead mouldings, which had not been melted by blow torches, and sent it off to a leading plasterer to quote for 12 new ones. The figure that came back was of astronomical proportions. I began to think that there must be another more economical solution, and so wandered up to the College of Art and spoke to a friend of mine who taught sculpture. The pleasing result was

---

53   Partners' Minutes

that the medallions you see today were made by students; some of the festoons were at another time made by the college's technician.)

A photograph from the 1890s shows the full extent of the previous steps; what is also interesting, for professors of paint colours, is that the fenestration is not brilliant white. Dividing the two doors there is a central full height bay with balustrade and associated parapet to the roof with decorated and bracketed cornice. In the basement there are a number of brick wine bins. On my desk to this day, acting as a paperweight, there is part of a green bottle, inscribed intriguingly 'G. C. Fox Falm'; but that and the wine bins are not foolproof evidence that the firm might once have been in the business of brewing. In fact, what happened in those days was that you would purchase wine and have it put into your own bottles, suitably stamped, or what is now called personalized, and then stored in your own wine bins. There is also in the cellars a vaulted safe which could be opened by use of a water lock situated in the main attic, as described in Chapter 8.

Some modern historians believe that the Fox family came to Falmouth and in a flourish, perhaps more sub-conscious than conscious, had Number 48 constructed in brick, which in Cornwall was often a sign of affluence, as their new and prestigious offices. I do not believe this was the case, any more than I believe a tour guide overheard, standing one day outside Grove Place, waving her hands around and saying 'All this belonged to the Fox family' (this is one of the more modest assertions I have wit-nessed over the years). It is more probable that the Foxes' attitude was one of pragmatism and that tentatively they

The main elevation of 48 Arwenack Street
Photograph, inscribed verso: 'Howard Fox on top of steps,
George Henry Fox halfway down steps, Wm Hy Daniell at
bottom of steps. U.S. Consul, Vice & Deputy U.S. Con[sul]s &
Chancellor of the Consulate at Falmouth, taken May 1896 on
the steps of the Consulate at G. C. Fox & Co.'s Counting House
Falmouth, by order of the U.S. Government who required
photos of all consular officers to be sent to Washington.'

had a lease on the building in the early days. Bank House nearby was, on the other hand, a commissioned house: it was built for Robert Were Fox (I), grandfather to the Barclay who wrote the *Journals*. But again it was a pragmatic choice, so much so that Robert Were never saw it until, on completion, the key was handed to him by the builder. It must have been much like handing over the keys to a car, and in contrast to today, when owners prefer to become fully involved in the realization of their creative ideas. It was also a tribute to the construction business that he should have had in it so much confidence. It has to be borne in mind, however, that this once was a modern house, and really no different in that way from large houses which are currently being built on the edges of any seaside town.

Before it was acquired for the Foxes' business, 48 Arwenack Street was a private residence, and the evidence of that is seen not just in the structure of the rooms, but in the number of artifacts that the family has had the wisdom to remove to non-commercial properties, artifacts such as paintings and furniture which are better suited to a domestic environment.

I have a distant memory of coming here as a child, from the hot and dusty streets of post-war Falmouth, entering through the cool colonnades of Doric and Ionic columns, made of wood and painted the colour of mahogany. The dark brown paint continued to decorate the glazing bars of any interior fenestration, and behind such a window, which might even have been the vernacular sliding sash, resided the switchboard with its terracotta-coloured dolly switches. This was part of the ship agency office as I understood it then: a dark austere place where men would gather and smoke tobacco, and speak in gruff voices. One in particular, Mr Tong, whose name amused us because it was pronounced to rhyme with 'sung', and who used to wear a thin grey double-breasted suit, would say 'Now then young men'; and still with his pipe in his mouth, he would take us two doors along the street to buy the most delicious vanilla ice creams, from a woman whose hair was the same yellow as the ices she sold. In the winter it would be a bar of milk chocolate, which to us, was the size of a cricket bat.

The only female voice I can recall in the office downstairs, indelibly ringing in my ears even today, is the telephone operator who enabled my parents to keep in touch, frequently:

'Which Mr Fox, Mrs Fox?'
'One moment Mrs Fox.'
'Mr Fox, I have Mrs Fox for you, Mr Fox.'
'Mrs Fox, putting you through now – one moment.'
'Mr Fox, Mrs Fox for you Mr Fox.'
'You are through now Mrs Fox'.

Then there was the noise of a lot of clicking, as various telephone cables were pushed into little holes on the vertical board, and others flew around and shot back into other little holes. Then, apart from a clock ticking, and the operator of the switchboard doing her endless knitting, the office would revert to a sort of reverential silence … until Mr and Mrs Fox had finished conversing, and the cables were all disconnected and had shot back into their little holes once more, and the rubber eyelids of the vertical holes would flutter, as if from over exertion.

POOR Mrs Fox …

I accept that this was no different from any other family business in the country at that time, but future social historians might be amused by this fascinatingly ridiculous verbatim account from the switchboard of a small family-run business.

The office in those days had the appearance of the sort of Western-style saloon bar designers strove to contrive in the 1960s and 1970s, but it had none of that contrivance: it just was what it was. Here there were bare boards, stoves to burn the sawdust from the timber yard, and the high-up Davenport desks with porcelain inkwells, wooden pens with scratchy nibs, blotters and blotting paper.

The only concession to a seven-year-old was venturing up the stairs and into his grandfather's room, which had a dark green carpet, set in parquet flooring made in the timber yard, and the most elegant grey wallpaper sporting monochrome sketches of roses, a million miles from the engine room downstairs.

My grandfather's secretary was called Miss Gummow, to him of course known as 'Gummie'. Her hair was done up in a farmhouse loaf, rather than a bun; and as if to accentuate this, her eyebrows were severely arched in pencil. She had a very sunny disposition and, like the switchboard operator, she also knitted. She wore a necklace made up of what I believe are called 'poppets'. With serious intent and often rather chocolatey fingers, I much enjoyed disconnecting these: the little plastic spheres would bounce about all over the floor of her office, and out on to the landing.

Then there would be a commotion: my grandfather appeared, like a bear rumbling out of its cave, and I got shooed down the stairs just as my mother, vaguely apologizing, and with her smile, came up the stairs.

Years later I saw Miss Gummow in the main street of Falmouth. She had two Pekingese dogs with her, and a Zimmer frame.

During the 1960s the ground floor received a face lift and centuries of unchangingness were swept away, ironically as it now appears, to celebrate the bicentenary of the company's existence in Number 48. In came something called Formica, lowered ceilings and suspended ceilings, and suspended lighting and the latest in office furniture; and as an extension of the ship agency, the first of the four travel agencies was updated. My father's idea of the specialist holiday was the new dynamism and brought with it everything that the 1960s had to offer in terms of the modern office, in particular glass doors and glass panels. Among all the wire chairs, wire wastepaper baskets and wire filing trays was the internal telephone system, much loved by me. On each desk sat a sort of shoe box, beautifully veneered in some rare wood with on one side an illuminated panel and switches; and in those days switches, as in cars, were not labelled. But the rare wood was. On top of this shoe box sat the resplendent telephone. In due course labels were introduced, and in the case of personnel their title and position within the firm were given, as well as name. There was a pleasing sense of power and efficiency with which you decided to flick your interlocutor on, or off (hence, perhaps, that new transitive word to 'disappear' someone). The helpful illuminating panel either waxed or waned in accordance with your executive decision.

Everyone loves labels: the three gentlemen's lavatories survived several makeovers with, discriminately, on one door 'PARTNERS', the next 'STAFF' and the last 'GENERAL', whatever that meant, and however relevant these distinctions were in cases of urgent need. They were no more to be observed than the small shiny white tiles on the walls, or the cupids supporting the high level cisterns. There was also in this area a notice which read 'PLEASE DO NOT DROP CIGARETTES IN THE URINAL – THINK OF THE CLEANERS'. This last phrase seemed an odd thing to say; and many preferred not to think of them.

By the late 1970s we were beginning to witness the noise and inconvenience of having to open three or four nose-squashing glass doors before reaching the British and American shipping department, or the Foreign shipping department, or, nursing our injured noses, going upstairs to the other offices. For this reason, and in keeping with the philosophy of the open plan office, the ground floor was converted into one big room. Away went peg boards, and grey and lemon yellow, and mahogany furniture, and in came the shop designer with worktops and storage units finished in oak veneer. Acres of glass set in black metal frames, and ceilings which remained suspended, but with a rusticated effect, completed this transformation to modernity.

This was in keeping with the nature of the business which had always kept abreast of the times: as has been mentioned in a previous chapter G. C. Fox & Co. was among the first in Falmouth to install a telephone, then a telex machine, then fax machines and finally computers. The company must also have been amongst the first to throw out telephones with dials, to the relief of secretarial finger nails, but no doubt also causing the sales of biros to plummet significantly.

In the early 1990s the building was re-roofed and a few years later the top floor was redecorated in order to let space to the offices of the National Maritime Museum Cornwall, whilst their museum was in the process of being built. Like so many businesses, and like so many homes, the partners were just responding to the demands of the time, using the building on an *ad hoc* basis, as had always been the case.

Before the museum people came, their initial office in the building had been the Gestetner room. It had on one of its walls a map of the world, so old that large areas were shaded in imperial pink. But this room was also (you could tell by the smell) home to the eponymous duplicating machine, cans, or tubes of ink, reams of pale green paper, rubber gloves and two nylon overalls, one sky blue, and the other café-au-lait, both with collars and cuffs checked with white. The colour of these garments proved to be irrelevant: it was impossible to leave this exciting office without tell-tale smudges all over your hands, face and hair, as well as clothes. Ink needs to be controlled but once the Gestetner machine had started to wallop away with copying, this could often be a problem.

It continued to be called the Gestetner room long after the Gestetner machine had been thrown out, and the Gestetner man no longer came in his Gestetner van, and no longer trudged up the two flights with his load of Gestetner ink. A new machine, yet noisier, and with a different purpose, was installed: the shredding machine. In a pre-delete and pre-permanent delete age this was used for the destruction of confidential files, probably now called 'document management policies'. It was a metal box on the top of which there was a sort of letter box set with menacing teeth. These you could noisily grind at a choice of two speeds. Into its hungry mouth you fed your documents; and because we had the de-luxe model you could also include, with a joyous sense of impunity, paper clips and staples. Lest you fed it something by mistake, there was a 'STOP' button, and a 'REVERSE' button; and when for fun you fed it telephone directories, it would regurgitate spectacularly, and with a suitably emetic sound. On the side of the machine, stuck with yellowing sellotape, there was a photograph, surely from Scotland Yard, of what to do if the worst should happen: you engage the services of two beautifully manicured females.

Endlessly patient, they are reconstituting shreds.

I wish I had kept that photograph; and whenever I come off an escalator I am always hopelessly reminded of those grinding teeth, and what might happen.

Often, waiting for the Gestetner machine to complete its work I would wander aimlessly through a warren of doors from one empty room on the second floor into the next, and in a desultory way examine the forever-peeling wallpaper, and the cupboards full of rubbish, etc. One of them contained a glass jar of pickled pilchards; they were not attractive.

Although it was probably psychologically good practice that the office staff had to dart about the building, up and down stairs, and along passageways, in order to photocopy, send telexes, make tea, etc., it was strange that the business was being carried on in such a complicated geography.

There was a cupboard in the partners' boardroom on the top floor, and at the back of it there was another door which led into the caretaker's flat, and out of his flat into another part of the building, up some stairs to an attic, or down five steps and up five steps to his bedroom, and then down further stairs to his bathroom, which was next to the office kitchen. This was very conveniently just next door to what was rather ambiguously called the female lavatories. On the way into the kitchen there was a filing cabinet, or two, of long term filing, which could also be found in the attics, or the cellars, or just outside – and at one time actually inside – what were known as the male lavatories on the ground floor. There were other rooms which hinted that they had at one time been used res-identially, with highly patterned carpets, Artex ceilings and Anaglypta walls, blocked-in fire places, candlewick lampshades, and mirrors from the 1950s. It was all rather vague, and no doubt very confusing for new employees being inducted.

There had always been this vision of utilizing all the square footage of the building rather than just a third, or less, as and when put to use; and I also had the concept of restoring one section of the building to its original residential purpose. Then there were the cellars, which was an area we visited as infrequently as possible. Armed with a torch you entered through the padlocked flaps of an abandoned coal hole, down some precipitous steps and into a roughly-hewn tunnel, four-foot-high, one foot wide. Along this ran some kind of sewer pipe, and off it were half a dozen wasted rooms, empty except for anything that was too heavy for the attics, such as a wire hawser, and, for the interest of those who live only in the paperless world of today, a few thousand travel files, which we had to keep for the requisite period of six years. Sometimes there would be the odd anaemic nettle growing from the floor; and like the interior of a submarine, running along the ceiling of the cellars were the countless cables of decades of different telephone systems, internal and external, many all covered in dust.

The electrician was often to be found in the cellars.

The longevity of G. C. Fox & Co. is very much due to the fact that being a family partnership there is the flexibility to discard one business and pick up another according to the changing economy. Examples of this in the past were tin mining and fishing. In later years similar decisions resulted in Number 48 becoming empty, or almost empty. Without the necessary funds to give the building the treatment it so desperately needed, and deserved, the partners reluctantly agreed in 2001 that it should be sold. This was a hard decision to take but one which arguably did a service to the building. The pragmatic approach seemed to be the one to take: a business is a machine for making money but if that machine is no longer being used there is no longer any need to keep it. I hardened my heart: it seemed that the building was about to be sold to become a steak house.

However, this did not happen. A man whose family

business belongs to the Tercentenarians Club became the new owner. This is a club for those businesses, such as G. C. Fox & Co. and its previous incarnations, which have exceeded 300 years of their lifespan within one family. Once a year it meets recreationally but apart from that has no other function. It had always been an aim of mine for this eminent group to be slightly more productive, and that aim was more than fully realised when the building was sold to someone whom the partners had met through the club, a man who had always had, necessarily had, a romantic notion of the building, and a man who was happy for me to continue having an involvement in its final renaissance.

Everyone was keen to avoid the pitfalls of Georgian look-alike, which so often descends into pastiche and worse than that, Disneyland. But in so doing, the conservation work followed that current architectural fashion where anything new has to show that it is markedly new, the great examples of this being the new glazed roofs at Greenwich Maritime Museum and the British Museum. Previous generations just progressed smoothly from one architectural style or period to the next without having to call upon the *avant garde*, the high tech or iconic. Indeed this has become such a fashion we may almost be in danger of losing proper conservation work where there is a place for it. At Number 48 a median line has been drawn.

The servants' staircase in the town house has been faithfully reproduced and extended from first to ground floor, but where a new staircase has been installed leading from the ground floor to the basement it is contemporary in design. A cast iron fan light, possibly made at the Perranarworthal foundry, was dragged up from the cellars where it had lain in desuetude, and installed over a principal doorway. Where there was a need for light and air to be let into the cellars, a hole six by four feet was punched through the boards of the ground floor; and immediately below this there is a restored section of cobbling. A well in the back yard was uncovered, and at the same time an equally ancient cannon. Extensive alterations were made to incorporate both a new entrance and a lavatory for the disabled. The architects have shown sensitivity over such issues, and in following the dictates of health and safety, even if the new porthole lights on either side of the staircase make me think of 'this way to the pool'.

But perhaps this was intentional, a visual pun on the shipping history of the building.

14

CROSSING THE BRINK

THERE ARE DIFFICULTIES in joining a family partnership, in running it, in handing it over, and harder than any of those, in selling it.

Family solidarity was always one of the great strengths of the firm. It is interesting that historically the most successful family businesses have often been those where the families in question are united by a common faith or religion, or by philanthropic ideals. This is borne out by the names you see on letterheads from the city: eminent members, for example, of the Jewish community. Equally, any investigation into the history of Quakers involved in company businesses reveals very quickly the enormous influence they had in the banking world; and how, perhaps unlike today, they used their wealth and influence for the benefit of others. In such companies there is less likelihood of disunity rearing its ugly head.

A random minute from the timber business in 1934 speaks for itself:

'It was decided that as we are now only 3 partners Fox Stanton Co.'s cheques up to £3000 could be signed by one partner.'

By law partners are jointly and severally liable for each other's debts: this entry shows the degree of trust for a liability of, in today's terms, over £150,000.

The parts that women had to play within Quaker businesses is an especially interesting subject. It is a topic in its own right and has been written about at length elsewhere. For centuries, women, not necessarily Quaker, have proved to be proficient at running either their own or their deceased husbands' businesses. Just because they have not been into power-dressing, flown around the world, stood on podiums and given high-level talks, does not mean to say that they have been any less effectual at running businesses: the bottom line has always been to make a profit. Often these businesses have been, and continue to be, the responsibilities of running a large estate. Somehow there is an impressive, and refreshing, honesty to the woman who rises early to do the cows and then comes indoors to sort out the accounts all over the kitchen table, attends to the expressed and unexpressed needs of tenants, and expectant ewes, before going out to a charity lunch, at which she says nothing of her morning.

As far as G. C. Fox & Co. is concerned, there is evidence from the early days of those unsung heroes – women, especially wives – taking a front seat in the running of the business. The wife of George Fox of Par is given a huge amount of credit, both financial and moral, in the letter books, mostly by her children. At one point she is described as 'Mother Fox'. Another astute merchantess, George Croker Fox (I)'s sister Tabitha, was clearly a good precedent for his widow Mary, who in 1781 succeeded (in both senses of the word) as a partner. When she died in 1796, she left to her five children £3,000 each, a not inconsiderable sum in those days. Years before equality of the sexes had even become a dream on a cloud, Quakers seem to have had an enlightened attitude to women in the workplace. Mary Fox was obviously a person of some standing, and it would be interesting to know what people thought of women filling such a role: was it expected of them and was it accepted?

My mother in her time was a director of a small private limited company owned by G. C. Fox & Co., and occasionally she would come up with some very pertinent remarks; once she noticed a mistake in the accounts. Much, much more than that, however, was the fact that she, as happens with husbands and wives, proved to be an excellent sounding board to my father as he droned on about his day at the office and all he had done, was doing, and would do. (He, again as happens with husbands and wives, also had to listen to her.)

As *On the Brink* should demonstrate, the successful company actually goes beyond merely healthy accounts; often it goes beyond today's archetypal image of the high-flying, profile-cutting business person, male or female. Two hundred and fifty years ago, before equality of the sexes and correlating gender confusion had become such political issues, and before discrimination had been spotted, it is probable that the role of women such as Mary Fox was not questioned. It just was what it was: survival.

Growing up, until well into my teens, I was unaware of the history of the family business. Its history, longevity or success was a subject never mentioned by anyone, not even in the press. In keeping with the Quaker dislike of self-aggrandisement, we were discouraged from talking about family history and I can recall, aged about 14, being ticked off by my mother in the car as I was banging on about the family from the back seat to some hapless guest sitting in the front. As a result, when I first joined the firm, it was without a very clear idea of what my role should be beyond the fact that I was expected to work my way up from the bottom.

My active involvement began in 1976, when I joined the firm of G. C. Fox & Co. as a junior partner. It grew during the 1980s as I gradually took over more responsibility from my father, eventually becoming senior partner; and it concluded at the turn of the new millennium with the sale of the two remaining parts of the business, the ship agency and Fox Travel. In this way, I was following in a tradition set when George Croker Fox (I) first established the firm in the 1760s, in an unbroken chain from father to son, with support and participation from cousins and nephews and, as we have seen, from time to time, wives, daughters and nieces.

Even my great-great-grandfather Alfred Fox (1794–1874), who became such a renowned and accomplished businessman, started at the bottom of the family ladder. Here are some details from his apprenticeship to his father Robert Were Fox (I). Politically incorrect today, they were probably standard legal form in 1813:

'...3 years during which Term the said Apprentice his Master faithfully shall serve his secrets keep his lawful commands everywhere gladly do He shall do no damage to his said Master nor act to be done of others but to his power shall tell or forthwith give warning to his said Master of the same He shall not waste the Goods of his said Master nor lend them unlawfully to any He shall not commit fornication nor contract Matrimony within the said term He shall not play at Card or Dice Tables or any other unlawful Games whereby his said Master may have any loss with his own goods or others during the said Term without Licence of the said Master He shall neither buy nor sell He shall not haunt taverns or Playhouses nor absent himself from his said Master's cries day or night unlawfully.'

Until the 1930s, the management and directorship of the firm rested principally in the hands of Alfred and his brother Robert Were Fox (II) and their descendants, the firm's name changing in accordance with the partnership from Fox Sons & Co. (1816) to G. C. & R. W. Fox & Co. (1854) before settling in 1871 on the name G. C. Fox & Co. which it retained until it passed out of family ownership in 2000 (see Appendix for full list of partnership changes). Alfred's younger brother Charles (1797–1878), famous for his gardens at Tredrea and Trebah but in the context of this book for his involvement with Perran Foundry, was also active in the partnership but died without a male heir: his daughter Juliet – Robert Barclay Fox (I)'s favourite cousin – had, like her cousin, married into the Backhouse family. Gradually the line of descent through Robert Were Fox (II) also diminished. In the years immediately after the Second World War, the family partners were two of Alfred's grandsons, my grandfather Cuthbert Lloyd Fox (1885–1972) and his brother George Romney Fox (1898–1968), soon to be joined by their nephews, Anthony Fox Laity and my father Philip Hamilton Fox, and eventually by my brother William and myself as junior partners.

For a young person, joining an established organisation, the phenomenon of being 'thrown in at the deep end' is fraught with pitfalls. In the first place, it can encourage over-fraternisation with staff which is not good for exercising authority and not always good for gaining respect. But it is difficult: our natural disposition, for both partners and staff, is to be friendly. It is also unreasonable to expect an incoming partner to know (for instance) how to grease engine rooms, and faintly ridiculous, not to mention irrelevant, to expect him to learn. But the fact that a partner is seldom seen on the shop floor does not stop him taking an effectual part in the running of the business, as should have been more than evident from the foregoing pages. The irony is that when push comes to shove, and there is a really unpleasant job to be done, a job that no one else will do, or can be expected to do, it is a partner who does it, such as George Henry Fox's task of gathering up human remains (see Chapter 5). Mopping up the floors in the office after the seriously inebriated and incontinent visits of ships' crews was mild by comparison.

In those early years, during my lunch hour I would sometimes drive out of Falmouth and look down on the port from the high surrounding hills, listening to the noises which ships make when they are being moved and mended, and wondering what might be my purpose among them. Thankfully, in my case, there were exceptions to the general rule of keeping one's distance and I was able to gain some practical experience, which I hope also gained me some respect. On first joining the firm I was, as mentioned in Chapter 7, set to work in our paint store in the Docks. One of the storekeepers there, Frank

Barrett, was brought up by the Plymouth Brethren and his face radiated with the fruits of the Spirit: love, joy, peace, forbearance, kindness, goodness, faithfulness, gentleness, and self-control. He was also a beekeeper who taught me everything I have ever known about beekeeping, never mind marine paints or anything else.

Much of the work was very enjoyable. These days, I am grateful to look back on the years spent boarding ships and working in Falmouth Docks, disinfesting ships or inspecting the application of anti-fouling paint on ships' bottoms (known as the flats). Those who did not know me from Adam (and there were many) could wear neither airs nor graces. If I was the last one off a ship which was about to undock, I, in my bright blue International Paint Marine Coatings boiler suit, could get a lift in the toe of a crane's chain as easily as a 'dockee' – illegal and probably impossible now. I enjoyed working on ships both with paints and pesticides: those horribly fascinating cockroaches which had somehow invaded the dials on the bridge, and others which had made their homes in Kilner jars, each jar containing a different type of flour, sugar or curry. I have a dim memory of once being mistaken for a Dane at the time of a Tall Ships' Race and being hauled up into a lorry-load of cadets going on an excursion; and because there was no room in the back of the lorry I was told to hang onto the bonnet, in those pre-CCTV days. I had jumped off sufficiently well before we reached the policemen at the dock gates. But in any event in those days they would probably have turned a blind eye. They were our friends: I was never much of a drinker but one evening I came swerving out of the Docks in my car and a policeman came running after me. I thought the worst was about to happen, until I was politely asked 'Mr Fox, do you realise your fog light is on?'

Something else which kept me busy and seemed to justify my existence in the firm was charitable work: it is so easy to be flattered into situations when you are young and are trying to take over the mantle of your father. For example, I was precipitated at an early age, and with a large donation, into becoming a trustee of the Falmouth Maritime Museum, which had been formed from a splinter of the Royal Cornwall Polytechnic Society. Even though by far the youngest I already knew that in order to survive it was necessary either to sell or to expand, and therefore came up with two suggestions. The first was to sell some irrelevant maritime paintings – not popular; and the second, even more cheeky, was to trot off to Greenwich's National Maritime Museum where a friend of mine was the director.[54] Two of us went for the day and were probably a bit of a nuisance as we were shown around this august establishment, and as we tried to ask intelligent-sounding questions. It seemed like a wasted trip; the only thing I remember with clarity was a picture by Landseer of Nelson with a bear, and another exhibit featuring some polystyrene sick on the side of a bunk, in a replica of a storm-tossed nineteenth-century trading ship.

As a young person, joining an established organisation, it is sometimes easy to see what needs to be done, but

------

54   Although not a consequence of the excursion, its wisdom was confirmed decades later when the Falmouth Maritime Museum became a founding part of the National Maritime Museum Cornwall.

inappropriate to mention it; it can be harder still to expect any responsive action. The younger generation is expected to please, and therefore aims to please. The danger of this, when it comes to an outgoing senior partner, particularly if he is your father, is that one becomes conditioned into a self-imposed role of expectation. This means in the first place a quiet submission to the new and prestigious post of being a junior partner and in the second place to an attitude from the established staff that 'nothing will change'. In itself this represents huge difficulties in handing over, but also becomes dangerous after the handover, when both staff and clients are, despite the proclamation that 'nothing will change', actually expecting to see changes and find nothing; and as happened in my case, for fully understandable reasons, the outgoing partner also continues to behave as if there has been no change.

My great-grandfather, George Henry Fox, had similarly mixed feelings about that airily bandied-about phrase 'handing over the reins', as I have learned from reading his diaries. At the age of 81, and after over 55 years in the firm, latterly as senior partner, at a Partners' Meeting on 1 May 1926[55], he wrote,

'I said I thought the time is come to transfer my consular appointments to a partner quietly if possible &

---

55   As he also recorded in his diary, this date was significant nationally for the beginning of the coal strike 'in defence of miners' wages and hours' which would soon escalate into the all-out, nine-day General Strike.

to look to retiring next June [*as*] my physical powers [*are*] getting much weaker. They approved transfers of

Finland V.C. to R.B.F. [*Robert Barclay Fox (II)*]

Portugal V.C. to C.L.F. [*my grandfather Cuthbert Lloyd Fox*]

Greak [*sic*] V.C. to G.R.F. [*George Romney Fox*]

but hoped I shd not retire, but might be more away if I wished. C.L.F. saying for pilchard works &c, he hoped I shd not retire & R.B.F. expressed similar hope & I said then I wd carry on [*as*] I liked the interest of the office affairs but I doubted being good for much in a 12 months time.'

The reversal of roles between an outgoing partner and incoming partner is potentially a difficult and dangerous situation, and one which both may prefer not to confront. It could never be said that my father ruled with a rod of iron.[56] But the trouble was there were many who *thought* he did, and that unfortunately included myself. As sons

---

56 My father filled many people who did not know him any better with feelings of awe and trepidation. Both he and his mother, who was born not long after the telephone had been invented, would sometimes answer it by saying 'Yes?' in a voice which was enquiring and imperious, but also off-putting. My father was also of an imposing stature and size. But in truth there was nothing he liked more than a good laugh, even if at times his sense of humour was slightly disconcerting. A secretary, with spiral notepad and pencil in hand, once asked him, timidly, if she could see him for a minute. 'Have a look now, if you like,' he roared back at her. Young girls being interviewed for the post of a secretary were expected to take down in shorthand and then type, 'An embarrassed cobbler met a harassed pedlar in a cemetery gauging the axis of symmetry on a lady's waist with unparalleled ecstasy'.

grow up and leave home, and when a father is widowed, or, as in the case of my father, suffers a personal tragedy[57], a family firm more than ever becomes like a family support system. It was where my father had all his friends; but fraternisation, as we have seen, has its perils. So when, for example, a decision was made to cut a rather over-lavish distribution of Christmas presents, I found that the next day my father had, very understandably, undertaken to perform that kindness out of his own pocket. My brother and I had been passed the responsibility, but not the authority.

Some of these problems were skilfully, though not consciously, circumnavigated by my becoming, for the third time, and not the last time in my life, a mature student. I cannot to this day think how I managed to scrape through the exams to become an Associate Member of the Institute of Chartered Shipbrokers. It is still annoying that this qualification does not, and did not, give me any more arrows to my quiver. It is the best qualification you can obtain to be a ship agent; but never in my life have I brokered a ship, and nor would I know how to do so. On reflection, it might have been more beneficial to have spent those years of study mastering a skill: how to type would have been quite useful.

In 1991, only a few years after I had become senior partner, I had the bright idea (as I vainly thought) of persuading all the partners to write a report on what is commonly

---

57   In September 1991, his wife (my mother) was run over by a car, causing almost fatal injuries which had life-changing consequences for both of them.

known as 'the way ahead'. I did not know then that this exercise had taken place just over 30 years earlier. In those days the emphasis was evidently on how the senior generation of partners could retire in a way which was most tax efficient for them and for the company. Nor did I know in 1991 that the company had, on that prior occasion, sought the advice of a high-powered accountant in London. No one in either instance actually referred to 'the way ahead', or that it was being controlled by some traffic lights showing red, and others flickering amber. As for the current trends of being educated on how to pass through the red lights *safely*, that, in the 1960s, was relatively unknown.

My report which was about 30 pages long came in two parts: the first was 'recommendations' and the second was 'implementation'. But what has taken me a long time to learn is that even if ideas are accepted, the real difficulty is the 'application' or 'implementation'. In other words, everyone says 'yes, brilliant idea; let's do it', but the next day they are back to their old tricks. I should have learnt from a previous experience when we had employed a sales marketing person who had some very bright ideas to impart. But the day after he had spent a long time showing the staff how to answer the telephone in an engaging manner, many of us had reverted to our old habits.

I have seen in my time a great many reports and feasibility studies, where a good 75% is devoted to describing the existing state of affairs; and I am probably guilty of doing this myself. But some of the worst culprits are management consultancy teams; and the underlying reason for this is that no one really wants to give the bad news, and no one really wants to discover that the best advice is the least palatable. (Many of these company doctors, from first-hand experience, know how it feels.) When it came to G. C. Fox & Co. (and the only reason we employed a company doctor from a firm of accountants was to give professional credibility to our own ideas) I had the sense to ask for a draft. This was duly returned to the doctor with a request to include one or two metaphorical words and expressions such as 'sacrifice' and 'major sea change'. None of this had been necessary in the 1960s.

The value of these reports and of meetings with the bank manager, was that, over a period of years, they all became a steadily dripping tap. But there was never a pressing need to sell. The two main strings of the firm worked reasonably well in a cross-subsidising way: in times of slump people travelled less but ships were laid up and made money for us; in times of boom ships traded and people travelled more. Property owned by the office meanwhile acted as useful, although potentially harmful, collateral.

As described in Chapter 3 (The Meeting House), responsibility towards the staff has traditionally been a hallmark of G. C. Fox & Co. In the old days, and in the absence of a decent welfare state there was a genuine concern for the finances of employees; and there were also various relatives who were able to expect dividends from the company. There had evidently been enough at various times for five partners to live in reasonable comfort, some with two homes – as described in the book of that name 'Two Homes'. When my brother and I joined the business, that luckily had ceased, but after tax there were still, I quickly realised, tenants who were effectively being subsidised more than members of the family. There was still this notion of an almost divine (and in this context the word is used with its intentional sarcasm) right for partners' drawings, and that 'the office will pay': every day the accountant was fed with little bits of green paper indenting for some quite surprising expenses. Worse than this, it became increasingly apparent as a result of all these meetings and consultancy reports that there was a small number of employees with far too little to do. We could not be so heartless as to ask them to resign, but this did not prevent one from observing the firm was in danger of acting like a charity.

Despite those who viewed G. C. Fox & Co. as an historic relic, the Foxes were, if nothing else, progressive. In the 1960s, and with all the enthusiasm of that era, the partners worked hard at dreaming up other forms of business into which they could diversify. Because the ship agency represented such a large percentage of local taxi business, this was investigated until it was realised that we would have put several perfectly adequate cab and hackney people out of a job. But a hire car business called Holicars ran with moderate success. The partners looked at the idea of aeroplanes and helicopters, which had been used with some success in the ship agency, and also at the possibility of purchasing some land near Newquay airport. They thought outside the box, in the case of Fox Stanton outside the production of just egg boxes, and into the rather unrelated (well, unrelated to shipping) world of full-scale poultry farms. My father, who had no time for hens, but loved a good drink, at one time thought that the wine-bins in the cellars of 48 Arwenack Street were the incentive for becoming wine merchants; and another partner, who eventually emigrated to a better climate may well have thought that his idea of investing in a villa in the Mediterranean could be tied to the advantages of cheap travel, and luxury holidays. There were endless meetings to discuss all these, and many other, possibilities, often involving accountants, and solicitors who, admittedly at our invitation, came purring down to Cornwall in their company Rovers to proffer advice.

Before the end of the century, however, those words from 1962 – 'the pension position and future of the Partners when they grow old' – were of little relevance, although the partners would have liked them to have been. In recounting the history of the business, it would be a serious omission not to include a few nails which have been used in the coffin of the ship agency. The most significant of these is undoubtedly the global changes in the shipping industry in the second half of the twentieth century. Older residents of Falmouth, as no doubt was the case in other working ports, will recall that in the 1960s the Docks were packed with shipping, often three deep to each wharf: and G. C. Fox & Co.'s quay punts waited in large numbers for their orders. By the 1980s the picture was very different: the rise in the use of container ships, together with an increasing tendency to send freight by air, meant that fewer ships were coming into port and there was far less demand for the work of ship agencies.

The same period saw the decline of G. C. Fox & Co. holding virtual monopolistic control of ship agency work in Falmouth. In 1886 George Henry Fox had noted

'At present competition is not so keen between the three ship agents – all representatives board in Fox and Co.'s steamer 'Norman'. We have shares in Fishery Co.'s tugs Triton and Briton. More interest centres in the tugs when there is not a proper living for all.'

The company was prepared to accept the competition and wherever possible use it as a way of generating extra income. For years the company had held a sweet-sour relationship with Broad and Company. There are many references to the two companies working together, albeit with restrictive covenants; and there are equally many references to contradict this. It all came to a head in 1936 when my grandfather pithily records

'Thus appears to end a competition between Broads' and Fox's which has lasted over 150 years, with various degrees of keenness, appreciation, and antipathy.'

But this monopolistic reign was to change with the advent of the cowboy ship agents. This is a ship agent who works on a system of obtaining discounted prices for the ship owner or charterer, but not passing them on in their entirety. This was in direct conflict with professional ship agents who made their money by charging a set fee, according to a scale recommended by the Institute of Chartered Shipbrokers. Unfortunately, in Great Britain it is not necessary to be a member of this august body in order to practise as a ship agent. Membership was impressive but it was not imperative, and for a small ship agency in Falmouth, in the face of increasing competition, it lacked any real teeth. Yet it also tied our hands: we had the context but increasingly, and unavoidably, not the content.

I would be failing in my task of recording the history of G. C. Fox & Co. if I did not also mention, in as forgiving a way as possible (in fact there was nothing to forgive), that during my time a new ship agency was started in Falmouth by a man whose surname was also Fox, but who was not related; and although he was legally entitled to do this it must have been misleading for some.

In the context of the travel agency, there were two other things which concerned me. One was that although cross-subsidising with the ship agency had its value, there was part of me that wanted to see each business stack up in its own right. But maybe you cannot do that any more than you can expect some exotic, or indeed non-exotic, fruit to stack up in its own right in a greengrocer's. The other thing which perplexed me was that because we owned the buildings from which we traded as ship and travel agents, there was no rent to pay. We had the increasing capital value of the property but that was academic and, compared to other companies where rent reflected a business cost, and helped to establish viability, we were giving ourselves a false picture in the profit and loss account. On top of everything else, although the turnover of the travel agency was impressive for a small business in south west Cornwall, the actual profit by comparison was minimal. Nowadays, with the internet, even less filters its way through to the high street travel agent. The only way to make money was by volume, something my father realised in the 1950s when he started the travel agency, and something that the purchaser of Fox Travel also realised when he entered the business.

For those who expressed surprise at the sale of Fox

Travel, the business was sold just before the tragedy of 9/11; and since that time, it cannot have been profitable either to sell or buy a small family-run travel agency business, let alone run one. With the tremendous advances in information technology, in which we could not make any affordable investment, airlines were beginning to pay less and less commission, if at all. There was for us an added problem, which paradoxically increased in line with our increase in business: the air returns. In order to retain our licences, these had to be paid out each month and gave our valiant accountant many sleepless nights, and an appreciable talent for juggling. On top of a sizeable wage bill, and any loan or overdraft facilities, and the availability of working capital, these air returns frequently amounted to hundreds of thousands of pounds; and significantly, unlike manufacturing, agency work could not, and cannot be factored.

In the end, as is so often the case with relationships, outside events pointed the way to the path which was followed. There was a rumour that Curnow Shipping was wanting to relocate its business from Porthleven to Falmouth. At that stage it was difficult to see clearly *how* it would work out; all I knew was that there was some synergy for arranging a meeting, at least to ascertain if they might be interested in moving to 48 Arwenack Street, a large building of which we only used a third. There were several subsequent meetings and, as is now well-known, the outcome was that Curnow Shipping bought the ship agency, which then moved to its new office in Killigrew Street. Meanwhile the travel agency became part of Let's Go Travel, remaining at 48 Arwenack Street.

All this involved a mass of inventories, compromise

agreements and solicitors' letters, and was not achieved without considerable soul-searching.

Since the day on which we made the decision to sell, thousands of other family-run businesses of repute have followed the same route, as well as the demise of much more important companies, revered institutions, and countless inheritances. Their fate has led me to realise that not only was it the correct decision but that it was the *only* one, though for a long time it did not feel that way. One morning, while I was shaving, I prayed that there would be a sign from the Heavens that the sale of the business had been the right course of action. Suddenly, or immediately, as it says in St Matthew's Gospel, I witnessed the most alarming scene outside the bathroom window. It could not have been closer or more directly in my line of vision: a pigeon being attacked in mid air by a buzzard. Seconds later my wife appeared, asked if I had seen the attack, and then said, 'You have to go and deal with the situation'. I found the half-dead pigeon fluttering around in the flower bed. It had no chance of survival. In wringing its neck, I took its head off in my hand; and then had to carry the two still pulsating parts of the pigeon to the dustbin. As I did so, I thought that this was a very accurate reflection of the situation at G. C. Fox & Co. I had separated the two living parts of the business and dispatched them. I returned to our kitchen and told my wife that I felt as if every bird in the garden was regarding me as an arch murderer. 'They knew what you had to do,' said my wife; and again, I thought how much this reflected what was going on with the business. For anyone who appreciates the world of nature, this was a very powerful symbol, with the additional message that the greater you love something the easier it is to put it out of its misery.

I longed for someone to say either, 'You have made the correct but difficult decision; let me help you get through it' or, 'You cannot let this happen; let me help you find an alternative way.' But no one did, until one day I turned on the radio in my car and hoped that the first words I would hear would be some kind of encouragement or confirmation that this had all been the right decision. That prayer was answered in the form of the opening words of Sir Hubert Parry's famous Coronation Anthem 'I was glad'. God, I believe, speaks to us all in many different ways, not just on Sundays or through the voice of the ordained clergy.

In the late 1980s I had a dream. In it, I was driving back to Cornwall from London late at night, which in real life was something my wife and I often did. In the middle of Bodmin Moor the car broke down; I got out and saw that the car was a Rolls Royce; I opened the bonnet; and inside there was nothing, just a bottomless pit of emptiness.

I welcomed this dream, for although I did not fully realise at the time, it transpires to have been prophetic. There were some nice touches of detail. First, my father always wanted a Rolls Royce, and was often going to London, or sending others, for meetings which today would be conducted by conference calls and emails. Secondly, the bonnet of the car opened sideways, and widely, one side at a time, which always seems to me a more objective, gentler way of examining an engine, rather than the confrontational and conventional under-the-bonnet approach; and there were fundamentally two sides to our

The restored staircase and stairwell at 48 Arwenack Street

business. Thirdly, as everyone knows, there are very few signposts to be found on remote moors, and in the dark.

Years later, when the destiny of this engineless car was being resolved I had another dream. It was a picture of the stairwell at 48 Arwenack Street, and out of the sombre depths of the ancient building, floating up and into the sun, came one brightly coloured balloon after another. This dream also turned out to be prophetic. Let's Go Travel and Curnow Shipping have both moved on and their respective businesses of travel and shipping have been absorbed into much bigger empires: G. C. Fox & Co. is now part of Denholm Wilhelmsen[58] which maintains an office within Falmouth Docks.

Everything has a life: civilisations come and go and so too do businesses, families and individuals: we 'blossom and flourish' but are equally liable to 'wither and perish', as the well-known hymn declares. If the family tree of just the partners of G. C. Fox & Co. is examined, it can be seen how in reality this has happened. First of all, in the middle of the nineteenth century the Wadebridge branch went in different directions, followed in 1934 by the last of the Penjerrick Foxes to be involved with the firm, and then, in the late 1960s and early 1970s, the last uncle and the last first cousin. At various times attempts were made to graft on some interest from more distant relations, but to no avail. It had been much easier 200 years ago to do this with cousins William, and Thomas Were senior and Thomas Were junior. But in the economic climate of today, and with Quakers no longer being the powerful empire they once were, and the old-fashioned type of partner not such an entity, it has been more difficult.

---

58 Pleasingly, but coincidentally, the stated ethos of this company very much reflects the Quaker sentiment. 'Every company and employee within the J. & J. Denholm group of companies is required to sign up to meet the Denholm standard', which proclaims integrity, fairness, respect and upholding the law.

There is a tendency to look at history with all the rosy-tinted vision that the distance of time will inevitably produce, and to see things from the past as quaint, or extraordinary, or unbelievable. But what so many of us forget is that history consists of the accumulation of moments in time; and as has already been inferred, the Foxes of previous centuries were not living in the past, but in their present. They made realistic decisions. From this point of view, it is interesting to observe the successful careers of those members of the family who during the last 50 years either left the firm or chose not to join it. They went off to plant flags elsewhere possibly in the same way that, in the seventeenth century, Francis Fox left Wiltshire to seek his fortunes further west; and they were successful. They were perhaps the first to observe that times were changing in a way which had never happened before, and that old-established family businesses were becoming increasingly unsustainable.

As it has turned out, if it had not been for some turbulent times at G. C. Fox & Co. I doubt very much if this book would ever have been written. The beginning of this book describes my early days at G. C. Fox & Co., and how one of my first tasks was to clear out an attic. In recent years this was followed by two auctions of redundant office furniture and effects, and, according to the receipts, the purchase of 500 black plastic rubbish sacks. I cleared up 300 years' worth of history; one day I sat on a step on the staircase and was led to the brink of despair: despair at things which I had done and thought perhaps that I should not have done, and despair at things I should have done but had not done. But on the other hand I came into my destiny, did what had to be done, tidied up – and then wrote a book about it.

I hope the redeeming product of that initial work in the roof spaces of 48 Arwenack Street, and everything that followed in a period of over 30 years, is this memoir; and I hope it will be read as a tribute to all those who made G. C. Fox & Co. the success it became.

15

THE LONG WALK HOME

IF I WERE going to select a golden age from the history of the firm, I might well choose the 60 years or so from the 1870s up to the late 1930s. It is true that the cataclysm of the First World War fell in the middle of this period. But as has been suggested already, whilst true Quakers abhorred any idea of fighting, the inconvenience and distress of war are paid little deference in the archives. As far back as the mid-eighteenth century George Croker Fox (I), writing from Fowey in 1755, talks about the desirability of a convoy:

> 'if any prospect of a convoy to the Mediteranian would make some difference of wch shall be glad to know, the near approach of war has stagger'd the resolution of some of the concernd, in the vessel proposed to send to Naples...the thoughts of warr occasions a great Indifferency to adventuring this season and hurts trade a great deal'.

It has been said that Quakers like to see the good in every person, and no doubt also in every situation. Wars in this way did not seem to impinge on either the path of their souls, or in fact on the business; they remained busy with ships and with timber, and in many respects became busier. Many Quakers did fight: my grandfather kept a record of numerous cousins who had died in battle, and in a dark green book entitled *Supplement to the Photographic Pedigree of the Wilson Family, a Quaker dynasty*, there are 76 pages of 'Memorials of those who gave Lives for the Country in the Great War'.

Looking back, however, it seems to me there was an era between the wars when, relatively free of anxiety, they were able to enjoy Cornwall perhaps in its most glorious undiscovered state, well before it became Fulham-by-the-Sea. This is borne out most of all by a collection of albums, typical of that time, but showing very squarely how much, mellowed by the horrors of war, they valued and appreciated the gift of life. The friends and relations in the photographs are not just Bohemians, or intellectuals, but much more of a type of person who is distinctly unstuffy, and at odds with stiff Edwardian formality, except perhaps for the inevitable presence of a few great-aunts.

If I try to recall in my mind past Christmas Days, they all seem to merge: I remember only those which were noticeably different. One year, when there was not a cloud in the sky, I drove into Falmouth. There was ice over the lake at Swanpool, and frost glistened on the hedges. When everyone else was doing, or not doing, all the frenetic things that happen on Christmas morning, I boarded a Norwegian tanker. Its colour was pistachio green, the sea was palest blue, and across the stillness of the water came the sound of bells, bells from churches all around the bay. It was a matchless winter's day, and one which will be remembered forever.

But most Christmas Days merge into a blur. The same is true of the partners of G. C. Fox & Co. in the early twentieth century. Obviously, each had his own idiosyncrasies, but for me they all merge into the same character. They all wore beards and moustaches; they were keen and knowledgeable gardeners and ornithologists, and were well informed on all matters of flora and fauna. Some became serious geologists and scientists. They cared for people, and worked tirelessly for the amelioration of the impoverished. They were quiet, gentle and wise, and happy to listen. The following quotes could be said about any one of them:

'Mr F was a wise adviser and took great interest in helping anyone and any course for the good of town, mankind, and of the world.'

'He loves beauty as well as that knowledge which to the uninitiated seems dry-as-dust.'

'To a rock-like firmness of will and stability of character was joined an absolute straightforwardness.'

As described in the previous chapter, the Foxes who were active in the partnership at this time were descended from Robert Were Fox (II) and his brother Alfred: they included Robert Were Fox's grandson Robert Barclay Fox (II) (1845–1934); Alfred's sons Alfred Lloyd (1829–1885), Howard (1836–1922) and George Henry (1845–1931); and Howard's son Charles Masson (1866–1935). Robert Barclay Fox and Charles Masson Fox were thus first cousins to George Henry's sons, my grandfather Cuthbert (1885–1972) and my great-uncle Romney (1898–1968), which brings us into what is called living memory.

It is clear that all these Foxes, and no doubt their predecessors, liked being outside, especially at sea or in the mountains. They loved picnics, and enjoyed walking. In 1874 Wilson Fox wrote that he was one of a small party which

'started from Glendurgan on a pollacking expedition to the Manacles'

and then rather definitively,

'than which under favourable circumstances there is not a finer day's sport in the United Kingdom for anyone to whom being on the sea is a pleasure and hauling in a big fish is a delight.'

(For those who are students of etymology, when the circumstances were unfavourable, the word 'pollocking'[59] – although differently spelt – according to the *Dictionary of Slang*, and thanks to the artistry of Jackson Pollock, can today assume another meaning for those who observe, or suffer, from sea sickness.)

All the family rode but if they could not find a horse, they were happy to walk (though perhaps Barclay Fox, from what we read in his *Journals*, found travelling a frustrating inconvenience). In the days when people walked

---

59   Pollack and pollock are two different fish.

four or five miles, or more, to work, Howard Fox would set off on foot to the Lizard, there to do a weekend's stint in the Signal Station, the subject of Chapter 4. He carried his binoculars; and it was a lovely walk, for three seasons of the year.

He would rise early on Monday mornings and be back in his Falmouth office before it was time for opening.

These men had a very sharpened awareness of the concept of stewardship in this world, and a never-ceasing sense of wonderment and appreciation for all that they felt had been given to them by God, not just in nature, but in families, in professions, and in opportunities to do good. In their homes, every day started with a reading from the Bible and with prayers; and everyone in the house, including the servants, was expected to attend.

It is no wonder that the Foxes were in demand – but not necessarily for their prayerful attitude. Nearly all the partners at one time or another became involved, often as founder, chairman or president in the following organisations: the County Council, Falmouth Chamber of Commerce, Falmouth Harbour Board, Falmouth Docks, Falmouth Working Men's Club, the Cornwall Sailors Home and Hospital, Falmouth Grammar School, County High School for Girls, Falmouth Art School, the Royal Cornwall Polytechnic Society, the Royal Institution of Cornwall, and many other charities. Mountains of paper-work were generated in this respect of these concerns. Most of it makes tedious reading but occasionally there is the odd gem such as,

'This chamber event should prove particularly appealing to lady-members of the Chamber and the ladies of our male members. They are particularly and cordially invited.'

Round about 1900 I feel that the firm, without knowing it, entered a new phase. From being merchants and ship agents, the family had already had business ties with some of the old established families of Cornwall; and as well as being closely related, they also had business connections with some of the great Quaker families such as Barclay, Buxton, Lloyd, Gurney, Pease and Backhouse. The ancient banking names of Hoare –another Quaker family – and Baring also crop up every now and again in the archives. But they had risen to prosper in other spheres, and with this had come, as is natural, all the palaver of new houses and their embellishment: a run of reproduced Pre-Raphaelite paint-ings, and photographic portraits framed in Gothicized style, or mounted in dull purple pocket-sized albums with clasps. Genealogical piety came creeping in as the gentry rose. This was hardly self-aggrandisement, but still a progress; and certainly, with their gardens, it was hardly laurel-resting but laurel-planting. Quakers did not go to church, but it would have been true to say 'the carriage and pair goes but once past the church door' for them to be accepted in society. Much of this was because the subjects which interested the Foxes were socially very interactive: for example, science, religion, economics, geography, geology, flora and fauna,

'bringing together kindred spirits whom a foolish class distinction might otherwise have kept separate.'

A passion for plants brought the Foxes into close friendship with, for instance, the Lemons at Carclew; it was not, as far as we know, because of the curious coincidence that Sir Charles' wife was a member of the allegedly related Fox-Strangways family.

There exists a letter from Charles Fox to Henry Williams, written in 1848 from Perran Cottage, which subsequently became Goonvrea, and which overlooked the Perran Foundry. In it he says

> 'It will be a pleasure to give thee some of the young Pinus plants which John Masterman[60] gave me the seed sent…from the East Indies'

and in the early part of the twentieth century George Henry Fox was given some olive trees which had come to Falmouth on a ship. Not to appease disappointed garden historians but more to illustrate what sort of person Charles was, he was clearly not above putting his hand to the spade, as in fact was true of all the gardening Foxes. At this stage Charles must have been renting from the Williams family, for he writes:

---

60 As well as the Foxes, John Masterman knew John Forbes Royle (1799–1858) who went to Calcutta in 1819 as an assistant surgeon for the East India Company. Over the next 12 years, Royle collected and studied 'economic' plants in India, bringing his collections back to England in 1831. He subsequently published his findings in *Illustrations of the Botany and other Branches of the Natural History of the Himalaya Mountains and of the Flora of Cashmere* in 1839. He dedicated this two-volume work to John Masterman.

'there are some branches of shrubs & trees encroaching either on the walks or on more valuable shrubs which I may advantageously cut back this winter, be assured that I should do it with much more caution than if they grew on my own property.'

But as far as I have been able to discover, and contrary to popular belief, there is not one reference in the archives to any of the partners commissioning captains to bring them seeds from around the world. This does not mean to say that this did not happen: it might well have been an informal request made outside the perimeters of the shipping business. In fact, if the importing of seeds was not part of their trading, it is likely that any commissions of this nature were treated as a separate item, and more significantly for historians, not documented. Quakers were ethical in their business dealings and would have kept any private pastimes out of the office; they were also astute and might have decided that this sort of thing was best kept unminuted, at any rate until they could tell if their gardening exploits were going to succeed, or not. Certainly there is plenty of actual evidence in the mid-nineteenth century that all sorts of tropical and semi-tropical specimens were beginning to appear in the Fox gardens, but some of these were coming from Kew, some were being presented by shipping companies, others came from the plant-hunting expeditions to be tried out in the favourable micro-climate of Penjerrick, and some were purely and simply because the Foxes had made friends with people like the Lemons, and John Masterman.

In this story there was a passage of about 50 years

when, as fast as they could, the Foxes ploughed back their rewards into the community. They immersed themselves into the world of the worthy citizen, as much as that of the entrepreneur. Yet, from their outward appearance and demeanour I do not believe that members of the family deliberately gave the impression of either of these two familiar types of person; and certainly they were totally unlike some of their predecessors who came from the ranks of Cornish aristocracy. I have in my mind a picture of a dutiful, methodical man in rather a wide cap or Homburg hat, driving all over Cornwall with the aid of linen-backed maps, in what are now known as veteran cars, to sort out the wrecks of ships, and at a time when there were not many cars on the roads, not many white lines, no yellow ones, and a paucity of road signs. Where today's sign might say 'Discover the hidden Lizard', there, at a thatched lodge, once began the private drive from Gweek to the mansion of Trelowarren, and beyond that, on a remote promontory, at the end of a track dented with potholes, there stood the Signal Station.

I have enjoyed writing this book, but there is one part which has been difficult: the selfless contributions that the partners made in the early twentieth century make me feel embarrassed at my own inadequacies. There are those little voices whispering into my ear: 'but it was expected of them', and 'but it was a different age' and 'no one else was around to fulfil those roles' and 'there were in life many things which they did not have to think about in those days', such as housekeeping or cutting the grass. Robert Barclay Fox (II) and his wife were childless; and so, rather like his aunts Caroline and Anna Maria, much of his energies went into serving the community – as well as running Grove Hill House in Falmouth and the estate of Penjerrick.

Similarly, the domestic life of my great-grandfather George Henry Fox was not without its trials: the loss of a son at an early age, three children with health problems, and a wife who left her family to follow the ways of the Panacea Society[61], might also have led him to have an altruistic view on life. Also, I do realise that this concept of worthy citizenship was no different from what was unfolding in other places in England at that time. It was what life was like; and, certainly with my family, there always seemed to be plenty of time for fishing, shooting, sailing, and playing tennis, cricket, or chess. Nonetheless I am full of admiration for those members of the family who stepped up to roles within the community.

As stated at the beginning of this book my intention was to paint a picture of the character of the firm, rather than that of the individual characters within the business. I have not dwelt on associated topics such as the building of Falmouth Docks, or the railway line reaching Falmouth. Nor have I lingered for long on the well-known story of the Royal Cornwall Polytechnic Society or on

---

61   The Panacea Society was a millenarian religious group which followed the writings of the Devonshire prophetess Joanna Southcott (1750–1814), in particular by campaigning for Southcott's sealed box of prophecies to be opened according to her instructions. My great-grandmother Rachel Fox was one of the four main founder members of the Panacea Society in 1919 and wrote its first official history, having been introduced to Southcott's writings before the First World War.

any what might be called 'extra-mural activities', which devoured the partners' energies. But my hope is that these few paragraphs by implication will give the reader an idea of what G. C. Fox & Co. was like in the early twentieth century.

As you drive down into the main streets of Falmouth you pass under a sort of bridge, which, although relatively smaller, can only be architecturally described as being inspired by three famous Italian bridges. On its facing side is part of the town's coat of arms, featuring the double-headed eagle from the coat of arms of the Killigrew family, of ancient but piratical character, and underneath that the word 'Remember'. This was one of the last words said by Charles I before his head was severed, and its relevance to Falmouth is mostly to do with the town's parish church, King Charles the Martyr, and the royal charter of a staunchly royalist town in 1661. But for many people this one word 'Remember' must be a mystery. A friend who was a well-known Cornish artist once told me that he was always tempted to take his can of spray paint and add 'your shopping list'.

Perhaps it is because the Foxes did not arrive in Falmouth until 100 years later that I tend to remember other things, rather than the Restoration era. It is preferable to think of the houses along Greenbank, and how they were once the homes of Packet captains and others who had prospered from the shipping business. It is an interesting exercise to wonder what Falmouth must have been like before there were buildings obscuring the view out to sea from Prince of Wales Pier; and within living memory there was a time when, during some demolition work, this was briefly possible. Perhaps best of all I like to imagine the town when, as is said elsewhere, properties such as the Foxes owned

'led delightfully from the centre of towns into the landscape beyond'

and what Thomas Carlyle in his *Life of John Sterling*[62] described as

'the mining world and the farming world open boundlessly to the rear.'

A few years ago, one Sunday morning in the summer, I walked home in the same way as the crow flies. I passed through the big gate posts to Arwenack Manor, and on past Grove Hill House, once surrounded by woods. It is still standing, as is so often strangely stated about properties, 'in its own grounds', if sadly diminished, and no longer supporting a rubber tree, and orange and lemon trees. Once, Falmouth was in a much more rural district. Susan Gay in her book *Old Falmouth* refers to a letter written by Mrs George Croker Fox in 1788 about Grove Hill House:

---

62   Published in 1851 by Chapman and Hall. The Scottish author and thinker John Sterling (1806–1844) was well-known to the Fox family and it is recorded in *Barclay Fox's Journal* that Sterling had proposed to his sister Caroline, who reluctantly turned him down because it would have meant 'marrying out', entailing expulsion from the Society of Friends. See the Introduction to *Barclay Fox's Journal* and diary entries for January and February 1844.

'My husband is now digging the foundations of a new dwelling. I have been a little intimidated at the view of residing in the country.'

I then walked along Woodlane, past Fox's Lane, and Rose-hill, the home of Robert Were Fox (II), Barclay's father, and Wodehouse Place, the home of Alfred. I thought of their happy proximity and the absence of cars; and the words of one of Alfred's daughters came to mind:

'George has a raven which amuses us much, but the greatest addition is a graceful greyhound, that goes out with us in all our walks and drives',

no doubt each excursion a picture of Victorian elegance.

There cannot now be alive many who remember Rose-hill House before it became Falmouth College of Art, and at a time when its acclaimed garden stretched for seemingly miles towards the horizon of the sea; and there probably are not many who realise the role the Fox family once had in encouraging the arts in Falmouth.

Turning right into Western Terrace I passed the Falmouth Sports Club which was for so many years such a sporting, and social, centre for the family and its friends; before that it had been Arwenack Farm.

I dipped down into a leafy lane and thought how once this led to Marlborough House, the fine Regency home of a Packet captain, and also a property my grandmother's family had rented in about 1910, when she had first met a certain Mr Fox. To my right up the hill lay Penmere Manor Hotel, once the home of Alfred Lloyd Fox, and above that, and still in use, the Quaker Burial Ground: Quaker elders pushing up the ground elder. Moving into open country I walked through allotments and took a footpath which skirted around the southern side of Penjerrick, historically and horticulturally the most important of the three famous Fox gardens. From this high vantage point (much like one of S. R. Badmin's mid twentieth-century landscape illustrations, familiar to so many through the *Shell Guides*), there is a panorama of Falmouth Bay, beautifully presented by everything in between: Tregedna where Joshua had lived with all his dogs and 100,000 roses, and in the distance the pines of Treworgan, home of his formidable niece Lucy Anna Fox (1841–1934). She had married a Hodgkin of banking fame and owned an appropriate car, but it was so large that it could not negotiate the coast road, so had to make every journey through Mawnan Smith. Further to the south-west the woods of Glendurgan and Trebah were visible. I cut through Rosemerryn, once owned by Robert Were Fox, and down to Bareppa which belonged to a Hodgkin daughter and her husband.

It cannot ever be said that the vernacular architecture of Cornwall is its unique selling point. There seems to be a gap between mansions and everything else. But perhaps the Foxes picked up on the exceptions and were thereby blessed by homes in pleasant places: houses which are neither too large nor too small, and for the most part architecturally delightful. Rather like Ireland, the rare building of merit in Cornwall can be a masterpiece, and often designed and constructed when times are hard.

The walk home took an hour and a quarter. Hot and

thirsty, I walked into the vegetable garden and found my wife tying up peas. 'Ah, I have been looking for you,' she said; 'hold this string please.'

Howard Fox in the garden of Rosehill

ENVOI

(with acknowledgements to
Barclay Fox's Journal 1832–1854)

LOST AND FOUND

Old house, what did you yield from your store?
What treasure chests from the days of yore?
Ladders waiting to be made from old masts
Which were untabernacled from their pasts,
Conifers before in distant forests,
And flags that once unfurled from crows' nests,
From the ocean bed encrusted anchor chain,
And fishing nets from the purpled main –
What fish they've seen and sought?
What shoals of pilchards caught?

A two-inch thick snake of cable wire
Sleeps with a rope ladder in case of fire.
Between the ancient timber boards
Ancient documents in their hoards:
All gather here in the dusty gloom
Thus forgotten in this attic room.

Now today up here you'll meet
Above the noisy peopled street:
The seagull's place
A sense of place
Clear blue and bright,
And through the light,
And cloudless day,
A hopeful way

A hopeful way.

From Dream On – Poems Written &
Illustrated by Charles Fox, *printed 2012*

APPENDIX

MAJOR CHANGES IN THE FALMOUTH PARTNERSHIP

1780 (28 July)   **George C. Fox Sons**
George Croker Fox (I), George
Croker Fox (II), Robert Were Fox (I)

1781 (August)   **George C. Fox & Sons**
Mary Fox, George Croker Fox (II)

1810 (August)   **Foxes & Sons**
Robert Were Fox (I), Thomas Were
Fox, George Croker Fox (III), Robert
Were Fox (II)

1816 (October)   **Fox Sons & Co.**
George Philip Fox, Alfred Fox,
George Croker Fox (III), Thomas
Were Fox, Thomas Were Fox (Junior)

1821 (30 June)   Thomas Were Fox, Thomas Were Fox
(Junior), William Fox

1854 (1 November)   **G. C. & R. W. Fox & Co.**
Robert Were Fox (II), Alfred Fox,
Charles Fox, Robert Barclay Fox (I),
Alfred Lloyd Fox

1871 (31 January)   **G. C. Fox & Co.**
Howard Fox, Robert Fox, George
Henry Fox

1901 (1 October)	Howard Fox, George Henry Fox, Charles Masson Fox, Robert Barclay Fox (II), Robert Fox
1912 (20 February)	George Henry Fox, Cuthbert Lloyd Fox, Robert Barclay Fox (II), Charles Masson Fox, Howard Fox
1934 (29 March)	Charles Masson Fox, Robert Barclay Fox (II), Cuthbert Lloyd Fox, George Romney Fox
1946 (11 March)	Cuthbert Lloyd Fox, George Romney Fox, Frederick Graham Carter
1947 (1 May)	Cuthbert Lloyd Fox, George Romney Fox, Frederick Graham Carter, Philip Hamilton Fox
1951 (4 April)	Cuthbert Lloyd Fox, George Romney Fox, Frederick Graham Carter, Philip Hamilton Fox, Anthony Fox Laity
1957 (6 May)	George Romney Fox, Philip Hamilton Fox, Anthony Fox Laity
1970 (24 January)	Philip Hamilton Fox, Rona Fox
1975–1980s	Philip Hamilton Fox, Charles Lloyd Fox, William Barclay Fox

Family Tree

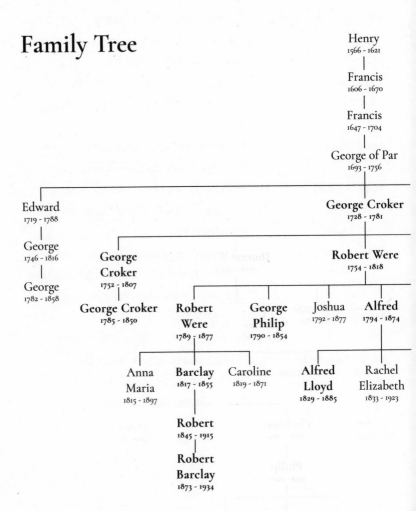

NB For the sake of clarity only those members mentioned in the book are included, with the business partners in **heavy type**. Marriages and further siblings have been omitted.

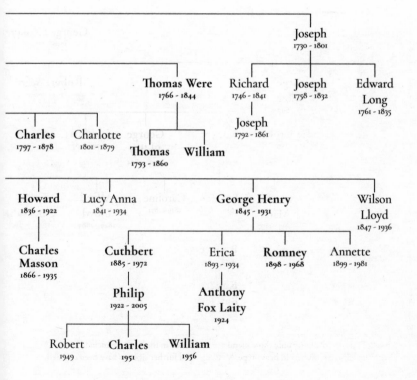

Cornwall & Isles of Scilly

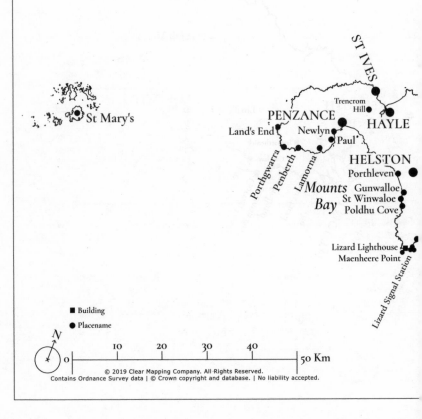

St Mary's

ST IVES

Trencrom
Hill

PENZANCE

HAYLE

Land's End

Newlyn

Paul

Porthgwarra

Penberth

Lamorna

*Mounts
Bay*

HELSTON

Porthleven

Gunwalloe
St Winwaloe
Poldhu Cove

Lizard Lighthouse
Maenheere Point

Lizard Signal Station

■ Building
● Placename

N

0   10   20   30   40   50 Km

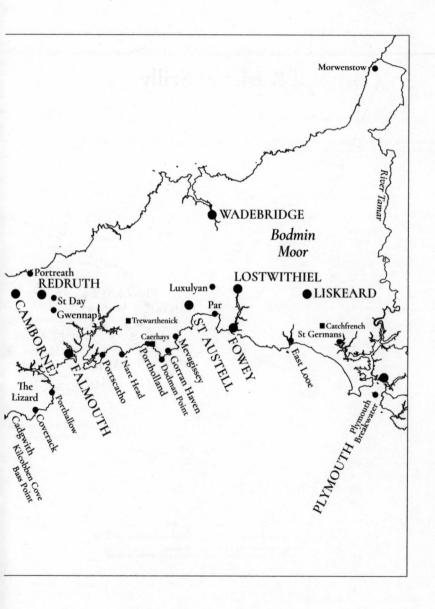

Morwenstow

River Tamar

WADEBRIDGE

Bodmin Moor

Portreath

REDRUTH

LOSTWITHIEL

Luxulyan

LISKEARD

St Day

Gwennap

Par

Trewarthenick

Catchfrench

CAMBORNE

Caerhays

ST AUSTELL

FOWEY

St Germans

Mevagissey

The Lizard

FALMOUTH

Portscatho

Nare Head

Portholland

Gorran Haven

Dodman Point

East Looe

Porthallow

Coverack

Cadgwith

Kilcobben Cove

Bass Point

PLYMOUTH

Plymouth Breakwater

313

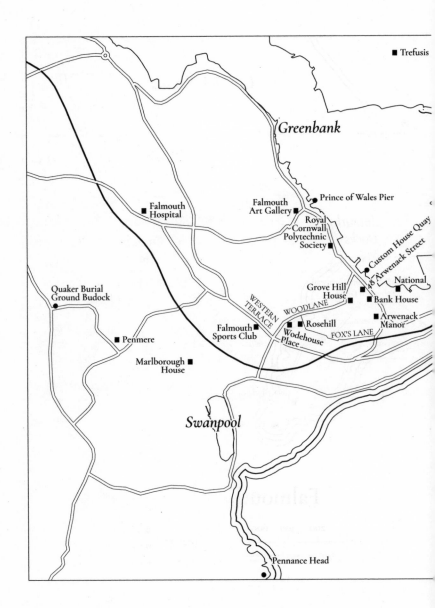

Trefusis

Greenbank

Falmouth
Hospital

Falmouth
Art Gallery

Prince of Wales Pier

Royal
Cornwall
Polytechnic
Society

Custom House Quay

48 Arwenack Street

Quaker Burial
Ground Budock

Grove Hill
House

National

Bank House

WESTERN
TERRACE

WOODLANE

Arwenack
Manor

Penmere

Falmouth
Sports Club

Rosehill

Wodehouse
Place

FOX'S LANE

Marlborough
House

Swanpool

Pennance Head

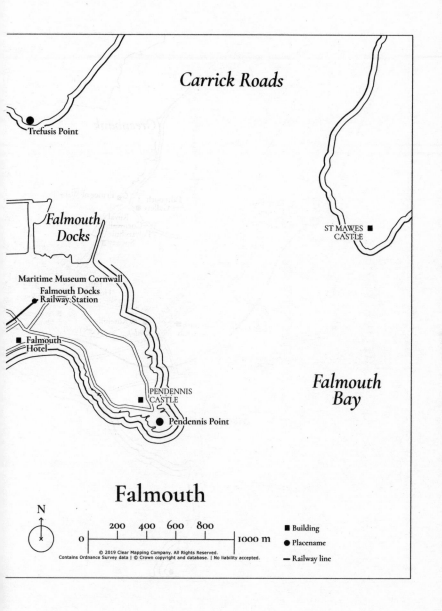

Falmouth

Carrick Roads

Trefusis Point

Falmouth Docks

ST MAWES CASTLE

Maritime Museum Cornwall

Falmouth Docks Railway Station

Falmouth Hotel

PENDENNIS CASTLE

Pendennis Point

Falmouth Bay

N

| 200 | 400 | 600 | 800 |

0   1000 m

© 2019 Clear Mapping Company. All Rights Reserved.
Contains Ordnance Survey data | © Crown copyright and database. | No liability accepted.

■ Building
● Placename
— Railway line

Carrick Roads

■ Building
● Placename

0   2   4   6   8   10 Km

© 2019 Clear Mapping Company. All Rights Reserved.
Contains Ordnance Survey data | © Crown copyright and database. | No liability accepted.

N

Grampound Road ●

TRURO ●
Malpas ●

● St Day

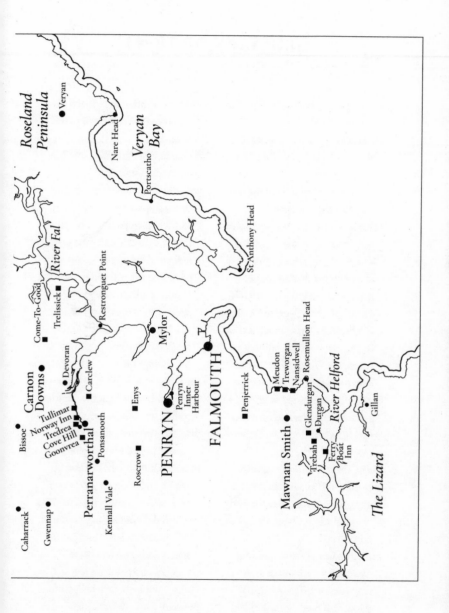

GLOSSARY OF TERMS

Aft At or towards the stern of after part of a ship.

Alum cake A porous sulphate of alumina mixed with silica, made from fine clay.

Amidships The middle of the ship, longitudinally or laterally.

Arsenic Poisonous chemical occurring naturally in the rocks and soil of mining areas in Cornwall, or as a by-product of copper mining. During the nineteenth century, Cornwall dominated the arsenic industry so much so that by the 1870s a small number of mines in the county produced over half of the world's arsenic.

Barque Three-masted sailing vessel, square-rigged on two foremost masts, fore-and-aft on mizzen mast.

Berth The station where a ship rides at anchor, or is tied up alongside a wharf; also the part of a ship where ships' officers and crew sleep.

Bill of Lading A memorandum by which the master of a ship acknowledges receipt of goods specified on the bill and promises to deliver them in the same condition as received to the consignee at the end of the voyage.

Binnacle Wooden case containing the ship's compass.

Blockade runners Ocean-going steam ships carrying weapons and other supplies (mostly from England) and used by the Confederates during the American Civil War to get through the Union blockade extending for about 3,500 miles (5,600 kms) along the Atlantic and Gulf of Mexico coasts and the lower Mississippi River.

Breakwater A wooden or stone wall built to prevent the sea from rolling inwards.

Brig Two-masted sailing vessel, square-rigged on both masts.

Brine tanking A new method of salt-curing pilchards introduced in the 1880s (possibly by Fox's) but which did not find general favour till the early 1900s. The process had the advantage of being quicker, and requiring less skill and manpower than bulk curing.

Broccoli Cornish word for cauliflower.

Bulk curing The age-old means of curing pilchards in dry salt by the cellar women.

Bulwark Planking or woodwork around the ship above the deck for safety.

Bunkers Compartments along sides and bottom of a ship for stowage of fuel (coal on steamers, oil on tankers). Filling or replenishing a ship's bunker with fuel is known as bunkering.

Buoy Float or block of wood fastened to anchor to show its location.

Bushel A measure of capacity equivalent to 8 gallons.

Chaise A horse-drawn pleasure cart or light carriage.

Charter party A deed or written contract between the owners and the merchants for the hire of a ship and safe delivery of the cargo.

Coburg A type of carriage.

Combings [Coamings] Raised lip higher than the decks, framing hatch openings to prevent water on deck from running down.

Conchologist Student of conchology (the study of shells and molluscs).

Consignee The party to whose care a ship or a consignment of goods is entrusted.

Container terminal A port where cargo containers are trans-shipped for onward transportation.

Cordage A general term for the running-rigging of a ship, also for rope of any size kept in reserve and for all material from which rope may be made.

Cutter Small, fast sailing vessel, originally with single gaff-rigged mast and bowsprit.

Deals Slices sawn from log of timber used for planking and decking.

Dinghy Traditionally a small open rowing boat used as a general work-boat in warships and merchant vessels, or as a tender to a yacht; the term is now applied more often to small open sailing boats used for racing.

Dipping needle Navigational instrument for ascertaining the amount of the magnet's inclination towards the earth, perfected by Robert Were Fox II (see Chapter 8).

Dockee Informal term for dock worker.

Donkey steam pump Small auxiliary steam engine used for providing power for lesser mechanical duties on board a vessel in harbour for which it would be uneconomic to produce steam from the main boilers.

Dracaena Old name for Cordyline, genus of evergreen plants resembling palms, originating from South East Asia and Australasia but much grown on the south coast of Cornwall.

Dragnet Fishing net used in seine fishing or for dragging along the sea- or riverbed.

Dredging A term used for fishing by dragging a dredge net.

Drifter Fishing vessel traditionally used to catch fish which normally swim near the surface in shoals (especially pilchards and herring).

Drift-nets Large net with meshes of one inch used for pilchard fishing.

Exequatur The official recognition of a consul by the government of the country to which he or she is accredited.

Firkin Small cask for liquids, fish, butter etc, originally holding a quarter of a barrel.

Fore-mast The forward lower mast of a vessel.

Fore-part All parts of a ship before the fore-hatches.

Fore-stay Large strong rope extending from the fore-mast head to the bowsprit end.

Founder, to The act of a ship when it sinks at sea through springing a leak or striking a rock.

Freight Goods transported in a ship.

Gig A light narrow galley or ship's boat.

Guano The excrement of sea-birds, a valuable manure.

Harness-cask A large conical tub for containing the salt provisions intended for present consumption.

Hawser A heavy rope or small cable with a circumference of 5 inches or more.

Heaving line A light-weight line used for the purposes of drawing a heavier line between ships, or from ship to shore.

Helm Another name for the tiller, also the general term associated with orders connected with the steering of a ship.

Hemp The plant *Cannabis sativa* the fibres of which produce the best natural rope.

Hewer The look-out for signs of shoals of pilchards off the Cornish coast. Also spelt 'huer'.

Hold Large compartment below decks for stowage of cargo or provisions.

Hulk General term for a large and unwieldy ship of simple construction.

Hull The main body of a ship apart from masts, rigging and internal fittings.

Hydrostatic Relating to the equilibrium of liquids and the pressure exerted by liquid at rest.

Jabot A decorative clothing accessory falling from the neckline of a man's shirt or collar.

Jib boom A continuation of the bowsprit forward to enable the jib (large triangular sail) to be extended.

Jigger top mast The aft-most mast in vessels with more than three masts.

Ketch A two-masted sailing vessel, with the mizzen or after-mast normally stepped before the rudder-head, giving extra space between the two masts.

Lugger Small vessel with four-cornered sails set fore and aft.

Mizzen The aftermost mast of a ship. Also spelt 'mizen'.

Note of Protest A declaration given under oath by the master of the circumstances beyond his control leading to loss or damage to the ship or cargo.

Packet Service The Post Office Packet Service for carrying mail and bullion (and some passengers) which began in the Tudor era to serve mainland Europe and the Mediterranean, later extending to America and the West Indies. Falmouth was the main Packet Station in England from 1689 until 1850.

Pilchards A fish closely related to the herring, which used to appear in vast shoals off the Cornish coast in July.

Pilot gig Small vessel used by experienced navigator to guide larger vessels into harbour.

Poop-deck Name given to the short, aftermost deck raised above the quarterdeck of a ship.

Port Left-hand side of a vessel as viewed from aft.

Privateer Privately-owned vessel armed with guns which operated in time of war against the trade of an enemy; also the men who sailed in her.

Propeller The rotating screw of a steamship by which she is forced through the water.

Prow Word used to describe the forward end of a vessel.

Quay punt A term peculiar to Cornwall to describe the fast sailing boats used to carry messages to vessels in the inner harbour.

Ria A long narrow inlet of the sea coast which deepens from mouth to head.

Rigging A general name given to all the ropes or chains employed to support the masts and arrange the sails according to wind direction.

Roaring Forties, The Strong westerly winds occurring in the Southern Hemisphere, generally between the latitudes of 40 and 50 degrees.

RMS Royal Mail Ship.

Salvage Originally goods saved from a wreck; the term now applies to an allowance made to those by whose means the ship or goods have been saved.

Schooner A sailing vessel rigged

with fore-and-aft sails on two or more masts.

Seine A long, large, shallow net used in fishing for surface fish.

Smack Originally a cutter or ketch-rigged sailing vessel, now used as a generic term for all small fishing craft.

Sounding pipes Small-bore mild steel pipes used to measure the quantity of fluid in a tank.

Spar A general term for any wooden support used in the rigging of a ship.

Stanchions Upright supports or wires along the side of the upper deck of a ship to carry the guard rail.

Starboard The right-hand side of a vessel as seen from aft.

Stay Part of the standing rigging of a sailing vessel which supports a mast in the fore-and-aft line.

SS Steam ship.

Stern The after end of a vessel.

Stevedore A docker employed in the hold for loading and unloading merchant vessels.

Tackle A purchase on which two or more blocks are used in order to multiply the power exerted on a rope.

Tanker A ship designed to carry liquid cargoes in bulk, particularly oil.

Tiller A bar which fits round the head of the rudder by which it

is moved as required to steer the vessel.

Tithes One-tenth of annual produce or earnings, formerly taken as a compulsory tax for the support of the Church of England and its clergy.

Trammel-net A large dragnet.

Turnpike A road on which a toll was collected at a toll-gate.

Tucking Part of the seine fishing process, whereby a manageable part of the catch could be separated from the main shoal within the seine net, by means of the tuck-net. This prevented waste since only as many fish as could be handled by the curers each day were tucked, while the remainder could be securely enclosed in the seine net for several days.

'Tween (or 'Twixt) decks The deck under the gun deck, where sailors usually mess.

Vulcanite A preparation of india-rubber and sulphur hardened by exposure to intense heat.

Winch A small horizontal capstan, driven by steam, electricity or by hand to provide power for hoisting or tightening.

ACKNOWLEDGEMENTS

Amongst those who need to be thanked, I owe a debt of gratitude to the County Record Office. The following deserve special mention for their skill in proof-reading specific topics: David Barnicoat, Master Mariner, for all things relating to ships; Diane Coffey for tug and towage matters; Tony Pawlyn for his information on ichthyology; Nick Johnson, former County Archaeologist, for mining history; Nicholas Keegan, author of *US Consular Representation in Britain since 1790* (Anthem Press, 2018), for his studies of the consular world; and my distant cousin Charles Beresford for his knowledge of the family and its businesses throughout the country. I also need to thank Freddie Reed and Jonah Horne who as students undertook some photographic and design work, and Paddy Dowling for the photographic portrait on the end flap. John Stengelhofen kindly allowed me to use a photograph of Robert Were Fox (II)'s hydrostatic lock, and the National Maritime Museum Cornwall equally has been generous with its resources.

I would like to thank Philip Marsden for writing the Foreword; Kate Dinn, my text editor, for her eagle eye and enthusiasm for the book; Caroline Robinson and her business Clear Mapping Company for their services; Dr Katharina Kaesehage for her encouragement; and finally Zuleika, the publishing company, and its director and commissioning editor, Tom Perrin, for their vote of confidence.